The Bargain 1

Reviews of the films

no one else wants to touch

Scot Nolan

A Chatters Production, published via CreateSpace Independent Publishing Platform, North Charleston, SC

First Edition, June 2016

Library of Congress Control Number: 2016904691

ISBN-13: 978-1530618132

ISBN-10: 978-1530618134

For more Bargain Bin Review goodness, check out the official Facebook page of The 'Bin at facebook.com/BargainBinReview.

Published in the United State of America

To my grandfather, Ken Nelson.

If your armchair hadn't been so comfortable,
this book would never had been written.

You are missed.

TABLE OF CONTENTS

ABOUT THIS BOOK

Back before the age of living through your phone and digital downloads, you had to go out to an actual brick-n-mortar store if you wanted to buy a movie. You'd get a physical DVD copy (and before that a bulky VHS tape) that you could hold in your hand, put on your shelf, and inevitably find some way to scratch, soil or ruin. Those stores would have all the hot titles, of course, but they'd also have a bargain bin: various copies of unloved titles at heavily discounted prices, sloppily tossed into a literal bin. You'd have to actually dig through the pile, hoping for hidden gems.

Those bargain bin titles are the kinds of movies you'll find in this book. I doubt you've heard of many of the movies I cover here, let alone seen them. It won't matter, because just knowing that these movies exist is its own kind of entertainment. These kind of movies – b-movies, straight-to-rental releases, cult films, titles you used to find in between the recognizable films in video stores back when video stores existed – are the ones that studios won't promote and proper critics won't touch.

Fortunately, I'm not a proper critic. I do have plenty of trial-by-fire experience, having taken on Bargain Bin Reviews since 2007. That's plenty of time to not only think about why a film is bad (and there are so many ways a movie can be bad) but to consider the most common question I get: *Why?*

To help you understand why I would do this to myself, each section opens with a quick tale of My Road to Bad Movies and a review of a film that led me down this particular path. As for the sections themselves, I've arranged the films in each section by chronological order simply because previously made films sometimes influence those made afterwards. If you want to find things alphabetically, I've included a handy index in the back, because that's where one usually puts an index.

Some quick housekeeping: Movies are rated on a scale of **0 to 5 asterisks**. Why asterisks? Because if the makers of these films can't be bothered with such petty things as character development or a coherent plot, then I'm not going to bother coming up with some kind of fancy doo-dad when I can simply hit [SHIFT]8 on my keyboard. The ratings break down like this:

*****	Bad movie bliss
****	Had a good ol' time
***	Liked it more than not
**	Disliked it more than not
*	Had a miserable time
0	Actively angry that I sat through this

Enjoy!

MY ROAD TO BAD MOVIES:
THE FIRST MOVIE I EVER SAW

Do you remember the first movie you ever saw? I do. It's one of my earliest memories, and I remember it vividly.

It was a Saturday afternoon, and we were staying at my grandparents' house for the weekend. I was maybe four years old. Maybe. Most everyone was upstairs talking and talking and talking – boring adult stuff – and I was down in the den playing with my uncle's abandoned Matchbox cars. They came in a heavy tin play-set with ramps and such. It was very cool.

So there I am, kneeling at the coffee table and playing with Matchbox cars. The only other person down in the den was my grandfather, who was watching me. And by "watching me," I mean he was taking a nap in his armchair. That's when the afternoon movie came on.

There was no way my grandfather, who preferred westerns, would normally watch a movie like this. I tried to make as if I wasn't watching – I had the sense that this was something I wasn't supposed to see – but I couldn't *not* watch. It was riveting. I understood that it was just a movie, but it had never occurred to me that there could be a threat of such scale, a threat of our own making. I'm positive this was the first time I'd seen people die in a movie. And it certainly never occurred to me that a hero could be both awesome and terrible.

I couldn't sleep that night. I was afraid that I'd be turned into a skeleton by the villain of the piece as demonstrated in poorly animated sequences throughout the film. But there was no denying that I was hooked.

That movie was *Godzilla vs. the Smog Monster.*

GODZILLA VS. THE SMOG MONSTER

Directed by Yoshimitsu Banno
1972, 87 minutes, Rated PG
"It probably came from a sticky, dark planet far, far away. Now go to sleep."

Some 30 years before Al Gore came out with *An Inconvenient Truth*, there was another slow-moving, unnatural behemoth stomping across the countryside to save the planet: Godzilla.

In *Godzilla vs. the Smog Monster*, an alien life-form called Hedorah drops by to feed on our pollution. Fortunately, neither Hedorah or the pollution sits too well with our softer, kid-friendly version of Godzilla, so the King of All Monsters comes wadin' in like John Wayne to take care of business. All of the action is witnessed from the point of view of a Japanese scientist and his short shorts-wearin' young son.

Let's start off with the Smog Monster himself, Hedorah. Godzilla has appeared in nearly 30 feature films, and for my money, Hedorah is by far one of his toughest opponents. Sure, Hedorah can shoot heat lasers out of his eyes and spit toxic loogies – he can even shift shapes (an ability later seen in such foes as Orga and Destroyah). That's all well and good, but Hedorah is also an entity of living sludge. This not only renders Godzilla's bread-and-butter – his atomic breath – fairly useless, it allows Hedorah to regenerate himself simply by consuming more pollution.

We're shown this through little animated interludes that show up in the film, illustrating all the pollution we're pumping out and how it's feeding the Hedorah. The animations are crude and accompanied by some hokey music, but the overall effect makes Hedorah even creepier.

But really, this film belongs to the hippies. The film itself was released just a couple years after Woodstock, and it really shows. What is mankind's solution to taking on the scourge of pollution? Hold a rock concert at the top of Mt. Fuji, of course!

This is, to date, the only Godzilla film to feature an acid rock music video (complete with trippy fish-headed dancers). Here is the chorus:

> *Save the Earth! (save the Earth)*
> *Save the Earth! (save the Earth)*
> *See the evil problem around us*
> *Save the Earth! (save the Earth)*
> *Save the Earth! (save the Earth)*
> *And the solution: stop pollution*
> *Save the Earth! (save the Earth)*
> *Save the Earth! (save the Earth)*
> *Save the Earth!*

No one said this film was subtle.

As if the movie's message wasn't heavy-handed enough, we have a villain that practically fellates those industrial smoke stacks just as world governments today tend to fellate the oil companies. We then see the unrestricted corporate monstrosity fly around the country, gassing and killing hundreds of people (of all the Godzilla films, this one may have the highest body count). Hell, *Godzilla performs abortions* on the little Hedorah egg-spore-thingies. Someone should notify the Catholic League.

Looking at the film critically, it's all pretty dark stuff. Well, it's not all dark. There is one other thing this movie is well-known for: Godzilla using his atomic breath to fly. I'll let you sort out the physics behind that.

I guess it seems silly to complain about the protagonist defying basic laws of science in a Godzilla movie, but there we are.

* * *

1: CRAZY FOR KAIJU

GODZILLA RAIDS AGAIN

Directed by Motoyoshi Oda
1955, 78 minutes, Unrated
For the first time for the last time at last once more!

Gojira may have been his debut, but *Godzilla Raids Again* was the first time the world saw a "Godzilla movie."

By that, I mean it's the first to have all the trappings one expects from a Godzilla movie: the handful of unassuming characters who somehow always seem to be in the middle of everything, the ineffective military, the hastily shoe-horned Message, and most importantly, a brawl between two giant monsters. *Godzilla Raids Again* was cranked out the year after *Gojira* became a surprise hit, and audiences were not impressed. In fact, Godzilla wouldn't appear again until 1962's *King Kong vs. Godzilla.*

Godzilla Raids Again opens with footage of a hydrogen bomb, because this is a Godzilla movie and that's how they roll. This kicks off a whole montage of Technology! Man and Machine working together towards a better tomorrow… which largely consists of launching rockets here and there.

But enough of all that. Time to meet our main man, Tsukioka. Get used to his clipped, whiny voice, because he narrates the film – and I do mean the *entire* film. It's a bit much.

Tsukioka is a pilot for a cannery company outside of Osaka. His job is to fly around off the coast of Japan and spot school of fish for fishing boats. Yes, apparently that is a real occupation. We also meet Tsukioka's special ladyfriend Hidemi who works as a phone operator for the cannery company, and his somewhat dim best friend, fellow pilot Kobayashi.

Kobayashi experiences some technical difficulties and is forced to land on a small, uninhabited island off the coast of Japan. Tsukioka flies in for the rescue, but by "rescue" I mean a beachside cookout. But then, zoinks! M-m-m-m-m-monsters!

It's Godzilla and fan favorite Anguirus – or "Gigantis" and "Angilas the angilosaurus," as they're known in this film – and they're fightin'. They fight themselves right off a cliff into the ocean, and the pilots decide to get out of Dodge and tell the authorities what they saw. This being a Godzilla movie, the authorities believe them without reservation.

This leads to what becomes tried-and-true beats in a Godzilla movie: scientists and government officials sitting around a table, discussing what should be done. There's never any debate – a scientist shows a film (often, like here, including footage from past movies) and Explains Stuff, and then gives a recommendation which everyone involved is immediately 100% onboard with. I was hoping the 2014 *Godzilla* would have a similar scene, but done American-style: half of Congress denouncing the scientist for his "obvious liberal agenda," refusing to pay for any reconstruction efforts without cuts in the national budget, and blaming the destruction on President Obama.

The next stretch in *Godzilla Raids Again* is a bit disorienting. We get lots of stock footage of the Navy leaping into action, and then we're told (but never shown) that Godzilla isn't heading for Osaka after all, followed by an extended nightclub scene in Osaka before oops, Godzilla *is* here! Everybody panic! The military comes up with the clever idea of luring Godzilla around with a light show, but when that inadvertently also attracts Anguirus, they switch over to what becomes the tried-and-true offensive assault via toy models.

During all this, there's a sub-plot involving some hardened criminals escaping prison amid all the monster-related chaos. There's a big chase scene, and it goes absolutely nowhere. Thanks for the filler, movie!

The Osaka fight between Godzilla and Anguirus is by far the highlight of the film, and it's one of the best fights in the entire franchise. Their fight is faster and feistier than the more pro-wrestling inspired action of later films, and both monsters are pelted relentlessly by the military throughout.

When all is said and done, Osaka is completely leveled – which sucks, because it's a great city and worth checking out if you ever get the chance. The movie does take the time to acknowledge this, not just in a Michael Bay-style spectacle but in the totality of the loss. The city's history, heritage, and countless lives, all gone.

Somehow, the movie continues on. All of the characters relocate to Hokkaido (the New England of Japan – also nice, by the way) and begin resuming their cannery-related activities when Godzilla shows up *again*. It's not as bad as having Godzilla chase their taxi around town, but there's a whole lotta land between Osaka and Hokkaido – kind of like if Godzilla followed you from San Diego to South Dakota – so it's pretty random. Maybe Tsukioka owes Godzilla money? Anyway, from here the film pulls out one more cliché-in-the-making, the ol' "trap 'em in ice" routine, but the attempt is not without sacrifice.

Looking at *Godzilla Raids Again* as part of a film franchise with nearly 30 titles (not including the American films), the movie is a bit of a conundrum. It's easy to pick out all the beats that become the kind of things you expect to see in a Godzilla movie, and it begins the transition from the intensely somber *Gojira* to lighter and more action-packed fare. It also boasts a fantastic kaiju fight.

But at the same time, *Godzilla Raids Again* is a pretty weak film, very dragged out in parts and leaning way, way too heavily on narration to tie the scenes together. I could see how *Godzilla Raids Again* might torpedo a potential franchise before it even got started. I'm just glad it didn't.

* * *

GORGO

Directed by Eugene Lourie
1961, 68 minutes, Unrated
Leggo my Gorgo

They say that those who don't learn their history are doomed to repeat it. Of course, "they" are always running their mouths with all sorts of homespun platitudes. Clearly, the main characters in 1961's *Gorgo* never bothered listening to a thing "they" say, cuz otherwise we wouldn't see a rehash of every bad decision ever made in a giant monster movie.

We open on a salvage vessel with a deck full of seamen. We're told that they're all very nervous, but they mostly just staring off-screen, looking like they're posing for a catalog. We're finally shown that in the distance, water bubbles. Okay... And then, A BIG STORM! Or EXPLOSIONS! I can't tell! The next day, Captain Joe and his "partner," Sam, survey the damage and decide that they need to go ashore. Wait, they're sitting in a harbor? Jeez, a proper establishing shot would have gone a long way here.

Joe and Sam meet the prerequisite Spunky Kid, who is all sorts of chatty and spunky, as well as the douchey and unhelpful harbor master who runs the area with an iron fist. Wouldn't you know it, the harbor master is hiding something from our salvage guys: sunken treasure! And also, a 65-foot tall Godzilla knock-off. Gorgo is somewhat Godzilla-esque with red eyes and big ol' mitts – all the better to smash landmarks with, my dear. Missing are the dorsal fins, the radioactive breath and the surly demeanor... as well as any sort of personality.

Now, if you were hanging out by the shore and a 65-foot tall monster came popping out like some sort of grotesque latex jack-in-the-box, you'd (understandably) see your life flash before your eyes. Not Joe. No, he see dollar signs. The dust hasn't quite settled, and he's strong-arming the harbor master into paying Joe to get rid of the monster.

Joe's big plan? *To jump in a cast-iron tank and use himself as bait.*

I know. I couldn't believe it either. Then again, it's just that kind of bone-headed gumption that put us on the moon.

Naturally, Joe's plan works because there wouldn't be much of a movie if it didn't. Loaded up with its big bag of monster, the salvage vessel heads back home to London. The Spunky Kid stows away because he wants to free the monster, which is understandable. It wouldn't be a giant monster movie without some tyke taking a shining to the gigantic, man-eating monstrosity.

In an awesomely presumptuous move, a couple of professors from the University of Ireland meet them at the docks in London to claim the monster. Joe blows them off with a laugh, because he has bigger plans: accepting a big-money offer to put the monster on display *at a circus in downtown London.* You know how those circuses are always throwing money around. Besides, I can't imagine what could go wrong with a plan like that.

Sure enough, while trying to get the freshly-named Gorgo into its holding pen, a photographer jumps the police line to get an extreme close-up. The camera flash drives Gorgo into a rage (even in the '60s, the paparazzi ruin everything), and one of salvage vessel's Red Shirts is killed before Gorgo is put in his pen. The death greatly upsets Sam, and the more Joe lives it up, the more Sam starts drinking and worrying.

Before things between Joe and Sam can escalate into a reality show on Bravo, the university professors call them in with some startling news: Gorgo is just a baby. Does that mean there's a Mama out there? Of course! Cue Mama trashing London harbor, looking for Baby Gorgo. Apparently Mam had one of those LoJack chips implanted in Baby Gorgo before the events of this film.

Everything goes pretty much as you'd expect from this point on: the British Navy throws everything at Mama Gorgo to no avail. She shows up in London and trashes some choice landmarks, etc. The only real surprise is the amount of time Joe spends running around the city streets with the Spunky Kid trying to get him to safety.

I would have been okay with *Gorgo* going as you'd expect if the creatures weren't so blah. I mean, Godzilla has loads of personality and King Kong has loads of pathos, but there's nothing to either Baby or Mama Gorgo outside of a guy in a latex suit.

And in these kind of movies, if you don't care about the characters (which I didn't) and you don't care about the monsters (which I didn't), then you just… don't care at all.

* *

KING GHIDORAH, THE THREE-HEADED MONSTER

Directed by Inoshiro Honda
1964, 85 minutes, Unrated
In which Godzilla learns the value of cooperation.

I can't help but feel bad for Ghidorah. Poor bastard.

Here we have a kaiju that has been set up to be the ultimate Big Bad, one who typically requires Godzilla to have some assistance in taking on. Since his first appearance in 1964's *Ghidorah, The Three-Headed Monster*, Godzilla has squared off against Ghidorah seven times… which means we've seen Godzilla kick Ghidorah's ass seven times.

It's to the point where I'm surprised anyone takes Ghidorah seriously – as soon as he appears on-screen, you know how things are going to end for him. They even started giving him the title of "King" Ghidorah in later films. Doesn't matter; he still gets spanked by Godzilla. Ghidorah's become the Washington Generals to Godzilla's Harlem Globetrotters.

Also: no arms? Really? I get that he's largely inspired by the kind of mythical dragons found in Asian lore, but all I keep thinking is that this is a creature that can be defeated by a doorknob.

Ghidorah doesn't even get that much respect in his own film. Sure, he's the title character and theoretical headliner of *Ghidorah, The Three-Headed Monster*, but the score and opening shots of an irate Godzilla make it very clear who is the star around here.

The obligatory human-centric story is a bit all over the place, but I'll try: First, there's a "shooting star" that scientists observe crashing in some nearby wilderness. Then we get a whole geopolitical thriller regarding the Himalayans, which are not mountains in this film but a sovereign nation run by people sporting those frilly accordion collars that were so popular in Shakespearean times. A Japanese intelligence officer is assigned to protect the Himalayan Princess during an incognito visit to Japan from assassination threats.

Unfortunately, the Japanese intelligence officer (I never caught his name, so let's go with "Jimmy") doesn't get a chance to have his Whitney Houston moment. During her flight to Japan, a shooting star hypnotizes the Princess and tells her to jump out of the plane, which she does seconds before the plane explodes. That's a talented meteor.

A day or so later, a crazy lady is addressing *hundreds* of onlookers, making predictions about The Future. It must be a slow news day, because the cute reporter gal from the opening (who just so happens to be Jimmy's kid sister) is sent to interview what must be the only crazy lady in all of Japan. Crazy Lady says she's from Mars but – gasp! – it's the Himalayan Princess!

The film takes a break from its regularly scheduled story for a TV variety show. Tonight's special guests are the Fairy Twins from Mothra Island. Cue the stock footage!

Jimmy realizes who Crazy Lady is, and while he and The Chief try to sort out what to do ("After all, it's no crime to practice demagoguery"), the bad Himalayans send some heavy hitters to go finish the job.

I know what you're thinking: Aren't there giant monsters in this movie? Where the hell are they?

Crazy Lady knows! She shows up to warn a bunch of scientists that the quasi-dormant volcano that's about to erupt is where Rodan is hiding. Everyone laughs at her – which is strange, in a country where giant monsters pop out of every other mountain – but sure enough...

There are more scenes featuring siblings squabbles and unintentionally hilarious '60s Japanese mobsters, and then finally – finally! – a Godzilla movie breaks out. Panic in the streets! Evacuations! Flaming harbors and slow-moving behemoths!

After an extensive amount of pyrotechnics, Ghidorah makes his first appearance. This is followed by more destruction, and then we get one of my favorite recurring moments in these kind of films: the National Broadcast System announcement that the space monster "has now been identified as Ghidorah." Okay, so *now* we can start evacuating!

Jimmy and his sister ask the Fairy Twins if Mothra can fight Ghidorah, but Mothra is currently in her larval stage. And that's when the Fairy Twins get the bright idea of having Mothra ask Godzilla and Rodan (currently duking it out by a backdrop of Mt. Fuji) to take on Ghidora with The Power of Cooperation.

Cooperation? Even Ghidorah thinks that's crap, and interrupts our heroes' pow-wow with some wholesale property damage.

Mothra shows up to the backdrop of Mt. Fuji and finds Godzilla kicking boulders at Rodan. Then Rodan starts headbutting the boulders back at Godzilla, who punches them back at Rodan... it's the strangest game of ping pong ever. And the strangeness is just beginning.

Mothra blasts Godzilla with some Silly String, which causes Rodan to *laugh at him*. Then Rodan gets the Silly String treatment, which settles him down. As Mothra crawls up a nearby hilltop, Godzilla and Rodan *sit down* so the three can have a chat.

Fortunately, the Fairy Twins spare us from a discussion consisting solely of roaring and pantomiming and insert their own commentary (the best being: "Oh, Godzilla! What horrible language!"). They reveal that Godzilla and Rodan agree on the general douchebaggery of mankind and don't really care if Ghidorah trashes the planet. The monsters also agree that they'd rather get back to fighting with each other, thank you very much.

Rejected, Mothra goes off to face Ghidorah alone. Fortunately, he's just a short crawl away.

Godzilla take exception to Ghidorah picking on little ol' Mothra and jumps in the fray. Rodan joins in as well, because what the hell else is he going to do? Before you know it, our monsters are winning the day with The Power of Cooperation. Oh, and the whole Himalayan assassination storyline is neatly resolved with a well-timed rockslide.

This movie is just damn weird, and it doesn't help that it's a too slow for kids and a too tame for adults. I know *Ghidorah, The Three-Headed Monster* is considered one of the better films in the series, and there's some great camp to it, but I think it's at best middle-of-the-road.

* * *

KING KONG ESCAPES
Directed by Ishiro Honda
1967, 96 minutes, Rated G
King Kong vs. Dr. Who

"So, Lone Star, now you see that evil will always triumph because good is dumb." Like many other things, Dark Helmet from *Spaceballs* had it wrong. Good isn't dumb, it's just dull. Evil, on the other hand, is inefficient at best and flat-out stupid at worst.

Consider: How many times have we seen a super-villain put the hero in an overly elaborate death trap and then talk his ear off about every detail of the scheme, allowing the hero to both escape *and* foil the plot? And how about those incredibly intricate and imaginative schemes? They're often foiled by some unpredicted bumbling by the comic relief, yet the entire scheme is scrapped afterwards – you never see the villain try again with an improved version.

Or how about the plot to *King Kong Escapes*: An unnamed country has tapped an evil genius to pull a massive amount of the highly radioactive "Element X" from a mining site, so the evil genus builds… A machine to excavate the area? A big crane? One of those cool exo-suits, like the one Ripley wore in *Aliens*?

No, a giant robot ape. Of course.

We get to see the giant robot ape in action almost from the get-go, as the evil genius sends it in to fetch the Element X. And why does this unnamed country want the Element X? To crank out a nuclear arsenal. Never mind that they've commissioned the construction of a *giant robot ape* that could do plenty of damage on its own. Unfortunately, the radioactivity shorts out the giant robot ape's circuits, so it's back to the drawing board.

But that's not the best part. The best part is that the evil genius's name is Dr. Who.

Enough about the baddies, let's meet our heroes: They are a couple of United Nations Research Council submarine commander-types – one American and one Japanese – who happens to be amateur Kong enthusiasts. When damage to their sub forces them to doc at Mongo Island for repairs, our commanders and the Cute Nurse take the sub's land speeder (somehow pre-dating the original *Star Wars*) into the jungle for some sightseeing.

And they get some sights indeed! Not only do they get to see (the Japanese) King Kong, they see him take on a pair of Godzilla D-listers (Gorosaurus and Manda), but the Cute Nurse gets herself a 60-foot tall admirer. Which, for Kong, is par for the course. He does have a thing for blondes…

The Japanese Kong is exactly as you'd expect: Cheap ape suit (you can see the seams and the flap covering the zipper), papier-mâché face, and bongo pectorals. It's delightfully cheap.

Once the commanders announce to the UN that they've discovered King Kong alive and well, Dr. Who has another brilliantly inefficient idea: Instead of simply fixing the giant robot ape he's created, he'll instead capture King Kong (like that'll be easy) and bring him back to the base to *hypnotize* him into doing his bidding. Yes, a much simpler plan… Naturally, Dr. Who is shocked – SHOCKED! – when Kong rejects the hypnotism after five minutes of digging in radioactivity.

When the commanders and their Cute Nurse return to Mondo Island and discover that Kong has been kidnapped, the American Commander immediately knows who did it. Sadly, that doesn't stop them from being kidnapped by Dr. Who just a few scenes later.

After some attempts at seduction, torture and chess, Kong and our trio escape and make their way to Tokyo. Our heroes manage to talk down the military (though I somehow doubt that "I'm with the UN!" would fly in the real world) as Dr. Who pursues Kong with his now re-functional Mecha-Kong.

Yes, it takes until the last 15 minutes of the film to see these two face off. At least it's an inspired battle as the two fight from on top of Tokyo Tower (sanity check: Kong and Mecha-Kong are both about 60 feet tall while Tokyo Tower stands over 1,000 feet tall). That's a big step up from the usual mysteriously flat and barren countryside where so many giant monster battles take place.

Between the battle up Tokyo Tower and the top-shelf camp of Dr. Who, King Kong Escapes turns out to be a delightfully bad film.

* * *

GAMERA VS. GUIRON
Directed by Noriaki Yuasa
1969, 80 minutes, Unrated
Come along and ride on my fantastic (intergalactic) voyage.

Gamera vs. Guiron was one of those movie's I'd often catch as a kid on the local channel Saturday afternoons. Gamera was the Daiei Films knock-off response to the King of All Monsters. The studio made eight Gamera films during my formative years, but somehow the only entry I ever saw was *Gamera vs. Guiron*. And while Gamera was no Godzilla, I was always happy to watch.

The film opens with lots of talk about the billeyons and billeyons of stars there are in the universe, and how all the astronomers are busy cataloging sound waves *from outer space.*

Man, you gotta love an era where droves of reporters show up to hear scientists give an elementary lesson on the planets in our solar system.

One night, young buds Akio and Tom just happen to see a flying saucer land in a nearby rock quarry. The next morning, the two and Akio's kid sister pedal off to investigate. When Li'l Sis balks at boarding the UFO, Akio berates her: "Scaredy cat. The spacemen won't hurt you. They flew here -- they're civilized. You're dumb." No debating that logic.

Akio and Tom start playing around in the UFO and are shocked when the ship takes off. Li'l Sis has no recourse but to shout, "Akio! You get out of there, or you'll get a good scolding!"

The UFO flies into space and towards a speeding meteor. Just when it's looking really bad for our lads... Gamera appears! Huzzah! And yes, this is exactly the kind of movie where the kids can talk to a giant monster from within a space ship in outer space without the use of a PA system and the monster understands perfectly.

That danger out of the way, they race. Watching the speeding Gamera, the kids have this conversation:

"He's really speeding up. Mach 3, I think."

"No, it's kinda deceptive out there. See Gamera's great jets? Mach 33 is what I would say."

"Really? I didn't realize."

The UFO lands on a miniature model of an alien planet, and after the customary discoveries of how the air and climate is so similar to Earth, we get our first monster fight. Flat-headed giant bat Gaos chirps a bunch, calling Guiron out of his secret underwater lair. It should be noted that Guiron is essentially a four-legged Ginsu knife.

The lads eventually meet up with a couple of sexy alien ladies who, believe it or not, aren't quite what they seem. When they ask the boys about Gamera, we get the equivalent of a clip show.

Gamera hasn't forgotten about the boys, and eventually shows up on Planet Papier Mâché. Unfortunately, Gamera is much more the Rocky Balboa type than Godzilla. Guiron emerges from his secret underwater lair to greet Gamera with a beat-down. It's a surprisingly bloody sequence, with Gamera spurting green pea soup early and often. Also, it turns out that Guiron can shoot throwing stars out of his nose, which just seems a bit superfluous to me.

Gamera comes back with a vengeance in their rematch, which includes some snazzy gymnastics work. Yes, really.

The exciting conclusion takes some major liberties with coherence, such as allowing Gamera to use his fire breath to weld the UFO back together. And when Li'l Sis is proven right about the whereabouts of the lads, we get this reassuring exchange:

`"We should have believed her."`

`"There are times, I guess, when our children are telling the truth, aren't there?"`

I guess we all learned an important lesson from *Gamera vs. Guiron*. I certainly learned that sometimes the knock-offs are just as good – or even better – than the big name brands.

* * * *

GODZILLA VS. MEGALON

Directed by Jun Fukuda
1973, 78 minutes, Unrated
Robots are magic!

It's strange. For a character that started off as a very grim avatar of nuclear holocaust, Godzilla somehow morphed into an incredibly kid-friendly by the 1970s. That kid-friendly Godzilla is in full effect in *Godzilla vs. Megalon*, which plays like one of the most dashed together films of the series.

Early on, we join an inventor on a lakeside picnic with his short-shorts wearin' son and racecar driving, uh, good friend? Suddenly, earthquake! The short-shorts wearin' son and his comically oversized paddleboat (a dolphin with dolphin-shaped paddles) are in danger, but fortunately, the inventor packed a rocket with 50 feet of uncoiled rope. The lad is saved, but the lake is completely sucked into the Earth's crust, never to be mentioned again.

Whatever! We learn the inventor has been working on a robot with a permasmile named Jet Jaguar. It is apparently a multi-talented robot, as we eventually learn that Jet Jaguar can:

- Fly
- Get out of people's way with its "avoidance system"
- Obey verbal commands through a transistor (except when it doesn't want to)
- Communicate with monsters
- "Program himself for survival"
- "Program himself in some way to increase his size"
- Get dizzy

With such an array of functions, it's no wonder that the great undersea nation of Seatopia wants to steal Jet Jaguar. This leads to a car chase between Seatopian agents and our racecar drivin' good buddy. I'm not sure that this is the most incompetently shot car chase, but it's definitely in the top five.

In case you're wondering, Seatopia is an Atlantis-like civilization that has existed under water near Easter Island for thousands of years. Unfortunately, the increasing amount of pollution in earth's oceans have forced Seatopia's toga-clad emperor to declare war and unleash Megalon! Our headliner is just like the Kraken, except it kinda looks like a giant cockroach with (as *Mystery Science Theater 3000*'s Crow observes) Chrysler Building arms.

That may be just as well, because during the obligatory army versus monster sequence, Japan's armed forces actually manage to drive Megalon out of the immediate vicinity. A short bit later, a now enlarged Jet Jaguar pretty much beats the tar out of Megalon — Godzilla wouldn't even be needed if Gigan didn't show up.

It takes about 20 minutes of screen time, but the King of All Monsters does finally show up for an epic tornado tag match. The battle in *Godzilla vs. Megalon* is much longer than in most Godzilla movies (perhaps to make up for the opening hour of incoherence) and it goes heavy on the pyrotechnics, but it's all very kid-friendly.

And so: the bad monsters run away, Godzilla declares it Miller Time, and the inventor announces that he'll "warn the scientists" about the danger they pose to Seatopia. The music tells us that'll work out just fine, just like it would in real life.

Yes, *Godzilla vs. Megalon* is a very silly movie... even for a Godzilla movie.

* * * *

GODZILLA VS. MECHAGODZILLA
Directed by Jun Fukuda
1974, 84 minutes, Rated PG
Identity crisis

By the 20th anniversary of Godzilla, the series had gotten a little... well, the previous outing, *Godzilla vs. Megalon*, featured a size-changing robot and a flying dropkick by Godzilla. That's pretty far astray from the sense of dread and Hiroshima imagery of *Gojira*.

So for the 20th anniversary, Toho wanted to put in some extra time and effort and money, and it shows in 1974's *Godzilla vs. Mechagodzilla*. After we get through the initial 15 minutes of incoherence, that is. Maybe it's just my version of the film, but those first 15 minutes play like it was edited in a blender: Ominous lightning storm! Happy bright opening credits! Pious traditional ceremony! Dire premonition! And a heap of characters thrown at us with no explanation of who they are or what they do! Seriously, it wasn't until the third act that I realized two of the protagonists were brothers, and don't bother asking me anyone's name.

But that's all good. You have to love the Godzilla universe. It's a place where "famous scientists" are immediately recognizable, a place where things like prophecies and "space titanium" are taken very seriously, a place where people are routinely robbed of a statue at gunpoint. It's a place where INTERPOL has intergalactic jurisdiction.

We only have to wait 17 minutes for Godzilla's first appearance, but when he shows up, he's a little... squeaky. Anguirus – who often plays the Boy Wonder to Godzilla's Dark Knight – pops up and the two fight. Though by "fight,"

I mean Godzilla beats Anguirus like a dirty rug. He even pulls a King Kong-style jawbreaker move, unusually nasty and gory for a Showa era (1954 - 1975) Godzilla movie.

Our (human) heroes are confused, as they thought Godzilla and Anguirus were friends. That's right: Big monster battle erupts in front of them, and they're not alarmed or freaked out but *confused*. Confusing to me was when our heroes discover a brick spray-painted silver at the site of the battle and declare that it too is "space titanium."

Later, during a late-night stomping of an industrial complex, Godzilla is surprised when a *second* Godzilla comes popping out of a factory like a damn jack-in-the-box. Godzilla #2 blows a chunk of skin off of Godzilla #1, revealing Godzilla #1 to be made of Terminator. Our famed scientist immediately deduces that Godzilla #1 is a cyborg, adding "You could call it a Mechagodzilla." Yes, let's do that.

The professor also deduces that Mechagodzilla must be remotely controlled by space aliens, which also turns out to be absolutely correct (we know they're evil space aliens by their metallic clothing and the way they sneer). Hey, the professor isn't a world-famous scientist for nothing.

In fact, the professor is so world-famous, the aliens kidnap him and a few others, tell the professor all about how they plan to conquer Earth with the now-broken Mechagodzilla, and force the professor to make the repairs. Meanwhile, Godzilla is getting repaired, too, by being struck repeatedly with lightning. Because that's something he can do now, I guess.

While all this is going on, there's a surprisingly engaging subplot where our some of our heroes are smuggling a rare statue back to Okinawa on a Carnival Cruise. An alien makes another attempt to steal the statue, and there's a big patio chair fight before an INTERPOL agent shows up and we learn that the aliens actually look like green apes.

The statue is key to waking up King Caesar, ostensibly Godzilla's ally in the final fight. I fully understand that King Caesar is based on the Shisa, but in reality he looks like an angry kabuki rabbit. But it turns out the statue only unearths King Caesar – to actually wake him, the girl from the opening who had the premonition must sing a song to King Caesar, Mothra-style. And she sings the whole song.

Sadly, King Caesar's contribution to the fight only lasts about half the length of the song. King Caesar is fast – very fast, by kaiju standards – and he has this neat ability to absorb and redirect lasers shot at him, which he only uses two or three times. After that, Mechagodzilla beats him like a rented mule.

Fortunately for King Caesar, Godzilla comes wading in, just like he always does. We get some more strangely graphic arterial spray before Godzilla unveils his Neat Trick For This Movie Only: the ability to make himself a giant magnet.

While it's certainly not as silly as *Godzilla vs. Megalon*, *Godzilla vs. Mechagodzilla* is definitely one of the stronger films in the Showa era. There's a nice balance between the somber and the absurd, the film moves along at a steady pace, and the human actions actually feel connected to the monster action. If it weren't for the jarring bits of gore, I'd say *Godzilla vs. Mechagodzilla* was a prime example of classic Godzilla.

* * * *

A*P*E

Directed by Paul Leder
1976, 81 minutes, Rated PG
"Let's see him dance for his organ grinder now!"

Right around the time the '70s was giving the world its first remake of the 1933 classic *King Kong*, Korea was churning out its own version. *A*P*E* has earned itself a spot in the Pantheon of Very Bad Movies, even making the cover of *The Official Razzie Movie Guide*. Reviewing it was just a matter of time.

The film opens on aboard a toy boat (yes, really), where two sailors share a smoke and talk about their cargo. They dance around the actual contents of their cargo, calling it "big boy" and whatnot. One sailor – who talks exactly like Squidward from *Spongebob SquarePants* – asks the mate if he was there when they caught him… so, we're doing a rip-off of *King Kong*, and skipping the 80% of the film that takes place on Skull Island? Swell.

Sailor Squidward hopes that their 36-foot passenger says asleep until they reach their destination, and the First Mate assures him that they used enough gas to keep their mystery guest asleep for "oh, another five days or so." On cue, a giant papier-mâché hand busts out of the hull.

"Oh shit," Sailor Squidward drones. Oh shit, indeed, as the entire toy boat blows up. Out of the water comes a very wet guy in a non-blown up ape suit, who immediately starts wrestling with a rubber shark. And by "wrestling" I mean "flailing around."

Yes, this film is very special.

Our Guy in an Ape Suit (GAS) then ape-walks on shore and starts trashing everything in sight. Also, he appears to have tripled in size. GAS starts throwing oil cans, which explode like grenades on contact. Just like in real life!

We leave that excitement for the next morning, when a famous actress (Joanna Kerns, Mrs. Seaver from TV's *Growing Pains*, in her first movie role) arrives in Korea and meets up with her reporter boyfriend, Mr. Rose. He badly wants to spend some time with Mrs. Seaver, but is pulled away to investigate reports of footprints "five or six feet across." I guess the trashed shoreline didn't warrant anyone's attention.

The film quickly falls into a routine: One scene of Mr. Rose/Mrs. Seaver, one scene of GAS trashing miniature sets and then one scene of an obnoxious, racist army colonel shouting into a phone. Those scenes with the colonel are strangely amusing at first. But after a half dozen or so scenes of a single, continuous shot of an army guy shouting into a phone, it gets real old.

No, the real action is with GAS. He scares off a bunch of unsupervised schoolkids in an abandoned amusement park. He interrupts the filming of a martial arts film, and the stuntmen respond by firing flaming arrows at him. Every now and then, we see a handful of people run across a field as towns are evacuated.

Yeah, the film is like that. There's one scene where I think I saw GAS's undershirt, and another where I swear the GAS is wearing sneakers.

So the GAS is taking a break from his death and destruction to sit (legs crossed!) and chew on a tree, watching Mrs. Seaver's film shoot. By the way, every scene we see of this film involves her being chased or about to be raped. I have the unsettling feeling that this was meant to be funny, but it's so poorly acted that it can't be taken too seriously. The GAS objects, and scoops up Mrs. Seaver. After an eternity of dubbed screaming, she quickly shifts gears and purrs, "Be gentle, big fella." Um, okay.

Mr. Rose and his Korean Police Captain buddy pursue and exchange stilted dialogue. In the film's most memorable scene, the two arrange a daring rescue where Mr. Rose runs in to retrieve Mrs. Seaver while the GAS is being attacked by helicopters. It works. Then, when the GAS takes out the last of the helicopters, he flips the audience the bird.

The GAS finally makes his way to Seoul and spends an insufferable amount of time smashing miniature sets. The army responds with lots of stock footage of vehicles zipping around. The GAS responds by throwing objects toward the camera, and yes, the strings are quite visible.

Colonel Shouts-a-Lot, who finally has authorization to take out the big ape, does so. "Let's see him dance for his organ grinder now!" the colonel shouts inappropriately. Everyone else feels bad as the GAS dies. Why? He was on a non-stop rampage of indiscriminate killing since stepping foot in the country. The whole humanity of Kong thing was apparently lost on the filmmakers.

Then again, general competence was lost on these filmmakers. I was expecting a lot out of the notorious *A*P*E*, which is probably why I was somewhat disappointed by it. The film is definitely worth seeing once – there are some great moments of cheese here – but it's all pretty tired by the end.

* *

THE MIGHTY PEKING MAN
Directed by Meng Hau Ho
1977, 90 minutes, Rated PG-13
I don't give a damn about your bad reputation.

Is there a more formulaic subgenre than the giant ape movie? It's as if ever since *King Kong* hit the theaters in 19-flippin-33, the only giant ape film to offer anything resembling an original story is *Mighty Joe Young* – and that's essentially an episode of *Clifford the Big Red Dog*.

Seriously. All I have to tell you is that *The Mighty Peking Man* is a giant ape movie, and you already know the following:

- Our main protagonist will be some kind of adventurer/explorer
- The ape will carry around a hot blonde
- The jungle will be filled with stock footage
- The ape will be dragged out of the jungle and shipped to a major city where it can be exploited by greedy corporate interests
- Said major city will be trashed when the ape runs amok
- The ape will fall off of a very tall landmark

All of that happens in *The Mighty Peking Man*, no surprises there. No, the surprises are in the details.

The Mighty Peking Man opens hot, with our title giant popping out of a Himalayan mountain like a hairy, rubber-masked stripper jumping out of a misshapen cake. The local natives think it's a swell idea to attack our Mighty Peking Man (MPM) with spears and catapults. It's not.

In Hong Kong, a Businessman reads about the incident in a newspaper on file at the library, and that's enough for him to send an exhibition in to catch the Peking Man. One of the yes-men recommends his buddy Johnny, a professional explorer. The yes-man reasons that since Johnny has just broken up with his actress girlfriend because she cheated on him with a TV producer, he'd be eager to march off into certain doom. I think we've all been there.

Soon Johnny, the Businessman, his yes-men and a platoon of expendable locals are marching into the stock footage jungle. There, they encounter stampeding elephants (where our heroes bravely stand aside and shoot at the endangered species) and a tiger that inspires a half dozen locals to jump into some nearby quicksand.

Eventually, enough expendable locals die for the Businessman to call it quits, which he does by having everyone ditch Johnny in the middle of the night. Johnny wakes up the next morning all alone... except for the giant ape! Johnny runs and runs and falls off things, but is suddenly rescued by Sheena, Queen of the Jungle.

Okay, it's not really "Sheena," but it might as well be. We learn via flashback that the aggressively Caucasian jungle girl was the sole survivor of a plane crash and was raised and nurtured by MPM. We also learn that MPM will pretty much do anything Sheena tells him to.

That's right: The Mighty Peking Man is voice-controlled.

The film downshifts for a bit to allow Johnny and Sheena fall in love. She nurses him back to health, he tends to her poisonous snake bite by sucking the venom out of the inside of her thigh. The run around the jungle and admire the stock footage. There's a lot of implied humping. It's essentially *The Blue Lagoon*, but set to a Musak version of Van McCoy & the Soul City Symphony's "The Hustle."

Yes, life is good for Johnny. Freed of the worries and heartbreak of modern life, it's just him and his sexy jungle girl and their pet behemoth, running around and eating mangos or whatever and having sexy jungle sex. So naturally, as soon as the montage is over, Johnny suggests that Sheena and MPM go back to civilization with him. A giant ape and a feral hottie in Hong Kong – what could go wrong?

Well, this:

- All the jungle animals cry, because Sheena is like a Disney Princess or something
- MPM is practically mummified in chains and taunted by the Businessman's sailors
- Johnny gives Sheena a "modern dress" that appears to be from Fredericks of Hollywood
- The Businessman forces the barge towing MPM through the heart of a typhoon
- MPM is put on display in a stadium where Hong Kongians can throw vegetables at him, and after the show handlers poke him with bamboo poles because… they're jerks?
- Sheena walks in on Johnny reconciling with his actress ex-girlfriend, because if there's anything people come to giant ape movies for, it's the love triangles

The final insult comes when the Businessman forces himself on Sheena (yes, he's a Bad Businessman) right by the big picture window so MPM can see. Predictably, MPM goes ape.

I have to say, I kinda dug this twist on the typical giant ape formula: Traditionally, everyone is trying to rescue the girl from the giant ape. Here, the giant ape is trying to rescue the girl.

So now the giant ape is rampaging like… well, that classic video game, Rampage, and it's time to bring in my favorite character in the film, The White Guy in Charge. TWGiC is having nothing of this rampaging business, and he's going to take down MPM – even if it means leveling Hong Kong in the process. After issuing "a personal order" for everyone to "get in position" and "stand by for attack," he gives his rousing speech:

```
"All units, you are to concentrate your
fire. And also intensify it. Anything to kill
```

Peking Man. Anything to kill Peking Man. Kill
the Peking Man by any means you can. Kill the
Peking Man by any means. That's an order!"

And here is TWGiC, problem-solver:

"I have an idea. I want you to fill the
water reservoirs on the roof with gasoline
and explosives. Use a timing device to
detonate it, okay?

"We could blow up--

"I don't give a damn about the [world-
famous] building. He's cornered now and easy
to kill. Get going! Carry out my orders!"

Clearly *The Mighty Peking Man* is a silly film – often
unintentionally so – but it's hardly as bad as its reputation. Yes,
this film was made on the cheap, so there's a lot of fun to be
had with the shoddiness of the ape suit, but the story tweaks
the formula just enough to make things interesting. *The Mighty
Peking Man* may have a mighty bad reputation, but I think it's
mighty okay.

* * *

GODZILLA AND MOTHRA
Directed by Takao Okawara
1991, 102 minutes, Unrated
a.k.a. Godzilla and the Caterpillars of Doom

There are only so many ways a Godzilla movie begins:
either with the sinking of a fishing boat or with a mysterious

meteor. This one goes with Option B as a meteor "approximately 96.25 meters in diameter" (which is big enough to wipe off all life on the planet, by the way) crashes into the Sea of Japan. The meteor not only wakes up Godzilla from his underwater slumber, but causes a typhoon that unearths... a giant egg! The Horns of Ominous Vibes tells us that eggs are *bad*.

We interrupt this Godzilla film for a Japanese knock-off of *Raiders of the Lost Ark*. There are so many similarities, it's like a ready-made drinking game. In the ancient jungle ruins of a temple, Japan's Indiana Jones (JIJ) carefully swipes a statue off its pedestal (drink!), causing the entire place to collapse (drink!). JIJ runs and leaps and tumbles into the next chamber, and into another booby trap (drink!). When JIJ finally crawls out of the temple, he finds numerous weapons in his face (drink!). Wouldn't you know it, Japan takes grave-robbing very seriously.

A Big Corporation, at the recommendation of JIJ's archeologist ex-wife, offers to bail JIJ out of the can if he'll help them obtain the giant egg from the opening of the film. Before you know it, JIJ, Mrs. JIJ and Big Corp's Suit Stooge are off to Infant Island. Amazingly, the filmmakers refrained from showing them travel across a world map via red dotted line.

The Suit Stooge is something to behold: He tromps through the jungle in his business suit and tie, despite having packed for the trip – it's not like this was a spur-of-the-moment excursion. Suit Stooge later mentions that he trained to be a ranger. Seriously? Like a park ranger? A Power Ranger? A Texas Ranger?

After pausing for a ham-fisted environmental message, our trio crosses a ravine via a rickety rope bridge that breaks halfway across (drink!) and enters an ancient vault where a beam of sunlight points out where they need to go (drink!).

And presto! They find the giant egg and the world-famous Tiny Mothra Fairy Twins.

The Fairy Twins aren't just there because of contractual obligations – they're dropping a big ol' exposition bomb. Their spiel inspires the Suit Stooge to let loose this nugget: "My company has killed many forests… I feel very guilty." But the big take-away is the existence of Battra, who can best be described as Evil Mothra. Sadly, Battra isn't just a Mothra puppet with a Van Dyke.

Our trio boat back to Japan with the twins and the giant egg in (literal) tow when Godzilla pops up hungry for a little soft-boiled goodness. Larva Mothra hatches just in time, and bites Godzilla on the tail tip for his efforts. Larva Battra shows up to get in on the action, and makes the mistake of blasting Godzilla in the process. Godzilla and Larva Battra go at it underwater and both eventually fall into an underwater volcano, as one is wont to do. The end.

Oh wait, no. There's still plenty more, with the Suit Stooge stealing the twins for Big Corp and a side order of divorce drama. Don't worry: There are still obligatory scenes featuring the rollout of ineffective tanks, of monsters plowing through model buildings and a musical number or two by the tiny twins.

It all builds to a triple threat match in an excellent model of Yokohama. And I'm giddy to report that the climax includes a moment where two of the monsters "talk" to each other – nearly a minute of eeking and growling while everyone looks on.

I love this movie. There are definitely campier and wilder Godzilla films, but few are as solid and well-made from top to bottom than this one. *Godzilla vs. Mothra* is an excellent starting point for Godzilla newbies, particularly for those wary of the campier '70s fare.

* * * *

GODZILLA VS. DESTROYAH

Directed by Takao Okawara
1995, 100 minutes, Unrated
The King is dead! Long live the King!

With 30 films under its belt, the Godzilla franchise has functioned mostly like the James Bond franchise. Both franchises ran through different "eras" with different mentalities. And both franchises generally release stand-alone entries, with the exception – like the Daniel Craig-era Bond movies – being the more serious and sci-fi minded Heisei-era Godzilla films of the 1990s. Each of those films tie directly into the previous entry with recurring characters and organizations.

By 1995, with the 40th anniversary of the original *Godzilla* and an American version on the horizon, Toho took the opportunity to wrap up the Heisei series and give the audience something they'd never seen before: the death of Godzilla. Yeah, that got Toho a lot of ink.

Godzilla vs. Destroyah opens with a quiet evening on Hong Kong getting upended by Godzilla. There's something immediately off about Godzilla – he's covered in pulsing red splotches, as if he'd been splattered with lava, and steaming. The effect seems to have amped up Godzilla. Even his nuclear breath seems powered up.

At a loss to figure out what's up with the Big G, the Japan Self Defense Forces hire college student Kenichi – the grandson of the scientist who created the Oxygen Destroyer to defeat Godzilla in 1955. Kenichi's theory (which, like everything Kenichi theorizes, is immediately accepted as fact by both JSDF and the film) is that Godzilla's heart is essentially a nuclear reactor and that he's experiencing a meltdown. As a couple of CGI simulations demonstrate, something the size of Godzilla having a nuclear meltdown is considered "bad."

Kenichi further theorizes that Godzilla's meltdown might be negated by an Oxygen Destroyer – the very thing his grandfather committed suicide over in the 1955 original to keep from being used as a weapon. Cue the staring off in the distance while hand-wringing over scientific achievement vs. moral obligation.

Now it just so happens that some other scientist guy has just invented "micro-oxygen," which is essentially an Oxygen Destroyer with a different name. Also, fallout from the O-G Oxy-D has created mutant lifeforms that have just made a big evolutionary step. Also also, humanity has just put the finishing touches on its latest mostly ineffective weapon against the kaiju, a beefed up jumbo jet called the Super-X III. Also also also, the psychic who has appeared in all of the Heisei-era films has discovered that some island has disappeared, and that's super-important for some reason.

Are you getting the sense that *Godzilla vs. Destroyah* is all over the place? Because the first half is all over the place.

Let's double back to those evolving mutant lifeforms, as they ultimately become one of the title characters… We get a pretty odd sequence that's kind of like *Starship Troopers* set in the Nakatomi Plaza from *Die Hard*. The creatures come wheeling out – because they're clearly on wheels – and someone tries to convince us that these bug-like things are "lizard-like." Did I mention that they're on f'n *wheels*? It's startling, like something out of a cheap '60s b-movie, and it doesn't at all fit in with the production values of the Heisei-era series. The end result is an amazing bit of unintentional comedy.

We then discover that these creatures have extendable mandibles straight out of *Alien*, but that still doesn't prevent the audience from thinking about all the production assistants just out of view pushing the thing around *on its wheels*. Somehow, all the not-lizardlike bugs combine to form what is either a bad-ass demon or a big pile of angry mushrooms.

Anyway, realizing that Destroyah is made up of Oxygen Destroyer… stuff (hence its name), the government comes up with a wacky plan to prevent Godzilla from melting down and destroying the planet: Let them fight.

"But how will we get Godzilla to fight Destroyah?" asks a character who apparently had been enjoying his very first day in Japan. Not convinced that Godzilla's general disposition would be enough to start the fight, they have the psychic call for Godzilla Jr. to use him as a decoy. And before you get all bent out of shape, relax: Yeah, no cutesy crap here. This isn't "Baby Godzilla," more like "Junior Varsity Godzilla."

From this point, it's "General, evacuate everyone within a 200-mile radius of Tokyo!" (and that's how many *millions* of people?), and we're off to the races.

I'm going to spoil the crap out of this movie. If you want none of that, hop on down to the end of the review. I put an extra line space in there so you can find it easily, cuz I'm helpful like that.

Still with me? Okay, you've been warned.

Despite being only half as big, Junior holds his own against Destroyah and even scores a TKO. Our lava'd Godzilla shows up just in time to see Destroyah jump back up and, sore over their last match, full-on kill Junior. You can imagine how well that goes over.

The title bout has some fantastic creature action, which is even more impressive given the bulkiness of Destroyah's design (and it's not like Godzilla is known for his nimbleness). In the end, Godzilla takes care of business because even though *his g-d innards are melting*, he's still the best there is at what he does.

And then, meltdown. Opera music kicks in as Godzilla literally melts before our eyes, and it's pretty damn tough to watch. But then, rather than destroying the planet or leaving Japan uninhabitable for centuries to come, all of the radioactivity disappears. Through the smoke, a freshly resurrected Godzilla Jr. – now all grown up – roars. The king is dead, long live the king.

Thus end the spoilers.

Godzilla vs. Destroyah is a tale of two films. The first half is a scattered mess, and so slavishly devoted to not just the continuity of the Heisei-era films but the minutia of the original 1955 film. Hell, you know how big a fan I am and I couldn't follow it all. But the second half gets it together and provides a climax and finish worthy of sending off one of the most iconic characters in movie history.

I toyed with giving this a split rating, but I think it makes more sense to call this one right down the middle.

* * *

ZARKORR! THE INVADER
Directed by Michael Deak and Aaron Osborne
1996, 80 minutes, Rated PG
As seen on TV!

As I've said again and again, I'm a sucker for giant monster movies. You'd think the sight of a rubber lizard suit smashing models of cities might get old after 40 years, but you'd think wrong.

Like this review, *Zarkorr! The Invader* gets right down to business: "Avalanche!" a local yokel drawls as a cliff collapses on the model of a small mining town. Out of the mountain comes Zarkorr!, and for what it's worth, they did a pretty good job with the monster. Zarkorr! looks pretty cool and not like an obvious knock-off. Zarkorr! makes short work of the two buildings in the town and then admires his work.

Eighty minutes later in Newark (or at least a soon-to-be model of a city, filling in for Newark), a postal worker named Tommy is visited by a teeny-tiny lady in go-go boots. She says that she's being piped directly into Tommy's brain or whatever, like a wee little Dean Stockwell (oh boy).

Anyway, Little Lady Go-Go is there to drop an exposition bomb: Tommy has been chosen by an intergalactic counsel to defend the earth from Zarkorr! Not knowing what the hell she's talking about, Tommy watches a good 10 minutes of "newscasts" featuring the worst acting I've seen in quite some time.

Why Tommy? Because he's the most average man on the planet. I kinda dug that.

Little Lady Go-Go mentions that no earth weapon can defeat Zarkorr!, but the means to defeat the monster are available to Tommy. Also, Zarkorr! is honed in on Tommy and making a bee-line for him. Go-Go, out!

Okay, so this is different. What would you do if you and you alone had to defend the Earth from a giant indestructible monster?

Well, if you're Tommy, you head down to the local news station and tries to enlist the help of the hottie crypto-zoologist that was on TV. Of course, Tommy sounds eight kinds of crazy, and the whole thing becomes a hostage situation. Unfortunately, the audience is taken hostage, too, cuz this little drama takes up an absurd amount of the movie.

It's totally stupid and kills any momentum the film had. Worse, the entire incident consists of various people yelling at each other, and I swear, it's like none of the characters have ever been in an argument before. The low point comes when the cops show up to evacuate the station and the news director fights them on it because the giant monster is such a huge story... overlooking the fact that a hostage situation at a news station is also a huge story.

Also, everyone assumes that Tommy has "gone postal" because he's a postal worker. These are the jokes, people.

Every so often, the hostage melodrama is broken up with quick scenes of Zarkorr! shooting lame eye beams at factories. That's nice.

Finally our long hostage nightmare ends, and Tommy, the hottie crypto-zoologist and their new cop friend head off to figure out what to do. And that's when we meet the Most Annoying Character in the movie, a "wacky" computer genius who is like every eccentric genius cliché wrapped up into one character. He's like cliché concentrate. I can't remember the last time I wanted to dropkick a fictional character so badly.

Once our heroes have a semblance of a plan in place, the film charges on through to its predictable conclusion. It all ends with the kind of final scene that makes it perfectly obvious that the filmmakers didn't know how to end the movie. The incredibly lame theme song playing over end credits almost makes it all worth it.

Almost.

* *

GODZILLA: FINAL WARS

Directed by Ryuhai Kitamura
2004, 125 minutes, PG-13
"This Godzilla guy is one tough dude."

For a franchise that's been running for over 60 years, there's been very little fan service in Godzilla movies. Even James Bond movies – the only other film franchise I can think of that has an equitable lifespan – make a point to throw in a souped-up sports car and "shaken, not stirred" into every film.

That's not the case with *Godzilla: Final Wars*, released on the 50th anniversary of Godzilla's debut. It's almost all fan service. They threw everything into this movie... including something none of the previous 27 movies had been able to do.

We open in the South Pole, where the crew of the *Star Blazers*-style *Gotengo* is doing battle with Godzilla. Things are looking bad for the crew of the *Gotengo* when an earthquake hits, opening up the ground underneath Godzilla. That gives the *Gotengo* a chance to bury Godzilla with few well-placed missiles and... it works?! Humanity has not only defeated Godzilla, but has done it before the title sequence?

Much of the film is spent following Ozaki, a mutant soldier with the power of *The Matrix*-style gun-fu and anime hair to match. He's been assigned to protect a sexy biologist with the U.N. (as if there's any other kind) as she investigates a tapestry of golden oldie Godzilla plots: a hibernating monster, the Tiny Fairy Twins and ultimately an alien invasion. Oh sure, the "Xiliens" claim to come in peace, but come on. Soon the Xiliens have unleashed a heap of monsters all over the planet – not just Tokyo but New York City, Paris, Sydney and Shanghai.

With the world in shambles, renegade Captain Gordon (mixed martial artist Don Frye) comes up with a wicked plan:

1) Boost the recently repaired *Gotango*
2) Hightail it to the South Pole and wake up Godzilla
3) Use the *Gotango* as bait to lure Godzilla into fights with the Xilien forces

If this sounds like one of the nuttiest ploys ever hatched, that's because it is – and the film is better for it. Godzilla pummels and blasts his way through nearly 15 other monsters, providing for some of the most memorable showdowns in the franchise's history. Even the brief scuffles, such as when Godzilla quickly dispatches a CGI creature that looks suspiciously like the 1998 Godzilla, are fun.

This nutty ploy is also the thing I alluded to that had never been done in the prior 27 Godzilla movies: it makes the humans an essential part of the plot. Sure, other Godzilla films had the human protagonists occasionally offer up some small way to aide Godzilla, but for the most part they're just spectators once the monster action starts. Not here. The actions of Ozaki, Sexy U.N. Lady and Captain Gordon actually *matter* – they intentionally lead Godzilla into battle and personally take on the head Xiliens in yet more sequences derived from *The Matrix*.

Seriously, this film is so steeped in *Matrix*-ness that I'm a bit stunned there isn't a slo-mo bullet time shot.

Still, if you're going to crib an action movie, you could do worse than cribbing *The Matrix*. Sure, there are still bouts of nonsensical silliness – this is a Godzilla movie – and the filmmakers still find time for our heroes to spout quasi-meaningful insights while staring off into the distance, but *Godzilla: Final Wars* is a very worthy celebration of venerable monster. In what was meant to be franchise's swan song (again), Toho has saved the best for last… at least until Toho decides to start it up again.

* * * * *

BIG MAN JAPAN
Directed by Hitoshi Matsumoto
2007, 113 minutes, Rated PG-13
Not "Big" Enough

My love of giant monster movies is well-documented. And in case you missed said documentation: I love giant monster movies. They help me make sense of the world, for there is no problem so big that can't be stomped out by a humongous radioactive lizard. Which is why I was so very excited to watch *Big Man Japan*, a mockumentary about a Japanese man whose day job is to grow many stories tall and fight off giant monsters. Do you have any idea how rare it is to be excited to watch the kind of movies I review here? It's Bigfoot-sighting rare.

You can imagine my disappointment at how mind-numbingly dull this movie is.

The film follows Daisato, a member of the Department of Monster Prevention. That may sound cool, but Daisato doesn't get to saunter around the halls of a dramatically lit office with a team of smartly dressed colleagues, like on every procedural drama on CBS. No, this sad sack wanders around the neighborhood, eating alone in ramen shops, moping on park benches and browsing for umbrellas. Daisato's wife and daughter have left him, he has no friends other than a stray cat and lives in a run-down little house that habitually has bricks thrown through the windows because everyone hates him. Sadly, that last bit is nowhere near as wacky as it sounds.

The filmmaker asks Daisato questions. Daisato strains to put together a complete thought. This goes on seemingly forever. It's a bad sign when I'm checking the time 15 minutes into a movie.

Part of the reason Daisato does little but putz around town is that he's constantly on-call. When he does get the call, he heads over to the local electric plant and zaps himself. This causes him to grow several stories tall (within a giant pair of purple briefs – nice nod to the Hulk there), and he goes off, hair standing on end and club in hand, to dispatch the monster.

I must say that the monsters are extremely cool. Presented in a crazy blend of CGI and claymation, the monsters Daisato must fight are the stuff Tim Burton might've come up with after a long night of drinking bleach. Unfortunately, the fight sequences are very brief, and the fact that Daisato takes on the challenge like a glum exterminator drains some of the joy out of it all.

For defending his homeland, everyone hates Daisato. The public hates him for all the property damage he causes and for his half-hearted fighting. His agent hates him because his lack of popularity makes it difficult to tattoo advertising space on his body. Me? I just hate him cuz he's boring.

But if you have the inclination, and you can tough it out, the last 20 minutes almost redeem the entire film. Describing what happens would not do it justice. By a long shot. All I'll say is that what happens is so strange, so bizarre, that I laughed my ass off the entire time, and all was forgiven.

Well, almost.

* *

MY ROAD TO BAD MOVIES: 2:35AM

There was a great movie podcast called The Demented Podcast where hosts Nick and Steve would ask their guest to identify the moment they knew they were a bigger movie fan than most people. That time for me came one summer night when I was about 10 years old.

After my experience with *Godzilla vs. the Smog Monster*, I became obsessed with Godzilla. For my first major art project in first grade, I made a giant papier-mâché Godzilla mask. I'd take out every book the library had on movie monsters in order to read up on Godzilla, and that introduced me to the classic Universal movie monsters and other creature features. And when the *TV Guide* would show up in the mail, I would scan the grids to see if any of those films would be on that week.

I could usually find something with giant insects or maybe even a Gamera movie on WTXX (an independent station out of Hartford, CT) on Saturday afternoons, but anything with the classic monsters was hard to come by. Then, late one summer, I found an actual Dracula movie listed in the TV Guide... at 2:35 in the morning.

So I did what any budding movie buff would do: Set my alarm for 2:30am so I could covertly watch...

SON OF DRACULA

Directed by Louis Gasnier
1943, 80 minutes, Unrated
"Pull it out! Pull it out, I tell ya!"

Believe it or not, there was a time when setting steamy, sexy vampires in steamy, sexy New Orleans wasn't totally played out. That time was the 1940s.

Unfortunately, *Son of Dracula* doesn't make much use of The Big Easy's setting. This 1943 film is Universal Studios' second sequel to the Bela Lugosi classic (consider that the next time someone starts bellyaching about all the sequels today), with a "Count Alucard of Budapest" (*sigh*) arriving in New Orleans to stay at Casa de Caldwell.

Yeah, "Alucard." I'm guessing the filmmakers thought this was a bit cheesy, too, because they have one of our protagonists, the long-winded Dr. Brewster, notice what that spells backwards in the opening scene.

Meanwhile, at a remote mansion in the swamps of New Orleans, the '40s version of a Goth Chick lectures us on the virtues of metaphysics. "You should allow your mind to explore the unknown, Claire. Then you wouldn't laugh at telepathy." I imagine you could read my mind during that particular gem. Turns out everyone else in the film feels the same way, and everyone lets our '40s Goth Chick know it again and again and again.

Yeah, the first 20 minutes or so is a bit of a slog. Finally, we meet Count Alucard in all his bat-transforming glory, and it's Lon Chaney, Jr.! LCJ is sporting a stylish little moustache for the role, which makes him look like a maître d' or a classy pornographer.

Intrigue abounds when Colonel Caldwell drops dead a couple scenes later, and 22-skip-skeedo, our '40s Goth Chick has jilted her long-standing fiancé to marry the Count. The Jilted Ex takes exception, naturally, and confronts the newlyweds. Alucard starts to get rough with the Jilted Ex, but this is America, baby! The Jilted Ex pulls a gun on Alucard, but unfortunately, the bullets sail right through the vampire and hit the '40s Goth Chick. Oops.

All of these events lead the Jilted Ex to the brink of sanity and Dr. Brewster to the conclusion that Alucard is a vampire. Why no one suggested that the Jilted Ex simply missed Alucard is beyond me, but that's just one of the many problems with this film. Almost from the get-go, Dr. Brewster assumes that Alucard is a vampire – he even calls in a professor from Budapest who is an expert in the legend of Dracula. They talk and theorize and talk and theorize, and when Alucard appears before them as mist and *confirms everything*, they continue to talk and theorize.

It wasn't lost on me that despite spending so much time with the professor and Dr. Brewster, neither one plays any kind of role in actually defeating the vampire.

Speaking of which, I hate to say it, but LCJ should never have been cast as Dracula. His rough, everyman features and demeanor gave great pathos to his iconic performance as The Wolf Man, but it makes him all wrong for our aristocratic bloodsucker.

In fact, if you're looking for good classic horror flick, go with *The Wolf Man*. *Son of Dracula* is one son who can't fill his father's shoes.

* *

2: VAMPIRES & OTHER CREATURES THAT SUCK

BLOOD FREAK
Directed by Gil Ward
1972, 86 minutes, Rated R
Only a turkey does drugs

When I first dug into *Blood Freak*, all I knew was that it is a grimy horror film from the '70s – though maybe calling it "grimy" is redundant. What is it about '70s films that make everything look like they're covered in nose grease? I'm pretty sure people bathed prior to 1980.

Blood Freak opens with a guy who looks Vincent Price's sleazy brother addressing the camera from his wood-paneled basement. He's in a disheveled silk shirt and smoking a cigarette, looking every bit like a guy who just came back from a key party. He takes a drag of his cigarette, looks into the camera and says, "We live in a world—

STOP. Just… stop.

I don't know what's going to come out of his mouth next, but this intro is already teed up like a rant from that one racist relative everyone has. Three seconds in, and this film is already completely ridiculous. That's how long it took *Blood Freak* to break my brain, beating the previous record of 30 seconds by *Garfield: The Movie*.

Anyway, Sleazy Price rambles on about how the world is always a'changing and full of unforeseen consequences, but there seems to be a grand plan behind it all, etc., etc. He also helpful defines a "catalyst" for us. I'm not sure what his point was, because I was distracted by him constantly looking down at his script just off-camera.

It really doesn't matter, because it's all a big wind-up to introduce us to Hershel, an easy rider with a discount Elvis vibe. He meets a leggy lady on the highway – as people tended to do in the '70s – and accompanies her to a party her sister is throwing. The leggy lady, Angel, warns Hershel that her sister, Anna, is "really into the drug scene." Sure enough, Anna immediately starts pestering Hershel to take a hit, because that's exactly how potheads behave.

Angel is not amused, telling Anna, "You know your body is the temple of the Holy Spirit." I did not know that.

Turns out that Angel is very religious, speaking almost exclusively in pseudo-Bible verses. It drives Anna crazy that Hershel is falling in line with Angel, so she begins plotting with her drug dealer, Guy, to get Hershel Hooked On Drugs.

Anna's elaborate plan to win Hershel:

> 1) Parade around in front of Hershel in a bikini
> 2) Physically throw herself at him, even though he clearly is not interested
> 3) Relentlessly nag him to smoke up with her until he relents.

This works. Watching the rather sleepy sex scene, I began to wonder whether or not this was actually a horror movie.

It is if you don't like turkeys! Hershel's night of passion (and drugs!) has made him late for his first day on the job, working at a turkey farm. You know what that means: turkey footage!

Not only will Hershel be working as a farm hand around the farm, he'll also be helping out in the lab (what?) trying out their sample meat (WHAT?). And just to sweeten the pot, the lab techs are willing to give Hershel some Drugs for eating their experimental turkey meat.

This is a good thing, because Hershel just barely makes hit back to Angel's and Anna's place at the end of the day. Why? Because he's wigging out, going through withdrawal because he's Hooked On Drugs!

Back at the ranch, the guys in the lab have roasted up an entire turkey for Hershel to eat. Hey, at least with all the pot Hershel is smoking now, he'll probably have the munchies! Hershel appears to eat the entire turkey, because by the next scene, all of the tryptophan causes him to pass out mid-stride out in the yard. Not so sure that tryptophan would cause the convulsions...

The bearded lab tech finds Hershel passed out on the lawn. He rushes over, checks on him, and then rushes over to... stroke his beard? Next scene, the farmer and the lab guys are talking about how they *dumped* Hershel's body? The hell kind of turkey farm is this?

Well, I'll tell ya: It's the kind of turkey farm that would turn Hershel into a were-turkey!

Unfortunately, that's not quite right. It seems that a combination of the drugs in the turkey and the drugs in the bird the lab techs roasted up have mutated Hershel's head into a papier-mâché turkey. Turshel stumbles off to Anna's place and writes her a bunch of notes explaining what happened. "Gosh, Hershel, you sure are ugly," Anna helpfully observes, and then goes about the business of imagining what their mutant turkey children would look like.

But Turshel has bigger problems than having a giant papier- mâché head – he's still Hooked On Drugs! This causes Turshel to go on a rampage, nabbing young ladies On Drugs and drinking their drug-enriched blood. Because he's On Drugs! And also, he has a beak. This leads to a particularly gripping scene between Turshel and a farmer's... let's say son? fighting to the death while someone impersonates a baby wailing off-camera.

I'd like to say it all builds up to some kind of out of this world craziness, but it doesn't. In fact, it leads to the type of cliché ending that makes me deduct an asterisk off my rating. But we do learn that when you're at your lowest, the best thing to do is to pray extra-hard to God to give you more faith. Because that's exactly how prayer and faith work.

Sleazy Price is back for one last appearance, telling us that the story we just saw was "based partly on fact, partly on probability." I don't know what that's supposed to mean, but I do know that *Blood Freak* is based entirely on crazy.

* * * *

SLUGS: THE MOVIE
Directed by Juan Piquer Simon
1987, 90 minutes, Rated R
Like Jaws, *but with slugs*

Every so often, you'll trip over an article on the web pissing and moaning about the lack of creativity in Hollywood today.

Those articles are the worst. Not only is the writer completely oblivious to the irony of how void of creativity it is to complain about the lack of creativity in Hollywood, it also shows a lack of understanding of how the movie business works. Producers don't give a fig about creativity, they care about making money. Know what makes money? Proven formulas. And when a newly proven formula comes along, they ride that thing all day long... no matter how absurd it is.

And just to prove my point of how long this has been going on, take *Jaws*. Summer of 1975, Steven Spielberg unleashed this gem into the theaters, causing the world to collectively wet itself. Everyone was afraid to go in the water, so they went to the movies and watched *Jaws* instead.

In the wake of *Jaws*, the studios started cranking out imitations with other animals. "Like *Jaws*, but with a [blank]" became the go-to elevator pitch. Once all the plausibly threatening sea life was used up, the formula was applied to land mammals. And once all of those were used up? Well...

Based on the 1982 novel that I wish was titled *Slugs: The Novel*, 1988's *Slugs: The Movie* stays true to form with a cold open featuring the underwater death of a nameless couple. Check that off the list! Post-credits, we meet all of our main characters at a nightclub for young Republicans. Among them is Mike Brady, the county health inspector. That's right: It's the story of a man named Brady, but he's not bringing up three boys of his own. Instead, this Mike Brady is accompanying the sheriff to evict the town drunk because... that's what county health inspectors do? Anyway, they find the find the guy dead and half-consumed. At least the eviction will go smoothly.

After some snippets of life in town, including complaints from the Crankiest Old Lady Ever and a scene of all the "cool" "teens" hanging out in the only diner in town, we get our first explicitly slug-related fatality. Harold is trying to enjoy his golden years tending to his greenhouse when A SLUG slithers/crawls/oozes into his gardening glove. Awesomely, when Harold puts on the glove, he's obliged to yell out,

"SOMETHING IS BITING MY HAND!" Rather than try to simply remove the loose-fitting glove, Harold flails about, knocking over an unfortunate combination of chemicals.

Then, seeing no other alternative, Harold chops off his own hand. Somehow, that doesn't provide him with much relief. Fortunately, his wife wanders in at that point, epically long ash dangling from her cigarette, and then everything blows up real good.

Shortly after, Mike Brady finds a slightly larger than normal slug in his wife's garden. When it bites Mike Brady on the finger, he freaks the hell out and does what any of us would do: bring the slug in to a British guy in a lab to analyze. Listening to the lab guy's Austin Powers-esque accent, Mike Brady starts to add it all up… half-eaten town drunk… explosion in a greenhouse… bit by a slug… our town must be infested with mutant, man-eating slugs! It's the kind of deduction that Adam West's Batman would love.

It appears that the slugs' mutant abilities also include teleportation. Just a few scenes later, a couple of "cool" "teens" head upstairs to have hot, drunken sex (this is a horror film, after all). They take a break from all the huffing and puffing to find that the bedroom floor is a sea of slugs! Maybe we should add the ability to detect premarital sex to the slugs' list of mutant abilities.

We get more deaths by slug, including a particularly memorable scene in a high-end restaurant, and soon, Mike Brady is running about doing a Chicken Little routine. Naturally, the good ol' boy sheriff doesn't believe him, suggesting there might also be "demented crickets" or "rampaging mosquitoes" – both of which sound like damn good movies to me. When Mike Brady warns the head of the water department and the mayor that their water supply has been contaminated, they both tell him to take a hike. Hey, why should they listen to him? He's only the county health inspector.

Mike Brady, his buddy in sanitation and Dr. Austin Powers devise a plan to take out the slugs. Amazingly, it doesn't involve table salt.

No, the plan is to head into the sewers on Halloween to douse all of the slugs with lithium ammonia, which apparently will make the slugs explode. Only the sanitation guy questions the wisdom of marching into a contained area filled with methane to make things explode. Of course, that only gives him pause before giving his wife the best kiss of death ever: "Hey, how about when I get back, you and I get naked and get crazy?"

Off our heroes go, where the central drama becomes less about Man vs. Nature (as natural as mutant slugs can be) and more about Man vs. Manhole. Unsurprisingly, given their master plan, the whole thing ends with about 800 explosions.

Yes, this film is glorious. Not that it should be: the premise is absurd, the dialogue is rickety, the music overblown and often inappropriate and the acting stinks on ice. Which, of course, only adds to the splendor and glory that is *Slugs: The Movie*. I can only hope I've done it justice in this, Slugs: The Review.

* * * *

BLOODSUCKING PHAROAHS IN PITTSBURGH

Directed by Dean Tschetter
1991, 89 minutes, Rated R
Death by Black & Decker

That's quite the title, eh? So let's get this out of the way: For reasons I can't explain, *Bloodsucking Pharaohs in Pittsburgh* fails to include 1) bloodsucking, 2) pharaohs, or even guys running around in pharaoh hats, or 3) anything involving Pittsburgh.

I usually penalize movies for this kind of thing, but I'm going to make an exception.

What *Bloodsucking Pharaohs in Pittsburgh* lacks in bloodsucking, pharaohs and Pittsburgh, it makes up for in cheese and gallons of gore -- though not necessarily in that order. Here's the skinny: Two sorry-sack homicide detectives are on the trail of a serial killer with a fondness for power tools. The daughter of one detective's former partner shows up to do all the heavy thinking, and there's this sub-plot about the other detective's wife trying to quit smoking, and they all end up in the city's Little Egypt district and, uh... Did I mention that Tom Savini did the special makeup effects?

Oh sure. NOW you're interested...

So why does this movie work where equally incoherent b-movies fail? For starters, the movie does its cheese very well. Just about every cop movie cliché finds its way into the film: Eating at crime scenes, the Cop On The Edge, the Detective Who Knows The Victims, the Screaming Police Chief, etc. It's the kind of humor where Don Adams would have felt right at home.

Secondly, this might be the most original serial killer I've seen in quite some time. For much of the movie, the killer tugs along a wagon with a generator to operate an array of power tools. No wussy gardening claw_for this killer, no sir! During the course of the film, the killer makes lethal use of hedge clippers, a circular saw, a jackhammer and a wet vac. A wet vac!!

As you might imagine, this movie is pretty whole-sale gross. Like Troma Films gross. The film revels in its grossness. How gross? There's a scene in the coroner's office where the medical examiner dig around the latest victim's body cavity (sans gloves), then head over to the snack table to celebrate a birthday with heaping scoops of tomato salmon casserole. Mm-mmm!

Also, there are ninjas. Okay, the ninjas don't play a major role in the film, but still: there are ninjas. I know some of you are suckers for that kind of thing.

* * *

CLUB VAMPIRE
Directed by Andy Ruben
1997, 77 minutes, Rated R
Don't get roofie'd

Club Vampire is the story of sexy vampires brooding and bloodsucking in sexy Los Angeles, which meant the film made me want to bash my own head in with a tire iron before I'd even hit the PLAY button.

The film stars John Savage, who you might know from such films as… Yeah, I dunno. IMDB.com lists over 200 movie credits to his name, but the best I can do is kinda remember him being in *The Deer Hunter*. Savage plays Zero, who admits in a trite voice-over opening monologue that he's "not human" and "is not allowed to use the V-word." As a century-old vampire who has lost his taste for blood and longs to see daylight again, Zero has the potential of being a compelling protagonist. That potential is immediately trashed by Zero's distracting lip piercing and the fact that he talks like Fenster from The *Usual Suspects.*

Zero is also smitten with a single mom who works as a dancer at one of those weird fetish clubs that features lots of glittery clothing, crappy jazz and performers trying really *really* hard to be sexy. Example: Topless women playing Twister. While I think it would be fun to *play* Twister with topless women, watching topless women play Twister is just... kinda weird. Also, note that the club in *Club Vampire* is not a club for vampires, which makes the film's title irritatingly inaccurate. Also also, the fetish-dancer single mom was apparently one of the inspirations for Elizabeth Berkley's character in *Showgirls,* as both characters behave like feral cats and lack any actual dancing talent.

Anyway, ShowMom gets accidentally turned by a member of Zero's "family," and Zero takes it upon himself to guide ShowMom into vampireness with lots and lots of bad poetry. Zero's vampire family, understanding the need to keep their numbers small, aren't thrilled about the accidental turning and decide to kill off ShowMom... and Zero, too, if necessary. In the meantime, we're treated to an extended scene where ShowMom eats her son's hamster only to vomit it up along with half her body weight, loads of fake blood and a whole lot of heavy-handed camera effects (because vampires are perpetually dizzy or drunk?). It's all the opposite of exciting.

Who was this movie made for? Goths? I'd wager that most Goths would rather shop at Abercrombie & Fitch than sit through this pap.

This movie is the film version of roofies: I passed out halfway through the film, my recollection is hazy at best and I felt used and violated afterwards. Falling asleep particularly pissed me off. One, how much does must a movie suck when I can't stay awake for the whole 77 minutes? And two, I had to watch the second half again. Again! Like it wasn't bad enough sitting through it the first time.

If there's one bright spot in the film, it's the casting of Michael J. Anderson as a vampire in Zero's family. You probably won't know him by name, but Anderson is best known as the backwards talking Man From Another Place in *Twin Peaks*. As awesome as a dwarven vampire might sound, it's not worth seeing this film for Michael J. Anderson (though he makes the most of his role). I'm just pointing him out because he deserves better.

*

PHANTOMS
Directed by John Chappelle
1998, 96 minutes, Rated R
It's a bomb, yo.

Any casual fan of Kevin Smith's films knows that "Affleck was the bomb in *Phantoms*, yo!" Any super-fan knows that line originated from what was clearly an inside joke in the *Mallrats* commentary (then again, at least a third of *Jay & Silent Bob Strike Back* is made up of inside jokes). It's been taken on face value ever since – why would Jay and Silent Bob lie to us? – but at some point, we have to turn our brains back on and look at things with a critical eye. So today, I power up and ask the question, "Is Ben Affleck really the bomb in *Phantoms*, yo?"

Turns out that Phantoms is based on a novel by Dean Koontz, which didn't bode well for me. I've always thought of Dean Koontz as a poor man's Stephen King, though that's probably unfair. Especially considering I've never been able to get more than 50 pages into a Dean Koontz book.

Anyway, we open with Rose McGowan and her sister, Dr. Jenny, driving through the snowy mountains of snowy Snowfield. We get some blah-blah about Dr. Jenny getting Rose away from Los Angeles and "Ronnie" as they pull into town, where everything is quiet – a little too quiet. Then, in a matter of just a couple minutes, the ladies discover that Dr. Jenny's housekeeper is dead, the phone is dead, their car (which was working perfectly just minutes ago) is dead, and the one cop at the police station is dead. Still not a soul in sight, not a sound. The ladies promptly take the initiative to arm up at the police station, so they can shoot at all the nothing that's around town.

And thus the first chunk of the movie consists of the sisters quietly wandering around town and occasionally finding some ridiculous bit of horror. We know it's supposed to be scary because all of a sudden, the movie makes a big BLAAARRR!! noise. Because that's how *Phantoms* thinks jump scares work.

Have no need to fear, Sherriff Affleck is here! And with him is Deputy Liev Schreiber (set to Dodgy Dork mode) and Deputy Copstache. Goodie, more people to watch slowly wander around. At one point, for no reason whatsoever, every alarm in town goes off all at once. Car alarms, smoke alarms, church bells, train whistles, frickin' pots and pans banging together… this too is supposed to be scary, but it's just stupid.

Shortly after, Sherriff Affleck finds a mysterious message for "Timothy Flyte" written on a mirror in an empty hotel room. Sherriff Affleck can't work it out: the room was empty, windowless, and locked from the inside, so how did the message get there. As for me, I can't work out what kind of hotel room doesn't have windows.

Later, the movie decides to stop being a town-wide haunted house movie and becomes *Alien*, complete with a giant CGI moth facehugging Deputy Schreiber. Meanwhile, in another movie… It's a dark and stormy night in the Big City, and Peter O'Toole is—wait, what?!

Screen legend Peter O'Toole is a disgraced scientist-turned-tabloid writer who just happens to be the "Timothy Flyte" from Sherriff Affleck's mystery mirror. The FBI picks him up and drags him into *Phantoms* very much against his will. Peter "*Laurence of Arabia*" O'Toole and the feds roll into town in full hazmat gear, changing the movie again from *Alien* to *Outbreak*. And then again to *The Thing*, as the whateveritis kills off all the feds with unidentifiable CGI tentacles and stuff.

Finally, the film transforms into a discount H.P. Lovecraft story as Peter "*Becket*" O'Toole explains the true nature of the whateveritis. According to Peter "*My Favorite Year*" O'Toole, this "Ancient Enemy" shows up every few hundreds of years to feed on a small town. While doing so, the Ancient Enemy absorbs the memories and experiences of everyone it feeds on and can assume any learned shape (hence the "phantoms," I guess). Consequently, it thinks it is the devil. And it has developed a massive ego, demanding that Peter "*Venus*" O'Toole "write [its] gospel" and that Sherriff Affleck, Rose McGowan and Dr. Jenny "witness [its] miracles."

And I'm going to stop with the recapping there, because I've already put more effort into this movie than the filmmakers did.

Here is, in no particular order, everything wrong with *Phantoms*:

- For a horror movie, the movie is unspeakably lazy. It has exactly one trick in its bag of tricks: cutting to gore or a killing with abrupt loud noises, and it fails every time. There's no atmosphere, no sense of dread and certainly no tension because…

- The Big Bad kicks off the third act by straight-up announcing that it doesn't want to kill any of the protagonists. After all, who would write its gospel and witness its miracles if it did? Way to lower the stakes, movie. Also…

- If Peter *"The Ruling Class"* O'Toole's hypothesis is right – and of course it is, it's frickin' Peter *"The Lion in Winter"* O'Toole – the Ancient Enemy is all done killing people for the next however many hundreds of years. It's not interested in conquest, so finding a way to "stop it" is really just preventing another mass killing some 700 years in the future. Again, pretty low stakes.

- Who did Peter *"The Stunt Man"* O'Toole piss off to get put in this movie? Wasn't it enough of an indignity for Peter *"Goodbye, Mr. Chips"* O'Toole to never have won an Oscar? Screw you, Academy.

- This movie can't figure out what it wants to rip-off (excuse me, "homage"), so it tries to rip off *all* of the movies. The end result is a mess.

- What's the point of putting the killer virus in syringes if most of the characters will just have the syringe contents splatter all over the phantom? If it didn't need to be injected, then why not just pick up some SuperSoakers and have at it? Why bore us with 10 minutes of Sherriff Affleck slooooooooowly trying to sneak a case of empty syringes across a road under the watchful eye of a phantom dog?

- What kind of doctor would load a virus-filled syringe into the end of a shotgun – like it's a damn minuteman's musket – to shoot at a phantom and think it would do *anything*?

- Speaking of the doctor, why are Dr. Jenny and Rose McGowan even in this movie? Their characters contribute nothing to the story. At all. You could remove both characters from the movie, and nothing would change.
- This is the most clothing I've ever seen Rose McGowan wear onscreen. Not to be a pig, but it almost seems like there was a dare to see how many layers they could get McGowan to wear during filming. The raciest this film gets is during a scene in a bathroom where McGowan is washing her hands – you can kinda see some forearm.

Here's the final verdict: No, Ben Affleck is not the bomb in *Phantoms*... through no fault of his own. His Sherriff Affleck is as generic a Hero Guy as they come – he even has a generic Tragic Past that, in a moment any view not in a coma will see coming a mile away, he has to face in the climax. For Affleck to even have a chance at "the bomb" status, he'd need material with at least a glimmer of originality to it. The guy's not a miracle worker.

*

BLOOD ANGELS
Directed by Ron Oliver
2004, 98 minutes, Rated R
Also known as Thralls, *except no one knows what the hell a thrall is.*

I had high hopes for *Blood Angels*. I saw the cover, read that the movie starred Lorenzo Lamas and a "bevy of fanged femme fatales," and had visions of a vampire film by way of Skinamax. Lovely, lovely visions.

I'm sorry to report that this is not that movie. Oh sure, there is a scene where one of the aforementioned fanged femme fatales unveils her fantastic fun bags for an unsuspecting victim… only to have CGI worm-thingies come busting out of them. I hate when that happens.

Here's the story: A pack of hottie half-vampires, and—okay, I have to stop right there. For all of you budding filmmakers, please note that the concept of a "half-vampire" makes no sense. It's like claiming to be "half-pregnant." So please, *knock it off.*

Anyway, a pack of hottie "half-vampires" run a rave while on the lam from their master, played by Lorenzo Lamas, straight off the set of *Are You Hot? The Search for America's Sexiest Person.* Yes, kids, that was an actual TV show. One of the lady vamps has just taken in her kid sister, who doesn't know about the whole vampire thing yet. Over the course of the night, an aw-shucks farm boy (tagging along with his cousin, "Doughboy") and Kid Sis meet cute, glowsticks are waved and Lamas shows up to chew scenery. In other words, this film is not so much Vampires on Skinamax as the rave-sitcom (ravcom?) version of *From Dusk Till Dawn.*

While lacking in gratuitous nudity, there's still plenty to like in this film. The ladies strut around fiercely in skimpy outfits, and the sparingly-used Lamas is good campy fun. The film also features the Necronomicon, an absurd scheme involving the winter solstice, even more absurd kung fu fighting stances, a magical CD, an indestructible toady named Remmy, a clip-show recap in case you lost consciousness, and a cameo by Hunter S. Thompson.

You'll want to come for all those things, but you'll stay for the Doughboy. Played by Kevan Ohtsji (Sub Zero in the *Mortal Kombat: Legacy* web series), Doughboy is an Asian brainiac posing as a hip-hop gangsta in a way I can only describe as "Vanilla Ice-esque." The character is meant to be comic relief, and for once, it works. Here is some of the Tao of Doughboy for you to enjoy:

- (his first line) "Yo, yo! Check out the hot booty on that bitch!"
- Later, as a bartender looks over Doughboy's ID suspiciously: "You're 36?" Doughboy: "Yo. I moisturize!"
- And later still, as one of the hotties makers her move on Doughboy: "This track is 11 minutes and 17 seconds... Think that's enough time?" Doughboy: "Ah yeah! I'll be done way before then."

My hope is that the folks who made this film, credited as – and I'm not making this up – "Vampire Production Productions," will soon come out with a sequel titled *Blood Angels II: Rise of the Doughboy.*

* * *

BLOODSUCKING REDNECK VAMPIRES
Directed by Michael Hegg and Joe Sherlock
2004, 108 minutes, Unrated
Not just any old vampires... BLOODSUCKING vampires!

This movie is well over 90 minutes long. That's usually a big red flag for me when I sit down to view these kind of movies. Face it: We're quite content to sit through three-plus hours of top shelf productions such as *The Godfather* or *The Lord of the Rings.* But I doubt even the filmmakers' mommas would call the movies featured here "top shelf."

So, how does a film with a title like *Bloodsucking Redneck Vampires* fill 108 minutes? Like this: We open to some Goth Chick, who's not nearly as hot as she thinks she is, sitting in an unfurnished living room, brooding and drinking wine (or is it?!?). Bluesy bar-band guitar music plays. She sits and broods. A guy with pubescent facial hair and a muscle shirt standing around in a hallway. She quietly broods. He stands around. I sit on my couch. Five minutes pass like this. Hence the red flag.

We eventually get to something that resembles a plot. The Goth Chick is actually some kind of Big-Deal Vampire (just ask her!), complete with an absurd Transylvanian accent. The muscle shirt guy is her human servant -- he's there to say, "Yes, Master," whine, and give our Goth Chick someone to talk at. The two are on the run from an unseen Vampire Hunter, and after a run-in with the World's Chattiest Redneck, our Goth Chick comes up with her master plan: Take over the small town (of rednecks) to be her undead army, and make her stand against the Vampire Hunter.

Having come to that decision, the Goth Chick disappears for the next hour or so of the film... and we launch head-first into sitcom territory. We meet the Poissier family (pronounced "pisser," of course), who has just won a contest to have their bathroom redecorated. With the arrival of interior designer Claude – who comes complete with beret, leather pants and *out-rage-eous* French accent – we get a full tour of the Poissiers' house and social circle. And I do mean full tour.

This tangent leads to further tangents including Ma Poissier's feud over the annual cook-off, the Tripe Days beauty pageant, an upcoming poker night, a redneck named Cletus peeping on a neighbor showering, a beer run, and numerous scenes of Claude, Cletus and Junior Poissier eating beans. Yes, there are more fart jokes per minute in this film than in an episode of *South Park's Terrance and Phillip*. Seriously, this isn't a horror movie. It's a comedy with vampires.

Speaking of which, from this point it takes nearly a half hour for the film to remember the "vampire" part of the title. We're then treated to various rednecks becoming vampires... and promptly bumbling into their own deaths. Turns out that redneck vampires aren't very bright.

The rest of the film is a showcase of laughably bad computer graphics and a jaw-dropping lack of any sort of pacing, leading up to the big battle at the Tripe Days Festival between what's left of the Goth Chick's redneck vampire army and Team Poissier.

Yes, it's the worst climatic face-off ever. How bad is it? When I was in high school, my buddies and I would sometimes make movies (not like that, sicko) of goofy little comedy sketches we called the Moron Movies. One such sketch was "Teenage Mutant Ninja Nerd." Picture two high school kids, one dressed up as a nerd, flailing around in a "kung fu" battle. Our unrehearsed and unskilled "Teenage Mutant Ninja Nerd" battle was still infinitely better than the final fight between the Goth Chick and the Vampire Hunter. Of course, after the first 100 minutes, anything less would have been out of place.

Your enjoyment of *Bloodsucking Redneck Vampires* – if you're somehow on the fence about watching this film – comes down to what you think of redneck humor. If you think *Hee Haw* is one of the greatest television shows ever made, you might get a kick out of this. But if Jeff Foxworthy's "You Might Be a Redneck" routine makes your stomach sour, run far, far away.

* *

DRACULA 3000
Directed by Darrell Roodt
2004, 86 minutes, Rated R
In space, no one can hear you suck.

Come on! "In space, no one can hear you suck" was pitched underhand to me. It may not be the official tag line of *Dracula 3000*, but it could have been. Either way, the end result is the same: Vampires!... In!... SPAAAAACE!!!

Need more of a sell on this film? Check out the all-star cast: Casper Van Dien and his Superhuman Jawbone, Erika "Ms. July '89" Eleniak, Coolio, and the ironically named "Tiny" Lister (Zeus from *No Holds Barred*) as the only guy fully aware of how crap this movie is and having fun. Personally, I was looking forward to the Dracula/Coolio showdown. World-famous vampire vs. the winner of *Celebrity Boot Camp*? Who can resist?

About the movie... First things first: Yes, it does indeed take place in the year 3000. Casper Van Jawbone plays Capt. Abraham Van Helsing (cuz it's not a Dracula movie without a Van Helsing), captain of a salvage ship, which is totally not like the one in *Alien*. Just like his crew is totally not an amalgam of the characters in *Alien* and, appropriately, *Dracula*.

Anyway, they find an abandoned freight ship that'd been drifting about for 50 years, the crew checks it out and – really, is it necessary for me to continue? You know where this is going:
the blurs of something scurrying by in the background, the interstitial clips of the previous captain's log, the ironic quips, the "surprise" "twist" that one of the crew is an android, etc., etc..

Now that I've beat up the plot, it probably goes without saying that most of the effects sucked, the sound mixing sucked harder and the cinematographer forgot to take his Ritalin while filming.

That's not to say this film is without joy. Coolio (who plays a character named "187," yo) was born to play a vampire. Erika Eleniak's acting is its own kind of comedy. And when Dracula finally shows up halfway through the film – despite the fact that he's from the *planet* Transylvania and it's the year 3000 – he's still sporting the trademark cape and Victorian duds. Awesome.

Ultimately, the film just... ends. Rather abruptly. Kinda like this review.

* * * *

MANSQUITO
Directed by Tibor Takacs
2004, 92 minutes, Rated R
Sadly, no giant-sized fly swatters are featured in this film.

Ah, 1990... The pre-dawn of the Grunge Era and Generation X, a time that definitely wasn't the '80s, but with its crazy silk shirts and C+C Music Factory, definitely wasn't the '90s, either.

My favorite TV show in 1990 was *Parker Lewis Can't Lose*. I'm sure you can find episodes floating around the Internet, but be warned that the show hasn't aged well. This cartoonishly surreal sit-com was about a really cool guy named NotFerris Bueller getting in and out of all sorts of high school antics. It did pretty well, running for three seasons – a solid 60 episodes better than the TV spin-off *Ferris Bueller* that debuted on the same night.

The title character, played by Corin Nemec and his perfectly sculpted hair, achieved a fair amount of fame and attention from the show. Since those days, whenever I see paisley prints or hear someone ironically quoting "Ice Ice Baby," I think to myself, "Whatever happened to Parker Lewis?"

Sadly, the answer is *Mansquito*.

Okay, so here's the situation: There's a new strain of the West Nile virus going around, and it's killing people off. An unusually hot scientist (are there any other kind in movies like this?) is close to developing an anti-virus, which she'll spread by introducing it into the mosquito population, but her douche bag boss wants her to test it on people *now*. So when a psycho killer previously put away by Police Detective Parker Lewis accepts reduced jail time to be the guinea pig, you know things are going to go pear-shaped. The psycho attempts an escape, he's caught in an explosion of radiation and mosquitoes... yada yada yada... Mansquito!

No, Mansquito isn't a junior varsity Spider-Man villain or a diminutive masked Mexican luchador. Though either would be awesome.

Predictably enough, Mansquito is a giant mutant mosquito. Or at least a guy in a giant latex cockroach costume. Mansquito also features a large, rigid proboscis that slowly extends out of his (its?) mouth before plunging it into his latest victim... I'm sure someone could write an entire dissertation on the subtext of *that*.

Speaking of Anvils of Obviousness, the Internets never fail me: In the whole three minutes of research I do in reviewing films, I quickly found a post from someone all bent out of shape over the unscientific portrayal of mosquitoes in this film. Because while having a federal prison release a homicidal killer for medical testing only to have the killer turn into a giant mutant mosquito that is bullet-proof and has bloodvision is fine, implying that male mosquitoes suck blood? That, apparently, is out of bounds.

So what does a Mansquito do? Pretty much what you'd expect: Mansquito flies about Los Angeles completely unseen and attacking people with its mouth boner. Fortunately for Mansquito, all of its victims think they're in an old-school horror movie: they just fall over and scream, as opposed to defending themselves or running away.

While that is going on, Det. Parker Lewis is sent to investigate the incident at the lab. The fact that he's in a romantic relationship with the Unusually Hot Scientist doesn't prevent him from working the case – no worries about a conflict of interests in this police department. Maybe it's just as well... after Mansquito takes out an entire SWAT team, Det. Parker Lewis is the only one smart enough to get himself a BFG.

Then again, our detective is also the only one able to survive multiple encounters with Mansquito. Looks like Parker Lewis can't lose after all.

* * *

VAMPIRES VS. ZOMBIES
Directed by Vince D'Amato
2004, 83 minutes, Rated R
The only loser in this battle is the audience.

I had such high hopes, even though the concept of vampires and zombies fighting doesn't make a lot of sense. Both are members of the living dead, and vampires drink blood while zombies eat brains. You'd think they'd want to work together and get a nice reciprocal relationship going, no?

The film opens with a guy and his "teenage" daughter driving down the road in "Idaho." The girl has been having recurring nightmares about a vampire – we know it's a vampire because she's dressed vaguely goth-like and trying very hard to be sexy. By the way, what's the deal with all the sexy vampires? I never understood it, because no matter how you dice it, a vampire is *a walking corpse that feeds on blood*. That's not sexy. That's a disturbing combination of necrophilia and cannibalism.

Anyway, we suddenly see a guy standing in the middle of the road up ahead, wearing what appears to be the world's worst black face. That appears to be reason enough for Dad to run him over. Cue the goth rock.

From this point – being the end of the opening credits – the rest of the film is incomprehensible. I'll try: Some GothMom pulls over Dad and Daughter and somehow talks them into taking her daughter, Camilla, with them. They go to a gas station, where the Daughter flirts with some goth chick named Bob. Camilla turns out to be a vampire, though hanging out in the daytime doesn't phase her. Dad is travelling to meet up with "The General," who has kidnapped some girl who isn't the girl he thought it was but turns out to be a vampire as well. At one point, The General meets up with GothMom, who somehow makes her car disappear. GothMom also appears later as a traffic cop... Or maybe it's just the same actress playing a different role? It's weird and none of the other characters notice or mention it. A few more zombies get run over by cars. And that's all before the scene 45 minutes in that is either an extended flashback or a dream sequence. Either way, it only succeeds in making the story even more confusing.

This movie made my head hurt. The main characters make decisions solely for the purpose of meeting the needs of the plot (as opposed to logic or common sense), yet from start to finish, *the plot doesn't make a lick of sense.*

If you're really on the ball today, you'll notice that something is missing. I've seen enough of these films now to expect very little from them. I don't expect the movie to be good in any conventional way. I don't expect competent acting, a clever story or good production values. And when I do encounter those things, it's a bonus.

Know what I do expect? THAT A MOVIE TITLED *VAMPIRES VS. ZOMBIES* FEATURE AN ACTUAL SCENE OF VAMPIRES FIGHTING ZOMBIES! What the hell! I sat through 83 minutes of that crap thinking to myself, "Well, at least I'll get to see some vampires fighting zombies." NO!!

I don't think I've ever been so angry in my entire life. I was mad enough to punch a nun. If I had a gun, I would have shoot my television, Elvis-style.

I was beyond irate, beyond outraged, beyond furious. I was so angry that my muscles froze up into a form of rigor mortis, leaving me a quivering mass of apoplectic ire. Come to think of it, enduring 83 minutes of full-body lockjaw would be better than watching this movie.

0

VAMPIYAZ

Directed by John Bacchus
2004, 83 minutes, Rated R
Suck it, beeotches!!

See what I did there? "Suck"? Vampire movie? That's why I'm the one with the book about bad movies.

My personal goal is to find the best and most enjoyable bad movies in existence, maybe even band them together in some kind of Hall of Poetic Justice. I now have another film I'd happily recommend. I present to you *Vampiyaz*.

Here are my unedited notes from the opening ten minutes of the film:

- Open on skyscraper at night, cheap Chyron of the movie title – not good sign
- F-bomb dropped repeatedly in 2nd line of dialogue -- also not good sign
- 2 guys practice opening safe, another guy wearing giant tinfoil(?) cross – are they connected
- more NYC stock footage
- was this shot in my garage?
- g'bye, Tinfoil Cross Guy
- if burglars enter through unlocked front door, is it still B&E?
- WHY IS HE IN A PINK BABY OUTFIT??
- jiggily camera = panic

Jakeem and Khalil are the burglars, and the job goes sour cuz Khalil is a gun-happy nitwit. Long story short, Khalil screws over Jakeem, Jakeem gets thrown into "jail" (played here by some abandoned structure in a state park) while Khalil gets attacked by a vampire.

Fast-forward eight years to Jakeem getting out of jail and reacquainted with freedom. Don't let the new tattoos and tuff facial hair fool you ladies! Jakeem is still a softie! He just wants that prostitute to hold him! An old contact, Ray, makes Jakeem an offer he can't refuse: get revenge on Khalil and get paid doing it.

Of course, it's a trap – Ray and VampKhalil beat the snot out of Jakeem and string him up, leading to one of the better lines in the movie: "So, you two clowns are vampires, huh?"

That line is bested just a minute later, when VampKhalil describes Ray as a "ghetto fabulous version of Renfield." Blacula would be proud.

The reason why Khalil doesn't just kill Jakeem is that he wants Jakeem to steal him an amulet. Really. This leads to the most asinine caper ever, featuring Jakeem listening to the tumblers while literally in the middle of a gunfight. There's plenty more running around, all building up to a climactic battle between the forces of good and evil, all taking place in someone's condo.

So what sets this movie apart? It's not just the bad acting or the corny dialogue or the pitifully choreographed fight scenes, or even the clumsy camera work or confusing editing... though all of those things are true. It's the comical, hilariously bad special effects.

One scene features a character "eating" a rubber hand. Little CGI explosions were added to the ends of guns during shootouts. That old school punching sound effect, used so often in westerns, is employed here. And the blood? I kid you not, it's like no one realized that they'd need fake blood *for a vampire movie* until a week into production. I don't know exactly what was used, but my best guess is fruit punch. Yes, it's that bad.

This film is a thing to behold.

* * * *

AGAINST THE DARK

Directed by Richard Crudo, 2008, 94 minutes, Rated R
Against the dark / Still runnin' against the dark
He's older now but still runnin' against the dark

Know how sometimes a movie will open with the definition of a word? That device can work nicely if the word has double meanings, or if the filmmakers want to introduce a new concept. This film opens with the definition of the word "infect." I don't think I ever been insulted by a movie so quickly.

Realizing that the definition of a word my four year old has mastered is a weak way to start a movie, we then move straight into the Exposition Montage Mambo. Infection, biting, panic in the streets, blah blah blah zombies. Everyone is either zombie-chow or has joined a vigilante group like "The Hunters" or the U.S. Army (more on them later).

Yeah, the film markets them as "vampires," but they're not very vampire-y. They crave blood and are nocturnal. No need for wooden stakes or holy water – a bloated '90s action star with a sword will suffice.

And here comes The Hunters: tuff types in leather dusters who are bad asses or whatever. Steven Seagal is their leader, the pompously named "Tao," who gets to stand in one place and hack up baddies as they come flying at him. Every now and then, he pulls out a shotgun and shoots them instead – just for the variety. There's also The Rock's Cousin, who has to do all the jumping and kicking and whatnot that Steven Seagal can't do anymore. And then there's a couple of sexy ladies who just stand around during the fight scenes. I'm guessing their main job is to make it look like sexy ladies enjoy hanging out with Steven Seagal.

Not content to sit back and be zombie feed, The Hunters walk the streets at night, taking the fight to the infected. Why they don't do this during the day, which would be safer and more productive is never explained.

After The Hunters dramatically rescue a young boy from a batch of infected baddies, Steven Seagal lets out this nugget: "Let's get the boy out of here. We're not here to decide who's right or wrong; we're here to decide who lives or dies." The hell? Maybe that would've made sense to me if I were also the reincarnation of a Buddhist lama.

So now we get to the actual plot, which has shockingly little to do with Steven Seagal or his merry band of *Matrix* extras: A quartet of survivors break into a hospital, meet up with another couple, and then spend the entire movie trying to get out of the hospital. Which is apparently the size of O'Hare Airport. There's some hackneyed explanation of how they need to go out through one specific entrance before the hospital's generator dies and the security system locks them in, which doesn't make a lick of sense as four of the survivors broke *into* the hospital through a broken window.

Then again, logic isn't our survivors' strong suit: Despite the fact that it's increasingly obvious that the hospital is full of zombies, at no point do any of the survivors arm themselves with *anything* – not even a folding chair or an IV stand. And there's a lovely scene in the cafeteria where the group bitches endlessly at the Stoner Guy for getting cut because the blood will attract the creatures. If only they were somewhere that had a generous supply of bandages…

So our survivors tip-toe around the World's Largest Hospital, occasionally bumping into creepy set pieces and/or non-vamps lying in wait. Frankly, it all plays out like a game of Resident Evil. In fact, the movie feels more like Resident Evil than any of the actual *Resident Evil* films. Take that for what it's worth.

Against the Dark feels like it's been stitched together, Frankenstein-style. While our survivors make their way through St. Zombieland Memorial, we get shoehorned scenes of the Seagal Squad randomly hacking up baddies and scenes from the fully functional U.S. Army base (!) run by Keith David (!!) talking about "sanitizing" the section of L.A. where the rest of the action takes place. I guess it's comforting to know that should the zombie apocalypse hit us, our armed forces will remain fully functional well after civilization has allegedly crumbled. Less comforting is the fact that Keith David has been reduced to making glorified cameos in direct-to-DVD Seagal movies.

Eventually, the survivors meet up with the Hunters, but they're still wandering around the World's Largest Hospital, so who cares. They do meet up in time to take out a crazed surgeon who I swear was channeling the spirit of Tommy Wiseau.

I'd love to tell you that the film builds up to a big, exciting conclusion, but that would be a dirty lie. It's pretty amazing: "Steven Seagal vs. vampires" should have been a pretty easy movie to make. I don't understand why I'm so surprised that they screwed it up.

* *

SUCK
Directed by Rob Stefaniuk
2009, 91 minutes, Rated R
Vampires rock.

The filmmakers of *Suck* have a lot of nerve. According to the Naming Principle of J.Lo's *Enough*, filmmakers should give their film a name that serves up the scathing review on a silver platter. So, naming your movie *Suck*? It'd better be good, otherwise the review pretty much writes itself.

Fortunately, the makers of *Suck* knew what they were doing.

Suck is the story of a struggling band named The Winners, rocking out in a club in Montreal and trying to claw their way out of obscurity. It certainly doesn't help that their manager (Dave Foley) just resigned so he could turn his attention to a J-POP band.

In the crowd is a missing member of Keifer Sutherland's *Lost Boys* gang. Seriously, this guy is so glam rocked out, David Bowie would suggest he tone it down. The Winners' comely bass player, Jennifer, catches Mr. Glam's eye... which starts glowing red. After the show, Mr. Glam takes Jennifer back to his place, where the World's Most Goth Party is taking place. Everyone stands around posing as dry ice pours down the stairs into the living room. Mr. Glam starts lip synching... You get that he's a vampire, right? Cool.

When Jennifer no-shows the next day, lead singer (and Jenn's ex) Joey makes the call to head off for Toronto without her. She abruptly catches up with the band in Toronto, but she's... different.

The band quickly picks up on the big difference in their set with New Jennifer. Audiences can't take their eyes off her, leading to a huge boost in the band's popularity. It probably helps that Jennifer's vampire powers include having her own wind machine.

Of course, New Jennifer has also attracted the attention of Malcolm McDowell's vampire hunter, and the chase is on. We follow the action through Toronto and into New York State, with each new locale introduced with a terrific little ink-soaked animation sequences – kinda like if someone mapped out the northeast of the U.S. *Lord of the Rings*-style, but on the back of a paper bag.

Obviously, Jennifer's vampirism isn't something she can keep secret forever. Soon, roadie Hugo is covering up for her on the promise of immortality (or else). Once she "comes out" to the rest of the band, Joey quickly lays out such ground rules as "no turning other members of the band." However, the other members of the band aren't quite sold...

Despite all the vampire action – yes, there's a healthy amount of blood and dismembered body parts – *Suck* is first and foremost a love letter to rock and roll. While not a musical per say, a great deal of time and attention went into the musical productions in *Suck* (it's tempting to say that The Winners sound far better and more polished than any bar band, but it's a very minor quibble). There's also a fantastic Motown sequence during the flashback that shows McDowell's origin story – bonus points for using footage of *A Clockwork Orange*-era Malcolm McDowell during the sequence.

And there's some fun casting. *Suck* features Henry Rollins as a shock jock, Alice Cooper as a bartender who is more than he seems and Iggy Pop as the veteran musician who has seen it all. Cheekiest of all is Moby as the arrogant lead singer of Secretary of Steak, a Buffalo-based band with die-hard fans who fling raw cuts of beef. Their involvement is fun, and drives home my long-held belief that all musicians want to be actors and all actors want to be musicians.

Yeah, there's a great sense of humor to *Suck*, too. Much of the humor comes in clever throwaway moments, such as McDowell wearing sunglasses over his eye patch or a shot in customs that mirrors the cover of Bruce Springsteen's "Born in the USA." And while not necessarily quotable, there are some great exchanges between the members of the band ("You can explain why you're chewing on a severed arm?" "Oh, don't be such a drama queen!").

But I think that is what ultimately makes *Suck* such a good film: along with some great music, it's funny and stylish without trying too hard. Even considering the final scene of the film – which reeks of not knowing how the end the film, *Suck*'s only major misstep – it's clear that *Suck* most definitely does not… stink.

* * * *

MONSTER BRAWL
Directed by Jesse T. Cook
2011, 90 minutes, Unrated
Fight of the Living Dead

What is it about fighting that we love? Whether it's giant radioactive lizards or grizzled action stars or a couple of hobos, we just can't get enough of fighting. Fighting, fighting, fighting. Fighting in our children's programming and our politics and our rap songs.

Why do you think that is? Is it something embedded in our DNA, something primitive that pushes us to be the alpha in any group? Is it something in our soul, a restlessness that yearns for something more, to set forth and conquer? Or are we merely attracted to the kinetic energies given off when two immovable object collide?

Eh, who cares.

Monster Brawl is an attempt to revitalize the ancient practice of pitting classic monsters against each other, with the modern twist of making the battles a pay-per-view event. With one very notable exception (more on that in a bit), Monster Brawl has the production values down to a T: the ring announcers and celebrity staff, the video packages, even the persistent Monster Brawl logo in the corner of the screen… this could have easily been something made by the WWE. It's fun to see "The Mouth of the South" Jimmy Hart in vintage form as himself, and getting comedian Dave Foley to do the play-by-play commentary was smart. The real masterstroke was getting Bargain Bin Review favorite Lance Henriksen to narrate the video packages.

But you want to know about the monsters, don't you? Competing in Monster Brawl are: A Werewolf, A Mummy (whose dialogue is accompanied by hieroglyphic subtitles), Lady Vampire, "Witch Bitch," a Cyclops (who, awesomely, is portrayed as a major kayfabe/babyface), a Zombie, Frankenstein (or as Sasquatch Sid says, "Technically, it's Frankenstein's Monster if you want to be a dick about it"), and Swamp Gut (which is like Swamp Thing with a giant beer gut).

A lot of time obviously went into the structure of the tournament, dividing up the monsters into conferences ("Creatures" and "Undead") and weight classes (middleweight and heavyweight). It's a credit to *Monster Brawl*'s concept that much of my time wasn't spent nitpicking the actual film but geeking out by nitpicking the placement of the monsters. I mean, the werewolf and the zombie are heavyweights, but the Cyclops is a middleweight? Please!

Monster Brawl soon falls into a routine. We get video packages of the next two combatants, pre-match commentary with "stats," and then the fight itself. The video packages are nicely varied, from origin stories to character motivations, with the best being the Discovery Channel-esque documentary on Swamp Gut. *Monster Brawl* gets a lot of mileage out of the "fight statistic," with a number of blink and you'll miss 'em gags. My favorite: the Mummy has "chronic arthritis" ("I'll be damned before I cheer for a mummy," says Dave Foley).

The fights themselves are... interesting. In a nutshell, they're wrestling matches with horror film effects.

Oh, they start off like traditional pro wrestling bouts – throwing opponents against the ropes, pinning each other in the corner, jumping off the top turnbuckle – and it's clear that the stuntmen and women playing the monsters all have in-ring experience. But these are monsters, so things quickly get ultraviolent (as guest referee Herb Dean quickly learns). When a monster goes for a foreign object, it's a lot more likely to be a hatchet than a folding chair. Matches eventually end with a Mortal Kombat-style finishing fatality.

Monster Brawl is a great concept with great action and more than a few priceless moments (the werewolf puts his opponent in a figure-four leg lock!)... but it still falls a bit short.

What happened? Well, the setting doesn't do *Monster Brawl* any favors. The tournament takes place in a cursed cemetery, which seems right... but there's no audience. I'm sure that was a logistical and cost-saving decision by the filmmakers, but the lack of audience sucks some of the energy out of the matches. It seems like a small thing, but it makes the action seem almost tedious by the last half-hour of the film.

If it were me, I'd replace the zombie – popular, yes, but not a very exciting fighter – with Bigfoot and have an audience full of zombies. Maybe for *Monster Brawl 2*?

* *

MY ROAD TO BAD MOVIES:
A WHOLE NEW WORLD

Junior high. I won't lie to you – there's a lot I've blacked out from my junior high years. As your parents will attest, something happens during that age where every kid becomes a bit of an asshole, and I reckon I wasn't any different.

I was still a big Godzilla fan, but those films were becoming harder and harder to find on TV. Around that time, my tastes started turning towards modern-day horror films. The *Nightmare on Elm Street* series. *Child's Play*. Stinkin' *Shocker*. Dark times, indeed.

One Sunday morning, my father surprising me with a movie he recorded the night before. He saw that it was going to run right after *Saturday Night Live* and threw a VHS tape in, figuring that I'd enjoy it.

My first time watching this, I was disappointed to see that Godzilla only made a passing appearance. But man, did this open my eyes to a whole world of bad movies.

I must've watched this film dozens of times, and watching it today, I can still recite some of the one-liners right along with...

IT CAME FROM HOLLYWOOD

Directed by Andrew Solt and Malcolm Leo
1982, 80 minutes, Rated PG
Hurrah for Hollywood!

It must have seemed like a strange and unlikely project in a world before *Mystery Science Theater 3000*: Assemble a few comedians at the top of their game and have them present a b-movie greatest hits clip show.

Note that *It Came from Hollywood* is not a documentary about b-movies. There's no narrative and nothing historical or educational about this film, with the possible exception of the segment on Ed Wood (and even that's a stretch). It's more like a catalog of b-movie absurdity, or a film adaptation of Michael Medved's *The Golden Turkey Awards*, which would certainly make sense as he served as a consultant on the film.

The set-up for *It Came from Hollywood* is very simple: Dan Aykroyd, John Candy, Gilda Radner, and Cheech & Chong take turns "presenting" various categories of b-movies: Gorillas, Giants and Tiny People, Troubled Teenagers… you get the idea. Each comic's segment opens in a way to play to their comedic strengths.

Aykroyd and Radner appear in assorted sketches as increasingly wacky characters, while Cheech & Chong simply try to take in a movie. While the sketches are funny, it's the latter approach that works best. Between the popcorn sizes at the concession stand and the unspoken social rules of sitting in a theater, Cheech & Chong have more than enough to work with.

After the segment's introductory bit, we go into a video compilation of various b-movies with occasional narration and/or snarky commentary from the comic. Their wise-cracking is used sparingly, but there's enough of it present to think of *It Came from Hollywood* as a precursor of *Mystery Science Theater 3000*.

What's really impressive about this movie (besides how well it holds up) is the breadth of films it covers. *It Came from Hollywood* features over 90 films, many of which appear in this book. Some might wish more time was spent digging a bit more into each movie, going into such particulars as the plot or even the title, but that clearly was not the intent of this film.

It's much better to think of *It Came from Hollywood* as a highlight reel, with some of the best comedians of the day showcases the best moments from vintage b-movies. Now that's what I call entertainment.

* * * *

3: VINTAGE BAD

BELA LUGOSI MEETS A BROOKLYN GORILLA
Directed by William Beaudine
1952, 74 minutes, Unrated
Old School Monkey Business

It won't surprise you to learn that there are a heap of films reviewed based on the title alone. *Death Bed: The Bed That Eats* was one; *Monster a Go-Go* was another. *Bela Lugosi Meets a Brooklyn Gorilla?* Absolutely.

The title was literally all I knew about the film. Oh, I figured there's be some kind of shenanigans with a potion turning some Brooklyn thug into a murderous ape and only Bela Lugosi's Van Helsing-esque figure can stop the crime spree. I figured so, so wrong.

The film opens in a cheap studio set of a jungle. "This. Is. The Jungle!" a narrator over-enunciates, just in case we weren't sure of what we were looking at. Turns out it's a jungle full of stock footage!

Also in the studio jungle: Two unconscious guys who look like Hassidic Jews. A bunch of doughy white guys in animal print pajamas pop up to investigate, and it's at this point where I start to wonder if this film is actually a comedy.

The locals bring the two unconscious maybe Hassidic Jews back to their tribe, where there's an extended argument entirely in "tribal language." Those doing the majority of the booga-boogaing are the Medicine Man, who is dressed up like a primitive San Diego Chicken, and a woman who turns out to be the chief's daughter. Naturally, she looks like a Hollywood starlet, complete with perfect hair, a tailored dress and hosiery.

The two clearly not Hassidic Jews wander onto the scene, freshly shaved and outfitted with Hawaiian shirts which they've strangely opted to tie up in front of their chests. Like tropical farmer's daughters, but guys. The sensible one, optimistically named Duke, starts asking sensible questions like "Where are we?" and sensibly flirting with the chief's daughter.

The other guy, Sammy, honks and sputters like a dime store Jerry Lewis.

Despite Sammy's every effort to annoy the tribe's chief, he still decides to hold a luau for the two New Yorkers. We're then treated to an extended sequence with Sammy being chased around by the chief's other daughter, who is overweight – ho ho! The luau turns into a real music revue – Sammy tells jokes, and Duke sings a swing tune.

Duke and Sammy need to get back to their traveling entertainment group (they were going to "play for the boys in Guam") so the chief's hot daughter takes them to see the scientist she's working with (Bela Lugosi). In a big, creepy castle, just like you commonly find in the jungle. They're doing "experiments in evolution," which leads Bela Lugosi to give a lengthy explanation of evolutionary theory. Simply hearing Bela Lugosi say the word "metamorphosis" is worth the rental cost.

There's actually some good classic comedy shtick in this film, particularly between Sammy and Bela Lugosi's monkey/experiment subject. The film flip-flops between Sammy's shenanigans and Duke's serenading the chief's daughter with numerous film-padding songs. Unfortunately for Duke, Bela Lugosi also has a thing for the chief's daughter.

Bela's solution? Feed Duke his de-evoluting potion to turn him into a guy in an ape suit. Mistaken ape identity ensues.

Let's bring it on home: The good news is that if you're a fan of vintage comedy, you'll enjoy the overall flow and vibe of the film – particularly once it settles in to the meat of the story. The bad news is that it takes a very long time to get to the meat of the story, what with all of Duke's crooning and Sammy's hijinks. And the intensely cliché ending. And did I mention that Sammy is really, really obnoxious? Yeah, *Bela Lugosi Meets a Brooklyn Gorilla* is a whole lot of bad news.

* *

GLEN OR GLENDA
Directed by Ed Wood
1953, 68 minutes, Unrated
"Pull the string!"

Glen or Glenda is Ed Wood's directorial debut, a film I was aware of long before I started reviewing bad movies. I don't think I'm any better off for having seen *Glen or Glenda*, but at least I can check it off my To Do List.

Glen or Glenda opens with an entire block of text. Naturally, it's all Ed Wood-speak: promises of "stark realism" and "all the facts," which makes the coming crapstorm all the more awesome. We then go to Bela "Don't call me Dracula" Lugosi reading a book, and the Horns of Horror tell us that we should all be peeing our pants right about now. I mean, it's *Bela Lugosi*! And he's *reading* a *book*!

I need to mention that behind Bela is a bookshelf with various books, knick-knacks, and a cheesy-looking skeleton hanging off the side. I can only assume that these scenes were shot in Bela Lugosi's living room. Bela babbles, and then LIGHTNING! and suddenly Bela is playing with his Mr. Chemistry set. I'd love to tell you what Bela is talking about in these scenes, but between his accent and Ed Wood's dialogue, I have no earthly idea. Something about being displeased with the world's hustle and bustle and the circle of life and hakuna matata or whatever. Bela then sets up the story we're about to see, already in progress.

A rather, ah, odd-looking lady is neatly resting on a day bed, pretending to be dead. About a half dozen cops spill into the room, along with a hard-nosed detective, a doctor and a newspaper photographer, because this is apparently the slowest news day ever. The suicide note mentions that the odd-looking lady had been arrested for the fourth time for cross-dressing in public (a-ha!). The hard-nose detective simply nods, as if committing suicide in this instance was a perfectly reasonable solution.

Later, the hard-nosed detective goes to his shrink buddy for advice on how to keep cross-dressers from killing themselves, and I can't tell you how bummed out I was to discover that [SPOILER?] the hard-nosed detective does not dabble in cross-dressing himself. Missed opportunity right there, Mr. Wood.

The hard-nosed detective and his shrink buddy talk in circles for a while, until even the shrink is confused and has to ask if they're talking about the suicide of the transvestite. "If that's the word you Men of Medical Science use for a man who wears women's clothing, yes." The shrink eventually agrees to tell the stories of two different transvestites. Our gung-ho detective quickly – a little too quickly, perhaps? – says that he wants to hear the stories "to the fullest."

The shrink gets all glassy-eyed, or maybe he just had gas, and says, "Only the infinity of the depths of a man's mind can really tell the story." Oh my. At least Bela approves.

The story of the first transvestite is, at long last, the story of Glen and/or Glenda. For those of you keeping track, that makes Glen/Glenda a story within a story within a story, and possibly the inspiration for *Inception*. Let that sink in a moment.

A newspaper headline reads WORLD SHOCKED BY SEX CHANGE, and the shrink asks us "Why is the modern world shocked by this headline?" Obviously, that's the wrong question to ask, for the world is shocked by the sex change, not the newspaper's headline. And since the world already knew it was shocked by the sex change, the headline shouldn't have been much of a surprise at all. The only thing shocking to me is the wholesale amount of personal health information that have been revealed in the article.

We spend a fair bit of time watching Glen (Ed Wood, credited as "Daniel Davis") window-shopping while dressed as Glenda. The narration is awesomely all over the place, at one point comparing sex changes to advances in aviation and later stating that the hats men wear cut off the blood flow to the head, leading to baldness. Later still, narration implies that men dress in women's clothing because men's casual attire is inherently uncomfortable.

So here's the deal with Glen: He's engaged to this real swell girl, Barbara (Dolores Fuller, Ed Wood's girlfriend at the time), but she doesn't know about his cross-dressing – or his desire to wear her angora sweater – and he's struggling to tell her. At one point, Barbara asks Glen if there's another woman, and that kicks us *Inception*-style all the way back up to Bela Lugosi. "PULL THE STRING!! PULL THE STRING!!" Bela bellows as stock footage of a buffalo stampede is superimposed over him. I don't know what any of that is about, but it's a pretty amazing moment.

Unfortunately, this is where the film falls apart. See, *Glen or Glenda* would have worked beautifully as one of those old school shorts that were so often featured on *Mystery Science Theater 3000*. But as a feature film, it struggles just to fill its meager 68 minute runtime. The plight of someone considering a sex change is hashed over repeatedly, and let me be the first to tell you that having the conversation accompanied by stock footage from an iron smelting plant doesn't help. Even after Glen confides in another tranny, who basically tells Glen to tell Barbara or shut up already, we have to sit through an endless dream sequence chock-full of interpretive dance.

Finally, *finally*, Glen tells Barbara about Glenda, and we're treated to some of the worst acting I've ever seen. Because the scene is narrated, we get lots of Big Acting Gestures from Ms. Fuller as she seems to physically wrestle with the revelation. Ultimately, she surrenders her prized angora sweater, so that all ends on a happy note.

The second story, of Alan/Anne, is barely worth mentioning. Long story short: Alan's parents didn't love him, his mom wanted a girl and made him do housework, blah blah blah, he's a tranny and ultimately gets a sex change. Amusingly, the shrink seems get himself a bit worked up when describing Alan's feminine attributes.

Leonard Maltin has said that *Glen or Glenda* – and not *Plan 9 From Outer Space* – may be the worst film ever made, and I'd have to agree. Yes, *Glen or Glenda* is surprisingly progressive for its era... but as I mentioned before, it's essentially a short stretched out to fill 68 minutes. The film is also genreless, plotless, overly melodramatic and, at times, completely random.

It's worth checking out. Once.

* *

ROBOT MONSTER
Directed by Phil Tucker
1953, 62 minutes, Unrated
A B-Movie Icon

Featured prominently in *It Came from Hollywood*, right along with the sections on teenage hoodlums and Ed Wood films, was a guy in an ape suit with a diver's helmet. I'm not being cheeky or hyperbolic – the creature was literally a guy in an ape suit, with a diver's helmet in place of the ape's head. I knew right then and there that my life would not be complete without seeing that movie.

Robot Monster opens with a young brother and sister playing in a rock quarry. Yay, rocks! They bicker over what to play, and then chat up a pair of archeologist chipping away in a cave. The kids are called away for a picnic, followed by a group nap.

When Brother wakes up, he wanders back to the cave. Suddenly: Lightning! Explosions! Stock footage of lizards fighting? Okay then! Brother climbs up the side of the cave, and out comes our diver ape.

The diver ape is Ro-Man. Ro-Man enjoys long walks around desolate locations, gesticulating wildly and young ladies in torpedo-shaped brassieres. Ro-Man has been sent to Earth to eradicate the "Hu-Mans," and has just about finished his task (it certainly helped that many countries started nuking each other). The Home Office informs him that eight humans still live, and to stop slacking off "…or I will sentence you for failure!" Home Office intones. It's definitely worth noting that Home Office sounds a lot like Kang from *The Simpsons*, which pretty much means our planet was destroyed by the Homer Simpson of Planet Ro-Man.

In the film's most disorienting moment – of which there are quite a few – we find out that the survivors include Brother, Sister and their Mom (now married to one of the archeologists from the beginning), and Big Sis (who is in a quasi-romantic relationship with the other archeologist). Our family of survivors – let's call them the Probsts, just for laughs – have so far evaded Ro-Man by living in an area surrounded by buzzing electric fences. It also helps that Papa Probst created an antibiotic to make them all immune to disease and Ro-Man's death ray. This doesn't stop Ro-Man from radioing in to their video screen to taunt them like a low-level wrestling villain.

The Probsts are all duly intimidated and begin plotting a way to get Papa Probst's serum to a garrison hiding out in a space station. This gives Big Sis and her hunky archeologist something to bicker about. "I'm bossy?" She asks. He incredulously counters, "You're so bossy, you should be milked before you come home at night!" Ah, young love.

Unfortunately for our hunky and sometimes shirtless archeologist, there's another suitor vying for Big Sis's attention… Yes, that's right: Ro-Man has developed feelings for Big Sis. In fact, when the Probsts call up Ro-Man to iron out a peace treaty, Ro-Man instead asks Big Sis out on a date.

And that's when we go to the INTERMISSION. Because the filmmakers clearly thought that 62 minutes of this film would be too much for the audience to sit through.

I could continue on with the plot of the film, but is there any point? You're not going to watch this for the deeply layered storyline or intricate characterizations. You're going to watch this for the cheaper than cheap special effects (like a bubble machine that doubles as alien technology), for the random stock footage of lizards fighting and for lines like "You look like a pooped out pinwheel."

But most of all, you're going to watch *Robot Monster* to see that, yes, that is indeed a guy running around in an ape suit with a diver's helmet.

* * *

BRIDE OF THE MONSTER
Directed by Ed Wood
1955, 68 minutes, Unrated
Bride of the Stock Footage

Giddy from the success of *Glen or Glenda* (if by "success," one means "ability to actually make a movie"), Ed Wood charged onward to make whatever it is you'd call *Bride of the Monster*. If Tim Burton's *Ed Wood* is to be believed, Wood pretty much created his tale based on the stock footage he had available to him – I can't verify if that's true, but it's certainly plausible.

To be fair, *Bride of the Monster* is a better film than *Glen or Glenda...* though that's hardly anything to brag about.

The film opens with a bolt of lightning. Man, Wood loves his lightning! If he were ever commissioned to make corporate training videos, he'd still find a way to add lightning. Two cops wander through a swamp, expositioning that this particular storm has been going on "for months."

Also among the Ed Wood Regulars is Dracula himself, Bela Lugosi. Here, Lugosi plays Dr. Eric Vornoff – no need to ask him his name, he'll tell you over and over – a mad scientist residing in a fully tricked-out mad scientist pad. Check it out: Varnoff's old mansion features a full laboratory with neon lights, a variety of levers and toggles, a full-sized fridge and a lumbering assistant (Lobo, played by Sweden's own Tor Johnson). The mansion is located deep in a swamp and guarded by Varnoff's attack octopus (played by Stock Footage). Pretty sweet, eh?

Tough break for those two cops. After being turned away from Vornoff's sweet lair, one gets attacked by a rubber octopus dummy and the other gets fried in Vornoff's failed experiment. Yet somehow, all of the headlines in the local papers scream that the monster has killed two more people. How would anyone know that? Did Vornoff hold a press conference to announce the murders?

No time for logic! It's time to meet our Protagonists: She is Janet Lawton, a tough-as-nails newspaper reporter, trying to make a mark in a Man's World. He is Dick Craig, a promising police lieutenant and Janet's boyfriend. And Dick's boss, the police chief, is strangely obsessed with birds. Janet and the Chief get into it because she's been writing article after article about "the monster" and he can't/won't comment on the investigation. In a huff, Janet decided that the only way to get any information is to go out to the scene of the crimes herself. Seriously? I did more research and footwork for the puff pieces I wrote straight out of college than this "star reporter."

Janet heads out into the swamp and promptly drives right into a ditch. Insert your own wisecrack about women drivers here. Fortunately, Lobo is on hand to carry her away. Dick, fully aware of Janet's ability to drive off the road, gets off his backside and goes looking for her.

Dick is joined by some of his colleagues and a visiting scientist, who allows Ed Wood to shoehorn in some talk about the dangers of atomic power with all the subtlety of a punch in the nose. The visiting scientist later has a sit-down with Vornoff and tries to lure him back to his home country so the government can make use of his mad scientist-ry. I suspect this was all an excuse to give Lugosi a Big Dramatic Monologue:

My dear professor Strowski twenty years ago I was banned from my homeland, parted from my wife and son, never to see them again. Why? Because I suggested to use the atom elements, for producing super beings, beings of unthinkable strength and size. I was classed as a madman, a charlatan, outlawed in a world of science which previously honored me as a genius. Now, here in this forsaken jungle hell, I have proven that I am right. No, Professor Strowski, it is no laughing matter.

So there you have it: An army of atomic supermen. Also, Vornoff can hypnotize women because he's double-jointed and Hungarian.

It all builds up to what you'd expect: shirts are torn, feeble attempts at fighting Lobo hand-to-hand are made and everything catches fire. Yes, Vornoff ends up rolling around with the rubber octopus, because as the old Hollywood adage goes, "If you show an octopus in Act I, it has to attack the villain in Act III."

Bride of the Monster isn't the movie that *Plan 9 from Outer Space* (released four years later) is, but it's a nice glimpse of the wholesale corniness to come.

* * *

IT CONQUERED THE WORLD

Directed by Roger Corman
1956, 71 minutes, Unrated
What is from Venus again?

This may be hard for you to believe, but there was a time in this country where intelligence wasn't looked down on as some kind of elitist ruse. Once upon a time, the scientific community was treated with actual respect. It used to be that when scientists announced that something was bad for you or that there was a global phenomenon taking place, people actually believed them.

Adorable, eh?

That's what I love about films like Roger Corman's *It Conquered the World*: The biggest suspension of belief isn't the silly looking alien or the wacky invention, but the mere fact that leading scientists would be taken seriously.

There are limits to that, of course, even in the '50s. And that limit is a young Lee Van Clef, who has traded in his 10-gallon hat for a science degree in this film. At the start of *It Conquered the World*, LVC is a controversial physicist who is desperately trying to convince the military to pull down its shiny new satellite. Okay, that part isn't particularly controversial. When pressed for a reason, LVC announces that "alien intelligence watches us constantly" and wants to keep Earth in its place. Yeah, he's patted on the head and sent away.

Three months later, LVC and his spunky wife invite a young Peter Graves and his better half over for dinner. Soon, the men are engaging in sexy, sexy satellite talk – seriously, Graves all but lights up a cigarette after musing about the technical achievement. LVC kills the evening by confiding in Graves that he's been hearing voices from Venus on his ham radio.

It's a testament to Mr. Van Clef's performance that he doesn't come off quite as bat-shit crazy as I'm making him sound. We do indeed hear LVC talking with his Venusian friend... or perhaps that's just one of the adults from *The Peanuts*.

Suddenly, word comes in that "the scientific achievement of the century has disappeared!" What? The TV? The automobile? Sugar-free gum? No, it's that satellite – again with the satellite! And guess who has hitched a ride to Earth on it?

Yeah, let's jump ahead and talk about LVC's little Venusian friend. It's a pretty shocking moment when we first see the alien, but not for the reason the movie thinks. Unless the filmmakers truly believed that audiences would find angry little foam pyramids terrifying. Of course this angry little pyramid of a creature is here to Conquer the World – we know this because it's right in the title of the film. Here is its master plan for world conquest:

1. Use its freaky Venusian powers to somehow make *all* of the world's machines stop working (except for LVC's)
2. Make exactly eight rubber bat-Frisbees, each one capable of mind-controlling exactly one human
3. Hang out in a cave until the conquest is complete

For such an "advanced" species, this seems like a really crappy plan. Everyone is strangely chill about the widespread power outage – even when it's blamed on the communists. Bizarrely, the rubber bat-Frisbees seem to work: The local sheriff gets bit by one, and merely drops it in the garbage and goes about his business. An army general actually sees a rubber bat-Frisbee, so he pulls his side arm and *waves the butt of his gun at it*. Unsurprisingly, that doesn't work.

Things eventually escalate to my favorite part of any film: the evacuation montage. People running in the streets! This one is particularly stellar, as it features a guy who had the wherewithal to grab his saxophone before running off.

During the evacuation, Peter Graves sees the brain-controlled sheriff shoot the town's newspaper editor for not leaving town. Graves is pretty casual about the local law gunning someone down in cold blood, and does a lot of righteous speechifying before socking the sheriff in the kisser. Then Graves is off to have a pillow fight with one of the rubber bat-Frisbees.

The speechifying becomes a regular thing by the third act, as Graves and LVC talk and talk and talk at each other. Their inactivity is a bit maddening – not just to the audience, but to the other characters as well. Eventually, LVC's spunky wife (Beverly Garland, easily my favorite character in the film) gets sick of all the flapping jaws, grabs a twelve gauge, and heads out to the Cave of World Conquest to take care of business herself. Sadly, once she gets there she remembers that she's a woman in a '50s movie, and things don't go so well.

So: Will Peter Graves and LVC stop talking long enough to defeat the Venusian? How many times will Graves cold clock the brain-controlled general? Who will surprise us with a homemade flamethrower? And what is a young Dick Miller doing in this picture? You'll just have to find out for yourself.

And you totally should. *It Conquered the World* is delightfully bonkers, and if you've never seen a vintage Roger Corman film, this is a great one to check out. As the write-up on the VHS cover puts it, "A creepy monster, blood-sucking bats, screaming victims and earnest men of science: now that's a Drive-In Classic!"

* * * *

WARNING FROM SPACE
Directed by Koji Shima
1956, 87 minutes, Unrated
That I found this movie on a compilation DVD should be warning enough.

This might be the first film I've reviewed that literally came from the bargain bin. I found this DVD on the dollar rack at a big box store... with three other movies on the same disc. After the world's hastiest opening credits, we're told by an alien race that "the Earthlings must be stopped" and "warned to stop their blundering." Two aliens are chosen to go down to the island of Japan and "warn the scientists." In theory, this should be a very simple task. It's not like scientists (even in Japan) are heads of state or reclusive movie stars.

No, the aliens' big hurdle is that they look ridiculous.

These aliens look like guys in giant starfish costumes made of flimsy pajama material, with a big eye in the middle (probably because they *are* guys in giant starfish costumes made of flimsy pajama material, with a big eye in the middle). Naturally, any Earthling who sees one of the aliens starts shrieking in terror. Seriously, Paul Stanley from KISS is scarier looking. The appearance of UFOs causes the standard movie response: screaming headlines. My favorite appears on the *Tokyo Times*: "Observatory Scientists Withhold Comment!" Exclamation point!

(Naturally, the second standard response is to launch ineffectual rockets at the UFO.)

So, we have starfish aliens trying to make contact, Japan launching rockets at UFOs and more footage of guys looking in humongous telescopes than you can shake a stick at... Time for a musical number! Yes, really. We get treated to one of those Old Hollywood bits where a woman in an evening gown tap dances with a platoon of guys in tuxedos. Can you say "padding for time," boys and girls?

After a scene of starfish aliens bickering in halting, monotone voices, one of the starfishes (using the power of Glowing Hula-Hoops) "transmutes" itself into the singer from the previous scene. However, Starfish-turned-StarGirl doesn't bother with any sort of backstory for herself, so she just wanders around confused for a while. Of course, all this means the audience gets to watch all the other characters try to figure out what her deal is. Joy.

Eventually, Star Girl tells us what the Starfishians are up to. This leads to some more screaming headlines (Tokyo Herald: "Experts Doubt If Space People Exist!") and some unintentionally hilarious scenes.

First, the observatory scientists need to verify that Star Girl is indeed an alien and not some crackpot. Science Stooge #1 successfully convinces Science Stooges #2 and #3 by producing Star Girl's fingerprints and cells on a slide, which they all examine *without the aid of a microscope*. No wonder Japan is so technologically advanced: Japanese scientists have superhuman vision.

Then, when the Science Stooges prove Star Girl's story is true after spending 36 straight hours starring into their large telescope, Tokyo's chief of police orders an immediate evacuation of the city. That's right: the *planet* is about to be destroyed – head for the hills! I suspect this was added in just as an excuse to include lots of sirens and footage of Japanese people running in the streets.

Unlike just about every other Japanese film made after 1945, *Warning from Space* doesn't have a clear anti-nuke message. Instead, the film blazes a different path, suggesting that nuclear weapons are ineffective and useless compared to the technology of fictitious aliens in cheap starfish costumes. So... yay?

*

THE GIANT CLAW

Directed by Fred F. Sears
1957, 75 minutes, Unrated
A case of classic Sci-Fi gone to the birds.

Man, I love these kind of films. The late '50s and '60s are littered with sci-fi thrillers about how some new-fangled science made some every-day animal 50 times its size. And then, after a few choice deaths and a significant amount of collateral damage, we all learn an important lesson in tampering with the Laws of God. We see this over and over and over again.

I'm tempted to say that *The Giant Claw* is much of the same, but it's a bit more special than that.

The new-fangled science in question here is radar (always referred to here as "ray-dar"). We start off in the Arctic, where hot shot test pilot Mitch (Jeff Morrow) is feeling the need for speed while his mathematician girlfriend, Sally (Playboy Playmate Mara Corday), figures out all the science-y ray-dar stuff. Mitch sees a UFO "as big as a battleship." Get used to that: the creature at the heart of this film is referred to as a "battleship" at least a half dozen times. It's kept intentionally out of focus for a while, making it look like a used Brillo pad.

Mitch reports the sighting and gets himself into all sorts of trouble for his efforts. That is, until other planes start disappearing... The movie spends some time with Mitch and

Sally bantering and trying to sort things out. Then, 27 minutes in, we get to see our Big Bad. And it's a Muppet of a vulture. I'm not exaggerating. Let that sink in.

I could try to be kind and understanding, and chalk this thing up to the limited special effects of the era. But even by 1957 standards, this ridiculous Vulture Muppet was a joke. Apparently, the plan was to have Ray Harryhausen create a stop-motion version of the bird, but then the filmmakers ran out of money. None of the stars had any idea of what the creature looked like until the premiere. Years later, Morrow said that the audience laughed so hard every time this thing showed up on the screen that he slipped out of the theater during the film so no one would recognize him.

The Army goes through its standard responses: 1) Fire everything, 2) Freak out when that doesn't work. Amazingly, there's no To Nuke or Not to Nuke conversation, but there is a lot of exciting Stock Footage vs. Vulture Muppet sequences. Awesomely, it wasn't enough for the Vulture Muppet to knock planes out of the sky – it has to swoop in and gobble up the people who tried to parachute to safety. When the Army fails to stop the Vulture Muppet, the only response is: "It's hard to come up with answers when you don't even know what the question is."

While you're mulling over that jewel of wisdom, let me note that there is a lot – *a lot* – of bewilderment over the inability to track the battleship-sized Vulture Muppet with modern-day radar. How can it fail? *It's radar.*

That means it's time to call in a Mr. Science Guy to science things up, and what better way to do that than to bring the action to a screeching halt with a lecture on anti-matter. Based solely on the Army's one-time experience and a feather that fell off the Muppet, our egghead theorizes that the Vulture Muppet is surrounded by an anti-matter shield. Of course, any high school biology teacher can tell you that's true of all giant vultures.

But wait, there's more! "That bird is extra-terrestrial. It comes from outer space… From some God-forsaken anti-matter galaxy billions and billions of light years from the earth. No other explanation is possible." Naturally.

As the laughable Vulture Muppet continues its "fantastic orgy of attacks," Mitch goes to work using his brain parts to develop "one of those cock-eyed concepts you pull out of Cloud Eight somewhere." Can you tell that I just loved the dialogue in this film?

The final stretch of the film is filled with attack orgy-goodness (so to speak), featuring the Vulture Muppet swooping down low to gobble up people, doing a Kong impersonation and even eating a Styrofoam U.N. Building (take that, world peace!). That's when our heroes put Mitch's plan into action – the world's best and brightest were stupefied, but a test pilot has all the answers – and there's time for one final cliché image that's so cheesy, it fits right in with the rest of the film.

So: A few choice deaths? Check. A significant amount of collateral damage? Check. The important lesson we all learn? Always budget accordingly for your special effects.

* * * *

THE GIANT GILA MONSTER
Directed by Ray Kellogg
1959, 74 minutes, Unrated
Versus the scourge of ukulele music.

I watched this particular film with a good friend of mine who teaches high school biology. I think it was an ideal selection: As a Man of Science, he was interested in seeing how the Gila Monster would be represented and explained; as a Man of Faith, I had the upmost confidence that this would be a laughably bad movie.

This story takes place in one of the many "uncharted," "unpopulated," "impenetrable" parts of our country (There were a few other "un-" words in there, but I didn't feel like pausing the tape twenty seconds into the film. Also, I was busy eating nachos.)... The kind of place where one has no idea of just how big a Gila Monster might grow. Like Wyoming. Regardless, the setting of the film looks suspiciously like southern California.

It's interesting to note that, unlike so many other films of the era, the filmmakers were *not* trying to explain away the Giant Gila Monster as a mutation or the result of a radioactive accident. Instead, the filmmakers are suggesting that Giant Gila Monsters are naturally occurring. Let that sink in a bit.

Here in one corner of our "uncharted" country is a couple of 30somethings – Pat and Liz, we'll learn later – nuzzling in their parked car. Suddenly, a big lizard arm! Blam! The car tumbles down a ravine and... sits there, failing to explode in an obscenely huge ball of fire. Hope Pat has AAA.

Meanwhile, the rest of the, ahem, "teenagers" are out doing what teens do best: listening to loud rock music, drag racing and dancing at the local pop shop. Go, Daddy-O! Pat and Liz fail to show up, so they miss out on the fun.

Pat and Liz? Still missing. Pat's dad and the Sheriff have an Argument of Exposition: they debate the possibility that the two ran off to elope (fat chance, says Dad) and the influence that Chase, Leader of the Pack, has over the couple (mostly good, says Sheriff).

Apparently eloping was a major social concern in the late '50s, cuz the Sheriff seems to pursue this for a good chunk of the movie. That's when he's not doing DUI checks by smelling people's breath, of course.

It's also apparent that the Sheriff is the only law officer in the county, cuz he never assigns the missing person's case to anyone else. With so much "uncharted country" to cover and breath to smell, the Sheriff quickly enlists Chase's help in finding Pat and Liz. Chase happily agrees to help, and the Sheriff thanks him by giving Chase an earful about his busted headlight. Nice.

Never mind all that – let's meet our Nameless Traveling Salesman. I'm sure we're about to learn all about your very interesting li— it's the Giant Gila Monster! And it's... a close-up of somebody's pet lizard in a sandbox! Roar, big lizard hand, bye-bye Nameless Traveling Salesman.

Chase is on the case – just as soon as he finishes up some automotive action for his shop. Tune ups! Towing! Auto maintenance! This movie was sponsored by Mobile Oil with all the subtlety of a poke in the eye. One redneck customer tells Chase that there's four quarts of nitro glycerin stored in some shack, which just might be important later.

Another customer, a drunk D.J., lays this line on Chase when asked if he needs a tow: "I'm suburb... Seven in a box, no corners. I'm a round house!" Ah, the days where drinking and driving was considered charming. The D.J. actually saw the Giant Gila Monster, but was so drunk that Chase can't believe him.

But that's okay, because the now-grateful D.J. just might be the big break Chase has been hoping for! Turns out Chase isn't just a hip auto mechanic – he also sings and plays the ukulele! The film grinds to a complete stop so Chase can play a song on his ukulele for his Very French Girlfriend and his polio-afflicted daughter/kid sister/young niece. The song is competent, I guess. Who can tell on a ukulele? The lyrics are a different story. It's like the kind of stuff Shel Silverstein would've come up with after drinking too much paint thinner:

```
My baby she rocks, and rolls
and rocks whenever she walks
my baby she rocks, and rolls
and rocks whenever she talks
My baby's a rock-n-rollin' tippy-toein
Never knowin' always glowin' baby
My baby she swings, and sings
And swings whenever I bring her things
She swings, and sings
And swings for little diamond rings
```

Turns out that the Giant Gila Monster HATES ukulele music, cuz it attacks the Big Party where Chase is playing later in the film. What happens from here I won't say, other than the climax doesn't involve any additional auto maintenance and ends exactly as you might imagine it would.

Afterwards, in order to complete his investigation, the Sheriff orders the entire party to stay put or be arrested. Hearing this, Chase and his Very French Girlfriend immediately drive off. That must be one of the perks of being the Sheriff's only friend. Or maybe the Sheriff was deeply disappointed that Chase would run off on him like that. I know I was rather disappointed with the listlessness and sluggishness of *The Giant Gila Monster*.

* *

SANTA CLAUS

Directed by Rene Cardona
1959, 94 minutes, Unrated
You'd better watch out / this film might make you cry

What better way to celebrate the holidays than with an aggressively horrible Christmas movie? Sadly, there's no shortage of these. Allow me to present Mexico's introduction to St. Nick, the 1959 film *Santa Claus.*

That's right: introduction. For many years, Mexico's Christmas focused heavily on the gifts of the Magi, so this film was meant to introduce the concept of Santa Claus to the youth of Mexico. Those poor Mexican children.

In *Santa Claus*, we learn that Santa lives in a castle in the clouds up in space. There are other castles in other clouds, which has me dying to know who Santa's neighbors are. The Easter Bunny? Jesus? Santos? The interior of Santa's abode looks somewhat like a mosque, and he has a sweatshop filled with child stereotypes from every country. In a hefty bit of padding, the film introduces us to the kids in just about every country. And I do mean Every. Country.

Santa plays the organ while his child workforce cranks out toys for all the good children of Earth. And just how does Santa tell who has been Naughty or Nice? With a wide array of nightmarish appliances that Terry Gilliam wishes he'd come up with. But all Santa can do is spy. For reasons never explained, Santa can only come to Earth on Christmas Eve, and must leave before sunrise or his cyborg reindeer (!!) will turn to dust.

A toy of the Devil (1959's must-have toy, perhaps?) abruptly transitions us to what I assume is Hell, where a platoon of guys in horns and red pajamas are doing some kind of interpretive dance. Yeah, definitely Hell.

Pitch is sent up to Earth to wage his War on Christmas. Sadly, his War on Christmas is waged not through the secularization of our nation but through minor property damage. A fair amount of time is spent trying to influence a Very Good poor girl into stealing a doll and three Very Bad boys into "kidnapping and enslaving" Santa. You can imagine the results of both schemes.

Most of the Santa vs. The Devil confrontations end up with the kind of slapstick shenanigans you'd expect in a really stupid sequel to *Home Alone*. When Pitch finally gets Santa in a pickle by stealing some of his magical gadgets – invisibility powder, a Daisy of Levitation +2, you know, standard Christmas stuff – Santa has to call on Merlin the Magician, for help.

If you really must see this film, I recommend a few stiff cups of eggnog first.

* *

THE WASP WOMEN
Directed by Roger Corman
1959, 73 minutes, Unrated
Bad jelly!

When I was in college about a million years ago, I took a bunch of mass communication courses. Each one would inevitably touch on body image in the media, and pull out one of those before 'n after pics of some name brand supermodel, pre- and post-airbrushing.

This has been going on forever. You knew that, right? I'd like to think you knew that. I assumed that *everyone* knew that, but I'm not so sure about these Millennial types, raised on reality TV and airing all their business online in the social media du jour. I even saw a reality show on the TV Guide Channel where people had plastic surgery to make themselves look like the celeb of the moment from a specific magazine cover. Not sure which was more horrific: the brainless self-mutilation or the fact that I was watching the TV Guide Channel.

Turns out that our obsession with beauty goes back to... well, at least the 1950s. That's when a film was released about a type-A whose obsessive drive creates a half-human, half-insect monstrosity. That film was *The Fly*. Unfortunately, that's not the film I'm reviewing today.

Roger Corman's *The Wasp Woman* opens in a world where grown men are absolutely obsessed with bees. Fiction! One particularly mad scientist-y guy with the positively mad scientist-ish name of Dr. Zinthrop has jumped the rails to study wasps. Instead of harvesting honey, Dr. Zinthrop has been extracting enzymes from the royal jelly of queen wasps – which is apparently a real thing – and has created an anti-aging formula.

An anti-aging formula – can you imagine the implications, the business opportunities? Because the rep from Honey Co. can't *at all*. That's not honey! And so, despite the fact that the anti-aging formula was developed completely on company time and with company resources, Dr. Zinthrop is promptly fired.

Later, in The City, we learn that sales for Starlin Cosmetics are plummeting. This is the first of many scenes of exciting boardroom action. Model-turned-business mogul Janice Starlin is mad as hell, but the Boys' Club that makes up her board is happy to put the blame on her. Take that, lady in charge of something in the '50s!

Yeah, she's mad. But is she mad enough to enter into a verbal contract with Dr. Zinthrop to perfect his anti-aging formula and begin testing it on herself, ultimately turning herself in a half-woman, half-wasp creature? Sounds like a safe bet.

It's not the predictability that bothers me – it's the lack of logic. I get the storytelling need for an economy of characters, but it's neither smart science nor smart business to test your highly experimental formula on the person funding the experiment.

And so: Office gossip! Corporate espionage! Executives flirting with secretaries! Yes, you'll have to wait until the last 20 minutes or so for a proper look at the Wasp Woman. But it's hard to complain as the film clips along at a good pace, and there's enough corniness and dated delights to make this morality tale all enjoyable.

Why yes, of course this is a morality tale. The moral is that there's a high price for chasing everlasting beauty, and that price is that you too will become a hideous half-insect creature. Don't say I didn't warn you.

* * *

THE BEAST OF YUCCA FLATS
Directed by Coleman Francis
1961, 54 minutes, Unrated
"Nothing bothers some people, not even flying saucers."

A bad movie that's only an hour long? Why can't there be more bad movies like this?

The Beast of Yucca Flats opens like a student film: Black and white, a girl looking at herself in a mirror meaningfully, with the only audio being the loud, relentless clanking of an old clock. Then a pair of beefy hands come out of nowhere and choke her to death. Oh well, at least the damned clock stopped.

Our narrator tells us – the film is almost entirely narrated – that Tor Johnson is a Big Deal Scientist who has just defected from the Evil Empire, and he and his aide have a whole briefcase of intel to hand off to some agents in Yucca Flats. That intel? Pertains to traveling to the moon. How cute. Sadly, I'm of a generation that only cares about the moon when Tom Hanks is involved.

As you might imagine, the KGB isn't too keen on any of this. A pair of agents try to get the jump on Tor Johnson and company, and we're treated to one of the more stilted shootouts I've seen in a while. Unfortunately, it's hard to sort out who is who when you have a bunch of non-descript guys in black suits shooting at each other. And it certainly doesn't help that all of the actors turn away from the camera when talking so that the dialogue can be dubbed in after the fact. This really is a student film!

So there's a shootout and a chase, and all I really know for sure is that it ends with Tor Johnson wandering around the desert with his briefcase when he finds himself in the middle of an atomic bomb test. What, no fridge to hide in?

If you're like me, you're looking forward to seeing Tor Johnson turn into the Incredible Hulk. No such luck. No cool mutation, not even much in the way of makeup. Just Tor Johnson walking around with a stick that he never uses to beat anyone.

The blast does give Tor's beefy hands the incredible ability to appear anywhere and choke people to death within seconds. And when he starts choking random travelers, the cops investigate. The press is all over it, too: BEAST KILLS MAN AND WIFE. What kind of "beast" strangles people?

And with the introduction of the only two police officers in Yucca Flats, we should talk about the narration. The writing is... wow. Everyone is introduced in choppy, hard-boiled fragments.

> "110 degrees in the shade... and there's no shade."

> "Nothing bothers some people, not even flying saucers."

I wonder what the narrator would say about me? I bet it'd sound like this:

> Film reviewer. Observer of the human condition. Looking for beauty trapped within the celluloid of terrible movies. A labor of love, with the emphasis on "labor."

Anyway, we get to watch these two cops conduct their search for the beast in what feels like real-time. As that is happening, a family stops for gas or whatever, and their two boys get themselves lost in the desert. Goodie, more people to watch wander around the wilderness.

The cops ultimately decide, and I'm not making this up, to fly around the plateau in a plane and shoot at anyone they see wandering around. Because anyone wandering around *must* be the killer. It really is "shoot first, ask questions later" for these guys, and dad is in for a big shock when he goes looking for his boys.

Just how bad are these cops? They eventually save the boys from Tor Johnson, fight and presumably kill him, and then *leave his body in the desert.* Cuz that's how they roll in Yucca Flats.

* * * *

CREATURE FROM THE HAUNTED SEA
Directed by Roger Corman
1961, 74 minutes, Unrated
Where's Scooby-Doo when the Cubans need him?

This came from an actual bargain bin. The DVD write-up describes the movie as an "outrageous comedy-horror parody from Roger Corman" that features "secret agents, Cuban loyalists and American gangsters." You can see why I couldn't leave this in the store.

Okay, the story of *Creature from the Haunted Sea*: Once upon a time, there was a revolution in Cuba. With Castro busy settling into power, the old regime was busy smuggling things out of the country with the aid of the U.S. underworld... things like the entire Cuban Treasury. Which is why after the opening credits (entirely made with construction paper), we find ourselves on the open sea.

Four gangsters, a half-dozen Cubans and a secret agent are on a boat with the entirety of Cuba's treasury. The secret agent is undercover with the gangsters, posing as a "notorious gum machine thief from Chicago." He runs down all the main characters for us in the kind of dead-pan style Jack Webb would approve of. There is the Boss, his moll, her brother and "Happy Jack," who apparently got his name because he "developed a muscle spasm in his cheeks from watching too many Humphrey Bogart pictures."

I think these are the jokes, people.

Oh, and Happy Jack is a master of animal calls – actually, the actor just pantomimes doing the calls while the sound editor dubs in the *real* animal noise. Happy Jack does this A LOT. Boy howdy, that doesn't get annoying!

The gangsters are hired to hang onto the Cuban Treasury until such time as the old regime can overthrow Castro (last I checked, that might take a while). Naturally, the gangsters would just assume keep the loot for themselves, but they need a way to get rid of all the Cuban soldiers on board without raising suspicion. The mob boss comes up with a scheme that would make any Scooby-Doo villain proud: Impersonate a sea monster. Wanna guess the chances of a *real* sea monster showing up?

As you might guess, there are some fine moments in this movie. Like when the Cuban Coast Guard approaches, the mob boss wants everyone to "act casual" by having his moll sing for everyone – a lounge tune, complete with accompanying piano music. Very natural!

Like when our secret agent tries to knock someone out with a fish.

Or pretty much any time we get narration from our secret agent. You can't beat hard-boiled lines like this: "It was dusk. I could tell because the sun was going down."

And we haven't even talked about the monster yet. Believe it or not, the sea monster looks like a hairy Homer Simpson. How awesome is that? I only wish the creature had more screen time. This monster was made with moss and Brillo pads and tennis balls for eyes. There are even a few shots in the movie where you can see the actor underneath the costume. Apparently, the biggest challenge the actors had during the shooting of this movie was *not* laughing at the creature whenever it appeared.

This is definitely one of those films Roger Corman made fully expecting young couples to ignore while making out at the drive-in. But if you like your narration extra hard-boiled and your Homer Simpson hairy, this might be worth checking out.

* *

EEGAH!
Directed by Arch Hall, Sr.
1962, 90 minutes, Unrated
The dangers of nepotism.

There are a lot of very bad movies that start with a pretty cool idea: A monster mash between a giant shark and giant octopus... Steven Seagal vs. vampires... A rock band terrorized by demons. It's not hard to figure out how someone was able to these movies made.

A woman and her father are abducted by a cave man? Not so much. Who thought this would be an interesting movie?

Arch Hall, Sr. apparently thought so. He helped write the film, he directed, he co-starred as the father, and he cast his son as the surf rock crooning romantic lead. And for his efforts, Papa Hall gave us *Eegah!*, one of the more famously bad films ever made.

And just so you know right off the bat that *Eegah!* will be a terrible film, the opening credits feature the kind of incredibly fake skeletons found in Disney's Haunted Mansion. We then meet Roxy, a hot-to-trot young lady who has just finished up some shopping and is speeding off to the club in her convertible when she nearly runs down "a giant." By "a giant," we mean Eegah!, played by a young Richard Kiel (Jaws from 007's *Moonraker*) in ridiculously fake facial hair and Barney Rubble's wardrobe.

The next morning, Roxy takes her dad (Arch Hall, Sr.) and her boyfriend, Tom (Arch Hall, Jr.) to the site of the encounter, and the group finds some Shaq-sized footprints. Also, someone off-camera shouts "Watch out for snakes!" – I thought that was pretty awesome.

That's enough to get Pop to rent a helicopter and don shorts, dress shoes, and a pith helmet in search of the giant. That doesn't work out so well for him.

Because *Eegah!* serves not just a cautionary tale of nepotism but of Nepotism Done Right [TM], we get our first musical number shoehorned into the film as Arch Hall, Jr. croons and croaks his way through a poolside song for his Roxy. It's hard to say what's more ridiculous: his singing or his gigantic blonde pompadour. With that detour out of the way, it's time for Tom and Roxy to pick up Pop in Tom's "dune buggy," which is really a repurposed Model T or whatever. Hey, I'm not a Car Guy, but that isn't any kind of dune buggy I've ever seen in the history of ever. Our lovebirds zip around pointlessly, with Roxy yelling out "Whee!" more than that kid in *The Phantom Menace*.

They take a break so the director's son can croak out another song. Unfortunately, the horrible crooning has drawn Eegah!'s attention (frankly, it nearly causes his fake beard to fall off). When he gets the chance, Eegah! takes off with the curvaceous Roxy, leaving Tom alone and confused.

We've now reached the painful middle *hour* of the film. Eegah! brings Roxy back to his place, where he's also keeping a mildly injured Pop captive. Pop makes absurd hypotheses, such as the sulfur water contributing to Eegah!'s long life — don't try that at home, kids. Eegah! shows off his cave paintings and very dead relatives to Roxy. Roxy shaves Pop and Eegah!, and Eegah! tries to eat the shaving cream. Pop lazily suggests ways for Roxy to avoid being raped by Eegah! It's pretty creepy, and not in ways it was intended to be.

That goes on for an hour. Every now and then, the action is broken up by scenes of Tom and his giant blonde pompadour stumbling around the same rock quarry where *Robot Monster* was shot.

The film finally builds up to a thrilling stumble around the rocks before Eegah! gets all Kong-like and follows Roxy back to civilization. It's there that Eegah! is mystified by such modern marvels as doorknobs and mannequins. The police eventually get the call of a "large man or giant" creating a disturbance, and you can imagine where things go from there.

Eegah! currently sits in IMDB's Bottom 100 and is a common fixture on bad movie lists, and *not* because it's so bad it's good. Recommended only for members of the Arch Hall family.

*

MARS NEEDS WOMEN
Directed by Larry Buchanan
1967, 82 minutes, Unrated
That's the Power of Love

Mars Needs Women is one of those classic b-movies I've been aware of for a long time. It just has one of those memorable titles that tells you the film will be cheesy as hell. But then I got an eyeful of the trailer, and realized this was something more.

Mars Needs Women isn't just some cheesy b-movie… it's a social science goldmine! I can easily imagine some budding film critic writing at length about how *Mars Needs Women* plays directly to men's fear of loss, of being bested by something more "alpha" then himself. I can easily imagine another budding critic taking a cheekier approach and claiming that *Mars Needs Women*, with its *Jetsons*-like Martians and genetic compatibility, supports the argument for an Intelligent Designer. And I can easily imagine a third critic saying how the

118 | T H E   B A R G A I N   B I N   R E V I E W

first two missed the point, that *Mars Needs Women* is an anti-feminist manifesto where women are merely things to be protected or stolen, and all that's important about women is that they're "lovely, built like goddesses and unmarried."

I will be making none of those arguments, because *Mars Needs Women* is just too stupid of a movie to warrant them.

Here, there and everywhere, women are blinking out of existence. This fires up the Strings of Suspenseful Urgency as we watch a colonel drive, drive, and drive some more to the NASA Decoding Center, enter the building and stride purposefully through an assortment of rooms and hallways. Exciting! The Colonel eventually runs out of rooms to stride through, and learns that we've received a message from Outer Space. First contact! An essential moment in world history! And what's the message? "Mars needs women." Oh. Well, nice of them to give us a head's up.

The Colonel is pissed. PISSED. Super TNT pissed. He's only in a handful of scenes for the rest of the movie, but every time is shows up, he's awesomely over-the-top pissed off. There's a confusing sequence where the Angriest Colonel in the World angrily discusses the message with a one-man press pool and *then* plans out a communication strategy with the Secretary of... they never say, so let's go with Agriculture. Somehow, it never occurs to these guys to, you know, just not tell anybody about the message.

Soon an actual Martian pops in (literally) to explain. The unfortunately named Dop (Tommy Kirk, a.k.a the kid from *Old Yeller*, in an prototype of a *Star Trek: TNG* uniform) calmly explains that he's a scientist here on a peaceful mission to save his civilization, and all he's looking for are a couple cute ladies to volunteer to help repopulate Mars.

I imagine there are lots of scientists who would jump at the chance, just to see an alien civilization. I imagine there are a zillion questions any of us would ask if faced with an honest-to-goodness alien who came in peace and just happened to speak our language. But none of us are the Angriest Colonel in the World.

After a parade of stock footage, the movie suddenly and strangely changes its focus to Dop and his Martian colleagues. Having been denied by the Angriest Colonel in the World, Dop and his gang have only 20 hours to each "survey, choose, examine the medical records of, and abduct a female meeting the exact qualifications." A key qualification? That the women are single. Because I guess abducting a *married* woman to help repopulate a planet is just beyond the pale.

And why only 20 hours? Because… Well anyway, the plan consists of obtaining some Human Currency, Earthling Attire and one of those machines that we Earthlings call an "automobile," and the Martians seem to have a working understanding of American slang and long-term parking at airports, so this should be a breeze.

First stop: a strip club!

While his buddy hangs out in the only strip club in the world to feature a non-stripping dancer in an evening dress, Dop catches a news report that there's a hot lady scientist meeting with all the Big Brass to discuss all the Martian stuff. Because in the '60s, "hot smart lady arrives in Houston" was breaking news. Dop is all over that, for he admires both "her credentials" and the fact that she's "blessed anatomically." It also helps that she's played by Yvonne Craig (the green-skinned alien Capt. Kirk makes out with in the original *Star Trek* series), who knows a thing or two about aliens.

The rest of the film focuses on Dop making time with the lovely Dr. Yvonne Craig while the other Martians attempt to find, stalk, and hypnotize lovely ladies. This mean the action falls somewhere between "slow-moving caper" and "slow-moving how-to guide for stalkers." And whenever it all becomes too fast-paced, we get another dollop of stock footage to bog things down.

It's too bad, because there's some really wacky stuff here. Like when Dr. Yvonne tells Dop that "it's presumptuous of us to believe that Martians are going to be any different than we are" – never mind the different atmosphere, exposure to sunlight, gravitational pull, etc. Or like when Dr. Yvonne practically throws herself at Dop, asking him to take her "as far away from scientific thinking as possible" so he takes her to a planetarium. Or that Dop's learning the Power of Love would make him not want to help his dying civilization anymore.

If only the film wasn't the visual equivalent of chugging cough syrup.

* *

MY ROAD TO BAD MOVIES: MOVIE SIGN!

I was in college when someone first showed me an episode of *Mystery Science Theater 3000*. You're gonna love it, my buddy told me.

No kiddin'. The show was a revelation — I was instantly hooked. It was fairly early in the run of the show, maybe around Season 4, on Comedy Central starring Joel Hodgson. I think because of that, I've always preferred the Joel episodes to the ones with Mike Nelson, the same way an old school Van Halen fan might prefer David Lee Roth to Sammy Hagar. There's nothing wrong with Hagar, but Roth was the real deal.

If you're reading this book, I doubt I have to elaborate too much on *MST3K*. But just in case: *MST3K* features a janitor and two robot buddies stranded on a satellite, where they're subjected to aggressively bad (and often in public domain!) films by a mad scientist. Silhouettes of the janitor and the 'bots, in theater seats, remain on the bottom of the screen where they lob wisecracks throughout the film. The show started out at a local affiliate in Minneapolis and was quickly scooped up by Comedy Central.

While the show has been off the air since 1999, it maintains a strong and passionate following. You probably could have guessed that *MST3K* was a big influence even before cracking open this book.

What I love about *MST3K* – besides it being one of the most hilarious and joyous television programs I've ever watched – is the show's central idea that comedy can be found in the most unlikely places. Even if it's not intentional, like in this film made famous by *MST3K*...

MANOS: HANDS OF FATE

Directed by Harold P. Warren
1966, 74 minutes, Unrated
The Master would not be pleased.

I'll be honest: I'd avoided reviewing this movie for a long time.

I don't think you have to be a bad movie connoisseur to know that *Manos: Hands of Fate* is a *baaaaaaaad* movie. Not delightfully bad or amusingly bad. Bad-bad, like spoiled pork.

Much of that notoriety comes from *Manos* being covered in one of the most famed episodes of *Mystery Science Theater 3000*. On an unrelated note, the film shares the name of the Manos Diner in Ithaca, New York, which we soon came to refer to as the Manos: Diner of Fate.

I'd only seen the *Manos* episode of *MST3K* once, towards the end of a very long day that included an all-morning TV shoot, drinking, an outdoor concert, drinking, *MST3K*, downtown for more drinking, and yes, the Manos: Diner of Fate. My memory is a bit foggy. What I do remember is that the movie seemed to wear down even Joel and the 'bots... or maybe I was the worn-down one.

Time to saddle up: *Manos: Hands of Fate* (or *"Manos": Hands of Fate*, according to the title cards) opens, the way all bad movies open, with driving. We're joining a family on a care-free vacation that involves driving, more driving, getting pulled over for a busted tail light, some more driving, driving again, and still more driving. At one point, Margaret asks her hubby, Mike, if they're almost there. "Only 12 more miles," he assures here, and then promptly drives what seems like another 120 miles.

They also encounter a "teenage" couple making out in their car on the side of the road. We'll cut back to that couple throughout the film, suggesting that they've engaged in a 36-hour make-out session.

They eventually stop at a lone, run-down house with a hillbilly out front. I'm assuming our family is only stopping to ask for directions, but before they can say a word, the hillbilly bleats out, "I am Torgo. I take care of the place while The Master is away." Torgo then mentions that The Master doesn't like children. Naturally, this causes Mike to insist on staying the night. Not that Torgo offered. Mike is kind of a tool.

We need to talk about Torgo. When I was a child, I had these inflatable Hulk "instant muscles." They were like water wings that you'd wear under your shirt. You'd then use a pump to inflate the "muscles," simulating the experience of "Hulking up." You always hoped to rip your shirt – sure, your mom would be annoyed, but it'd be worth it.

So not only does Torgo resembles a character from *The Beverly Hillbillies*, but he seems to have those instant muscles on his thighs. As a result, Torgo is super bow-legged... and super slow-moving. In fact, everything about Torgo is slow: he walks slowly, talks (well, bleats) slowly, thinks slowly, reacts slowly. By proxy, Torgo makes everything else slower, too – I swear, time came to a halt during my viewing of this film.

Or maybe that's because 57% of the film consists of uncomfortable staring. Upon entering the incredibly creepy house, Mike and Margaret spent about 40 hours staring at a portrait of The Master, who happens to look like an angry Freddy Mercury. Yes, I know *MST3K* makes a similar wise-crack, but it's uncannily accurate.

Shortly (for this film) after, the family's pet poodle is mauled, and Torgo comes on to Margaret, telling her that The Master wants her to be his wife. None of this seems out of sorts to Mike, who increasingly proves himself to be an aloof tosser. Maybe he's just too busy bossing Torgo around to notice what's going on. Mike certainly doesn't notice that his young daughter, Debbie, goes missing, launching the saddest attempt to find anything ever. Debbie eventually reappears with a hellhound in tow. Also, she's found some kind of pagan play set.

We get a fair bit of Torgo fondling unconscious women tied up at the pagan play set, which means we get way too much Torgo fondling unconscious women. Then, in a rare bout of initiative, Torgo coldcocks Mike to the delight of the audience.

And now, for my money, the best sequence in the film: The Master rises! Just in case the preceding tedium of *Manos: Hands of Fate* had you dozing off, we cut away quickly to the portrait of The Master to verify that yes, this is indeed The Master. After taking his hellhound for a walk, The Master performs a long and rambling spell to wake up his wives. Almost immediately, all the wives start talking at the same time. The Master stands aside, taking in the jabbering, and wishing he'd let them sleep.

Eventually, the jabbering is too much for The Master and he leaves. The wives start to argue about something or other, and then engage in some overly choreographed lady tussling. It's nowhere near as sexy as I've made it sound – and I don't think I made it sound very sexy.

I'd love to tell you that it's all building up to something, but it's not. The Master and Torgo argue in the most undramatic way possible. There's a murder via interpretive dance, and an oh-so thrilling "look around the desert at night" sequence. One of the wives slaps around an unconscious Mike. That part was pretty awesome, actually.

And just when it looks like the film is reaching its climax… we jump to some undefined amount of time later. Hey, no need to show the exciting parts of the story!

Do I really need to point out that every aspect of the film — the performances, the dialogue, the pacing, the cinematography, the effects, etc. – are terrible? No? Good. Because *Manos: Hands of Fate* definitely deserves its infamy. But unlike other famously bad films, to say you sat through *Manos: Hands of Fate* is a badge of honor.

*

4: COMEDIES, INTENTIONAL AND OTHERWISE

HERCULES IN NEW YORK
Directed by Arthur Allen Seidelman
1969, 91 minutes, Rated G
Schwarzenegger Takes Manhattan

New York City can be so pretty from a bird's eye view. It's an incredibly iconic city -- there truly is no place on earth like it. So it's no wonder why New York City is the setting for so many movies: *The Godfather, Annie Hall, Ghost Busters...* the list goes on and on. And because the city is so iconic, so unique, it makes for some great fish-out-of-water stories like *Crocodile Dundee, Brother from Another Planet* and *Cloverfield.* Long before either The Muppets or Jason took Manhattan, another world-famous character stormed the Big Apple: Hercules in 1969's *Hercules in New York,* starring a certain future Governor of California, credited as "Arnold Strong." As you can imagine, this film is not heavy on serious social commentary.

The film opens in a lovely garden party, where Hercules (Schwarzenegger) is grousing to Zeus about not being able to go down to Earth. Zeus, flanked by the usual handful of gods just standing around, isn't having it.

But that's not what would immediately jump out at you in this scene. No, it's the dubbing.

Consider: "Awh be bock," and "Get in da choppah!" and "It's naught a toomah!!" Doing terrible Schwarzenegger impressions is practically an American birthright. But the filmmakers of *Hercules in New York*, who may or may not have traveled back in time in an attempt to prevent decades of generations of bad Ahnold impressions, have all of Hercules' lines dubbed in. Apparently, they hired the same guy who voiced instant coffee commercials in the '70s. Needless to say, it's really distracting.

Anyway, Zeus finally gets sick of all the whining, so he throws a cast iron bolt at Hercules and explodes him out of Mt. Olympus. Herc is rescued by a fishing boat, and it's here that we learn that Hercules is a colossal brat. He refuses to do any kind of work around the boat that *saved him from drowning in the ocean*. Instead, we get the first of many scenes of Herc tossing a half dozen guys around like ragdolls. Ha ha, stupid sailors wanting the freeloader to help out!

Herc de-boats in New York City, and after tossing around some more seamen (uh, you know what I mean), he befriends a scrawny little pretzel vendor named Pretzie. No word on whether this is a nickname alluding to his vocation, or if he took up pretzel retail because of his name. Pretzie starts showing Herc how things are done in America (Pretzie just assumes Herc is from Greece), but that doesn't stop Herc from rolling a taxi cab because the cabbie had the audacity to demand cab money.

Herc later shows up a "champion" track and field team, which catches the eye of a local professor and his hot daughter, Helen. The professor invites Herc and Pretzie over for tea – why is never really explained – where Herc shows his gratitude by crushing Helen's boyfriend. Naturally, Helen finds such brutishness appealing and agrees to go out to dinner with Herc.

I'm not going to recap the entire film, but this next sequence is priceless: We fast-forward to Herc and Helen taking a post-dinner carriage ride through Central Park. They're laughing and having a great time. Meanwhile, a police officer hears this report: "All Central Park units: Escaped from zoo, one 600-pound grizzly bear. Take caution with animal. Known to be surly and dangerous."

Back to our carriage-drawn lovers, who spot something bearlike approaching them. Hercules (historically not the sharpest knife in the drawer) promptly hops out of the carriage to fight the bear, which is now clearly *a guy in a bear costume* – so awesome. Topping off the scene is Helen in the carriage alternating shouts of "No, Hercules!" and "Beat him!"

The movie kinda goes all over the place from there: Herc becomes a professional wrestler, and then the mob forces Pretzie to sign over managerial rights. A few gods make guest appearances to talk and/or goad Herc into returning to Mt. Olympus. Juno (Hera for those of you who prefer the Greek names – the filmmakers apparently couldn't decide whether to go with the Greek or Roman versions) comes up with a scheme to strip Herc of his demigod powers. There's a weightlifting contest, a chariot chase through New York City – which, by the way, would make a great Grand Theft Auto mission – and a big brawl at the end with little to no resolution. And after all that, it occurs to Herc that he's been kinda douchey, and he up and leaves for Mt. Olympus without so much as a goodbye to Pretzie or Helen (who pretty much disappears from the film).

This film is ridiculous. The story is all over the place, the acting ranges from fairly bad to awful and the sound effects are a joke. In other words, I really enjoyed it. And for what it's worth, it made me want to go to New York City. Now there's something you can't say about *Annie Hall*.

* * *

DEATH BED: THE BED THAT EATS

Directed by George Barry
1977, 80 minutes, Unrated
Yes, the title pretty much says it all

The movie opens on a blank screen with only the sound of someone eating a carrot. Or maybe celery? Hard to say, but as you might have guessed, the "title character" is not a vegetarian. I thought I'd be able to write this review based on the title alone, but no, this movie is even weirder than that.

The federally mandated opening scene casualties: A young couple hikes a long ways away to an old, abandoned estate for some picnic lovin'. The demon that possesses the bed (and how pissed must that demon be to be stuck in a bed?) steers the young lovers into its room. Not being the least bit suspicious that an old, abandoned estate has a pristine bed with immaculate sheets, the couple lays out the most pathetic picnic ever – two apples, red wine and KFC – on the Bed before going at it.

Here's the awesome part: While they're making out, the Bed begins to secrete what appears to be cream soda foam and ingests the picnic food, starting with the apples. We watch the apples sink down into the food's "stomach" to be "eaten" with a lighting filter that obviously inspired Serrano's controversial "Piss Christ." And then – ready for this? – the Bed spits out the apple cores. Hey, it's a demon, not a savage.

Finally, to the surprise of absolutely no one, the Bed eats the couple.

So here's the main gist of the story: Many years ago, th— ah, who cares? *It's a bed that eats people!!* You've either already added this movie to your "must-see" list or you've moved on to read something else.

Still with me? Cool. The film is narrated by a ghost forced to haunt a painting in the Bed's room, from which the ghost makes cynical remarks a faux-British accent. Our BritGhost narrator seems to have an odd relationship with the Bed, alternating between taunting it (sadly, he never busts out with anything like, "Hey, who has four legs and can't move?") and sympathizing with it. That's probably the kind of thing that happens when your only companion for decades is a frickin' bed.

If you can sit through the crappy film quality and sluggish pacing that are the trademark qualities of a '70s cult film, then this is a must-see for you. Though speaking of sluggish pacing, I have to confess that I fast-forwarded through one scene: a woman dragging herself across the floor of the Bed's room to the doorway. There's nothing gratuitous or horrific or upsetting about the scene — it just takes her damn near forever to reach the door.

But don't let that one scene steer you away from this gem. Need any more enticing? Then I have two words for you: "Skeleton hands."

One last note: Though this film was first shown in 1977, it wasn't officially released until 2003. Apparently, the brainiac who came up with the concept of a bed that eats people showed the film around, couldn't get it sold, and then *forgot about the film* until he discovered that pirated copies had been floating around Europe for 25 years. That's right: He forgot that he made the film. You know how common it is to completely forget that you wrote, directed and produced your own feature film — especially when it's the only film you've ever made.

* * * *

THE DRAGON LIVES AGAIN (a.k.a DEADLY HANDS OF KUNG FU)

Directed by Kei Law

1977, 96 minutes, Rated R

Could this possibly be more entertaining than a Bruce Lee movie?

First, some background: Once upon a time, Bruce Lee was The Big Thing. So the film industry, just as creatively bankrupt in the '70s as it is today, tried to fill the void left by Lee's untimely death with Bruceploitation films – cheaply made kung fu movies starring actors "named" Bruce Li or Bruce Le.

This movie, *The Dragon Lives Again*, is like the Sistine Chapel of Bruceploitation movies.

The film opens with the body of "Bruce Lee" being presented to a feudal Chinese lord. Since it is clearly NOT the real Bruce Lee, one of the ladies of the court helpfully explains, "It just so happens, when a person dies, their face and body undergo a change." Oh. And speaking of "oh," it appears that the body of Bruce Lee is in a state of, eh, rigor mortis – the kind that made me swear off wearing sweatpants when puberty hit.

So are those nunchucks in Bruce Lee's pants, or is he just happy to – nope, they actually are nunchucks. The feudal lord is pissed that Bruce Lee came in packing and won't bow to him and orders his guards to beat the hell out of Bruce Lee. But even in death, *nobody* beats the hell out of Bruce Lee, and he comes to life to engage in this asinine argument:

BRUCE LEE: Who the hell are you?!

FEUDAL LORD: How dare you! Get down on your knees before me! Or do you want to die already?

BRUCE LEE: HA! Is there something wrong
with you? You're weird! I'm going to die?
You're going to die!

FEUDAL LORD: Don't you realize who I am?
How dare you be rude to me!

BRUCE LEE: I know who you are -- a rat!

The feudal lord, after managing a retort of "pipsqueak," expositions that he's the King of the Underworld and that they're all apparently in some variation of Purgatory that resembles a pre-industrial China. But even calling this Purgatory doesn't make sense because – well, at this point, the story resembles something I would have written when I was ten-years-old.

Bruce Lee heads out into this new world and befriends Caine from the TV series *Kung Fu* and, I kid you not, Popeye the Sailor. It gets better: Bruce Lee then has a run-in with members of The Godfather's gang – yes, that would be Mario Puzo's Vito Corleone. Turns out that The Godfather runs a powerful gang that includes the blind swordsman Zatoichi, James Bond, French softcore icon Emmanuelle, Dracula and Clint Eastwood (as the Man With No Name). Also part of the gang is The Exorcist, who appears to be either Oscar Wilde dressed up as Elvis Presley or Elvis Presley dressed up as Oscar Wilde. Trust me, no copyright was left un-infringed.

Mixed in with such randomness as a talking skeleton, some gratuitous bath scenes, references to Bruce Lee's generous endowment and labored put-downs such as "He's really a pig-ignorant twit," we're treated to a healthy dose of kung fu fighting – the kind of fun, fast-paced kung fu that once ruled Saturday afternoon TV. All of the fight scenes (for reasons never explained) take place in the same location, and are often fights to the death. Never mind that all of the characters are in the Underworld and, one might think, are already dead.

These fights also feature quick freeze frames to announce when a character is unleashing their own special move. My favorite is a toss-up between Zatoichi's "Blind Dog Pisses" and Bruce Lee's "The Third Leg of Bruce."

The Godfather's gang, backed by at least a dozen guys in full-body skeleton costumes, plan on overthrowing the King of the Underworld. Their master plan? Send Emmanuelle to have energetic sex with the King of the Underworld until he has a stroke. Turns out that you really haven't lived until you've seen a badly dubbed sex scene.

All that stands in their way is Bruce Lee... And all he wants to do is return to Earth. Which, in case you ever find yourself in the pre-industrial China version of Purgatory, is accessible by zip-line. And just because I know the question has been burning in your mind throughout the review: Yes, Popeye does eat his spinach.

I've given this move five asterisks, but I don't think I could fit enough asterisks on a single page for what this... stunning masterpiece deserves.

* * * * *

ATTACK OF THE KILLER TOMATOES
Directed by John De Bello
1978, 83 minutes, Rated PG
What about the T.O.U.S.'s? Tomatoes Of Unusual Size? I don't think they exist.

Attack of the Killer Tomatoes is a stupid comedy.

I don't mean that as an insult, though it certainly sounds like it – I'm just describing the type of humor in the film. The jokes are the kind that will make you simultaneously laugh and groan, much like the humor in *Airplane!* or *Student Bodies*. But that's probably obvious from the title of the film. I mean, who could take the idea of a "killer tomato" seriously?

Then again, apparently people said the same thing about *The Birds*, until an army of blackbirds descended upon Kentucky's Fort Campbell in 1975, so what do I know?

Attack of the Killer Tomatoes opens in traditional horror movie style: A woman is alone in her house, washing dishes after a long day. She looks down and sees a tomato in the sink drain. The tomato starts muttering gibberish and rolling round, soon making its way out of the sink. The woman is in terror – which seems like an extreme reaction regardless of the horror music accompanying the scene. Then we hear chomping noises, and the woman screams. Cue credits, and that classic theme song.

Post-credits, it's quickly established that the tomatoes are revolting. No, let me rephrase that: It's quickly established that a government program to grow bigger, healthier tomatoes has gone horribly wrong, causing the tomatoes to gain sentience and eat people.

(It's worth noting that, unlike what is depicted on the movie poster, these tomatoes aren't mutated with monster faces and big teeth – they just tomatoes. I'm glad the film's budget didn't allow for the filmmakers to do that. It's funnier this way).

In an attempt to cover their butts, the government officials responsible for the tomatoes assemble a committee of obscure military generals to deal with the incident, and hand-pick a washed up agent named Mason Dixon (clearly, not all of the jokes land) to investigate. Dixon is given a team of mostly useless experts – including an "underwater expert" in full scuba gear and flippers. Once his team is deployed (the underwater expect is dropped off at a dusty meadow, with water nowhere in sight), Dixon rendezvous with Finletter, a paratrooper who never seems to get around to stowing or detaching his parachute.

While Dixon and Finletter wander around, we also follow the President's Press Secretary as he does damage control, and we meet Lois Fairchild, a cub reporter for the society section of The Times who gets the tomato assignment because no one else is around. For the first half of the film, we fall into a comfortable pattern of a scene or two of plot and then a scene of random people being killed by tomatoes. The best of these by far is the homage to *Jaws*, complete with underwater shots of the swimmers and tomatoes approaching from the depths of the ocean.

Then, about halfway through the film, we discover that the tomatoes are growing to unusual sizes. Strangely, it's around this time that *Attack of the Killer Tomatoes* drops any attempt of being a horror movie, shifting to a hybrid between a disaster film and a '70s-style political thriller. It all leads up to a final confrontation in San Diego Stadium – and don't worry, the San Diego Chicken does indeed make a cameo.

If it sounds like the film is all over the place, that's because the film is all over the place. Then again, *Attack of the Killer Tomatoes* isn't about plot, it's about dumb jokes. The danger of jokes that will make you simultaneously laugh and groan is that sometimes you just groan, and there are a number of those moments in this film, particularly anything involving the Japanese scientist (whose voice is badly dubbed over) or the loud advertising agent who works for the President.

The good news is that *Attack of the Killer Tomatoes* is pretty heavy on sight gags, and those work like gangbusters. There's a priceless scene early on where the military is meeting in a conference room so small, everyone has to crawl over the table to get to their seats. There are throwaway gags, like Dixon's car being marked "UNMARKED CAR" and establishing shots that are obviously San Francisco being labeled "New York." And really, the sight of someone running away from a tomato the size of a beach ball never gets old.

Nor does it get old to see the gung-ho, all-business Finletter march around with his parachute dragging behind him. In many ways, Finletter is a perfect representation of *Attack of the Killer Tomatoes*: energetic and not too bright.

* * *

STUDENT BODIES
Directed by Mickey Rose and Michael Ritchie
1981, 86 minutes, Rated R
Alternative title: Slasher: The Movie!

Horror-comedies can be tricky to pull off. The best kind play like love letters to the genre, by which I mean the film knows its particular subgenre so well that they can thoroughly skewer them and still work as good, scary entries into that subgenre. *Scream* comes to mind, as does *The Cabin in the Woods* and the Greatest Film of the 21st Century (So Far), *Shaun of the Dead*. And here we have a film that claims to be "The World's First Comedy Horror Movie" (their words, not mine): *Student Bodies*. The question is, can *Student Bodies* hang with the likes of *Fright Night*, *Scream*, *Shawn of the Dead* and *Cabin in the Woods*?

After a couple fumbled title card gags, we go to a very familiar setting: A young teenaged girl babysitting in a large house late at night, and the point-of-view of the fiend stalking her. This is our killer, "The Breather," so named because of his (or her? For my sanity, let's stick with "his") exaggeratedly heavy breathing. The Breather spies on the babysitter as she gabs on the phone (her friend spoils the ending of the Civil War for her by telling her the North wins) and checking on the dog (which meows and farts). Of course, The Breather isn't so slick either, constantly bumping into things and getting his galoshes stuck in wads of gum. Once inside, The Breather finds a desk full of deadly weapons and selects… a paper clip.

It's obvious before this scene is over – and you know where it's going: fake jump scare when the boyfriend shows up, upstairs for sex, she's killed while he's in the shower, etc. – that *Student Bodies* is trying to be the *Airplane!* of slasher films. That endeavor is fully on display near the end of the scene, when the parents show up to a seemingly empty house. "Where *is* that girl?" the missus wants to know. "I hope we don't find her murdered in our bed," her husband replies.

And when they do find her and her boyfriend murdered in their bed, the film helpfully tracks the body count for us.

The absurdity continues at the funeral, what with the cheerleaders performing and the parents of the deceased babysitter getting paid the money she earned the night she was killed – 65 cents an hour plus car fare "one-way, of course." The high school principal, who is also running the funeral for whatever reason, announces that due to budget cuts, the Big Parade, the Big Football Game and the Prom will all be held on the same day. And we're off.

Much of the film falls into a regular pattern (which must have simplified the screenwriting process):

> 1. After a minute or so of debate, a teenage couple slips away from a public place to have sex in increasingly unusual locations.
> 2. The guys is ready to go, but the girl begs off. The guy mentions that whatever it is that's bothering the girl gets him "hot."

3. The guy runs off to get something to aid in their sexy time: a blanket, birth control… usually birth control.

4. As soon as the guy runs off, The Breather kills the girl with the most ludicrous murder weapon imaginable. Seriously, The Breather uses an *eggplant* at one point.

5. The guy returns, finds his girl dead, and is promptly covered up with a black garbage bag by The Breather.

And then, more often than not, virginal Good Girl Toby discovers the bodies. The film actually gets a lot of mileage out of the mystery behind The Breather's identity. The faculty all suspect Toby, so naturally every faculty member behaves as suspiciously as possible. Standouts include the shop teacher strangely obsessed with making horsehead bookends and the amazingly lanky janitor Malbert, who appears to have double-jointed everythings.

But here's the thing about trying to be the *Airplane!* of… well, anything: With so many gags flying around, there are bound to be some stinkers. *Student Bodies* goes overboard with the sound effects at times, and it gets tiring. It being 1981, there are a number of less-than-P.C. jokes – they're more tasteless than mean-spirited, but I doubt they would have been deemed hilarious even in '81. And there are a few moments where the film is halted altogether for the flimsiest of reasons, such as an abrupt message from the producer of the film to tell the audience to f' off, thus ensuring the film would get an R-rating.

Then there's the last 10 minutes of the film, where things get really trippy. It plays out a bit like the filmmakers weren't sure of how to end the movie, so they threw in a bunch of cheeky twists. Again, some of the bits work and some don't, but the overall effect threatens to ruin what is a delightfully stupid movie.

And this is a delightfully stupid movie, one where I laughed out loud quite a bit. Is it scary? Absolutely not. But unlike the *Scream/Shaun/Cabin* films I mentioned at the beginning of the review, *Student Bodies* has absolutely no intention of functioning as a horror movie. No, this film is about as scary as *Attack of the Killer Tomatoes...* and about as funny.

I don't give half asterisk ratings – it's all or nothing, baby! – but this is a rare instance where I'm rounding *up* instead of down. Yeah, the end is weak and some of the jokes are clunkers, but pointing out that this movie was made around the same time *Porky's* was becoming a huge hit explains a lot. Most of the jokes do land, and some are brilliantly funny. So this may be a weak four-asterisk, but it's a four-asterisk movie nonetheless.

* * * *

KISS EXPOSED
Directed by Claude Borenzweig
1987, 90 minutes, Unrated
Lifestyles of the KISS and Famous

In addition to being an absolutely hilarious film that more or less created the mockumentary genre, *This is Spinal Tap* is notorious for hitting a little too close to home for many rock stars of the day. The only way to make sure a film isn't making fun of your rock band is to make your own mockumentary and let the band in on the joke. And hey, if you can move some product in the process, even better.

Thus *KISS eXposed* was born.

It shouldn't be much of a surprise that KISS came out with a feature like this: While their musical talent is questionable (and I say that as a fan), KISS has proven time and again that they are marketing geniuses.

The documentary opens with a stuffed shirt warning us that the following film may "disgust" or "titillate" us – I would have gone with "amuse with unintentional delight," but okay – and assures us that everything in the film is 100% true. Then he gets hit with multiple cream pies. Because *KISS eXposed* is going to be exactly like that.

In case it wasn't obvious enough that this takes place shortly after the band unmasked, here comes The Ultimate '80s Geek. He comes complete with high-waters, ill-fitting sports jacket, coke bottle glasses and his own cameraman to Paul Stanley's doorstep to film a documentary on KISS. Being an '80s rock star, the noontime guests woke up Paul Stanley who answers his own door (despite the presence of a butler) in nothing but a necktie and Hammer pants.

Paul begrudgingly lets them in, and we learn a few things about Mr. Stanley:

- His doorbell chimes the chorus to "Rock and Roll All Nite"
- His mansion is littered with scantily clad women in various degrees of consciousness
- He shares his bed with at least four women named Carol and a chimp dressed up as Sonny Crocket

Paul isn't too impressed with the proceedings until he learns that our Ultimate '80s Geek has an unedited copy of the "Who Wants to Be Lonely" music video. Roll film!

Yes, this entire feature exists largely to string together music videos and concert footage, though this particular video cracks me up. It almost plays like a parody of a rock video, complete with one sexy swimsuit model getting unexpectedly hit in the face by all the sexy water.

This is an era with KISS in full glam rock mode, a move that paid off at the time, but feels out of character now. Oh, the songs are fine and Paul Stanley is clearly in his element here – if there's any past or present member of KISS who would be at home in a sequined duster and pink gloves with fringe, it's Paul Stanley – but everything feels like a miscast Cinderella video. And it's increasingly obvious in the post-makeup videos that Gene Simmons wasn't comfortable letting go of his Demon persona, as he continues to glare into the camera, looking like he's on the verge of biting off the head of a toddler.

Speaking of Gene Simmons, it's good to see that he didn't lose his sense of showmanship along with the makeup. When we get to see his "room" – Gene Simmons can't afford his own place? – it's roughly the size of a school cafeteria and looks like an Ozzy Osborne album cover. Yes, I'm a little jealous.

Nestled in among all the obvious farce ("Paul Stanley's Workout Video"?) and the myriad of bikini models (who suddenly opt to go topless around the 56-minute mark) lying around the premises are nuggets of actual fact and KISS history. We get stories from Paul and Gene about the early days of the band, how they came up with the name KISS and more. Paul and Gene do a fair bit of bantering, including this bit which is even odder when you factor in Paul's slight lisp:

PAUL: I just want to make one point: You know, if we're into anything, it's not post-nuclear holocaust, post-nuclear war. We're into Post Raisin Bran, post nasal drip, the U.S. Postal Service, what have you.

GENE: Post Toasties?

PAUL: Post Toasties.

As I mentioned earlier, there's plenty of concert material in the film. Some of the best moments include a performance at a San Francisco club during KISS's early days and concert footage of Ace Frehley's guitar catching fire and Gene Simmons spitting blood.

Of course, not all historical material is good. For as mortified as KISS may be about *KISS Meets the Phantom of the Park*, they should be just as mortified by their hilariously dated video for "Lick It Up." And the ridiculous video for "All Hell's Broken Loose," perhaps the only rock/rap fusion video that features a swordfight between two random women. Also, I do appreciate Paul Stanley's absolute refusal to convincingly lip synch the lyrics.

Know what's not in this documentary? The other members of the band. I understand that Eric Carr and Bruce Kulick aren't founding members, but they were both long-standing members who probably deserve more than a cameo.

The film predictably ends with a performance of "Rock and Roll All Nite," followed by slow motion footage of Gene showing off his tongue. I can't tell you how many movies I've seen that would be greatly improved by ending on Gene Simmon's tongue.

* * *

BAD GIRLS FROM MARS

Directed by Fred Olen Ray
1990, 81 minutes, Rated R
"BOING-BOING"? Really?

"There's no room on Mars for limp dicks!" That, sadly, was one of the more inspired lines of dialog in this movie. *sigh*

Bad Girls from Mars opens with this cheesetastic narration: "Ladies and gentlemen, the motion picture you're about to see deals frankly with the subject of low-budget films. It contains sexually explicit scenes that may shock some members of the audience." The solution, our helpful narrator narrates, is to accompany sex scenes with a submarine dive horn.

If you think this is absolutely hilarious, then *Bad Girls from Mars* is right up your alley... and there's little I can do to help you.

Opening credits! Synthesizer! Outer space! And that planet must be Mar-- no. I haven't studied the solar system since grade school, and even I know that the planet with the big frickin' red spot is Jupiter.

We have to wait a whole three minutes before our first shot of gratuitous nudity. And it really is gratuitous: A Space Lady in a sadly unflattering "sexy" space outfit has Indiana Jones's Frumpy Uncle cuffed to a wall, and for his lack of cooperation in... uh, doing whatever, she takes off her top? I did enjoy the fact that she struggled with the fastener in the front of her bra – glad to see I'm not the only one.

Space Lady is about to examine Frumpy Uncle's "captain's log" when SURPRISE! It's a film within a film! Uh, this is such a tired storyline. So tired that Shakespeare did it three times. The only thing that could make this even more tired is if there's a killer on the loose, picking off people on the se—oh, never mind. This is so not the movie I was hoping for.

So the film within the film is called *Bad Girls from Mars*, and thanks to the Killer on the Loose, it had picked up a reputation for being jinxed – losing four female leads to "tragic deaths" will do that. To save the film, the producers have arranged for the world-famous author/madam Emanuelle, to take the lead role. Emanuelle is played by Edy Williams. I suppose that's a big deal to some people, but since I didn't hit puberty in the late '60s, I'm not one of those people. Anyway, the director picks Emanuclle up at the airport so he can take her directly to a cast meeting. Emanuelle responds, naturally, by changing her clothes in the back of his convertible (top down, 'course) as they drive through Beverly Hills – boobies AND "comedy"!

I'm guessing by the way all the characters react to Emanuelle, she's not just a world-famous author and madam, but a sex goddess to boot. I had a hard time seeing it, particularly since she sounds like a drag queen and delivers her lines like a Peanuts character.

And on and on it goes. Sitting through bad acting is one thing... sitting through bad acting with a script written by a 12-year-old's version of "sexy comedy" is another. Do we really need the "BOING-BOING!" sound effect whenever Emanuelle runs up stairs? Or the waaaaacky music whenever the director trips and falls over? Apparently you do if you're one of the makers of *Bad Girls from Mars*.

I've just barely mentioned the whole mystery of the Killer on the Loose. Is it Frumpy Uncle? The bitchy costume girl? The P.A. with a thing for the director? Or is it zzzzzzz...

Sorry about that. I just *bored the living hell out of myself* writing about the mystery killer plotline.

In short, this movie is miserable. There are actually a handful of flattering recaps in the User Comments section of IMDB that I can only assume were posted by family members of the filmmakers. If you really need some dated entertainment with lots of immature humor and softcore action, you're better off digging around for a copy of *Hardbodies* or playing one of those old Leisure Suit Larry games.

*

RUMPLESTILTSKIN
Directed by Mark Jones
1995, 91 minutes, Rated R
Once upon a time there was this movie that really blew…

You remember "Rumpelstiltskin," right? That's the one where some lady promises a little old guy that if he helps her spin a bunch of straw into gold to help her become queen, she'll give him her first-born child. The little old guy fulfills his end, but then the newly crowned queen uses the "I know your name" loophole to get out of handing over her kid. The moral of the story is that the rich and beautiful are always free to screw ugly little men out of oral contracts.

So of course, this is a horror film.

The film opens "Somewhere in Europe – 1400s." So, somewhere in a continent during a 100-year span? I guess the filmmakers didn't want to pigeonhole their film. Anyway, Rumpelstiltskin (played by Max Grodenchik in a bunch of his Ferengi makeup swiped off the set of *Star Trek: Deep Space Nine*) is scampering through the forest with an infant, and an angry mob in pursuit. A surly den mother comes out of the mob to confront Rumpy, and they immediately defuse any tension in the scene by throwing glitter at each other.

The surly den mother curses Rumpy for 1,000 years, but get this: *she builds a loophole into the curse.* Who does that? Why bother making a curse at all? And it's the vaguest loophole ever: "broken by a wish, a child, heartfelt tears." Seriously? I might've singlehandedly broken the curse the year I really wanted Rock'em Sock'em Robots for Christmas. Anyway, Rumpy gets torched, turned into a petrified turd and thrown into the ocean.

Fast-forward to present day Los Angeles, accentuated with the Worst Rap Music Ever. Officer Destined To Die gets killed in the line of duty, leaving behind single mom Shelly who finds the petrified turd in a curio shop… you see where this is going, don't you? The rest of the movie is just a series of scenes where Rumpy busts through a wall like the Kool Aid guy, makes wise cracks and then gets run over by a car.

Here's my beef with the movie… um, besides its overall lameness: In the fairy tale, Rumpelstiltskin and the maiden make a deal – spin straw into gold for the first born. Sure it's ethically challenged, but at least it was a mutually agreed-upon arrangement. But no such arrangement is made in the movie. Shelly wishes that her dead hubby could meet their son, he shows up (non-decomposed) for the weakest sex scene ever and then Rumpy gets all in Shelly's grill about how he wants the baby? Perhaps instead of brutalizing him in front of her baby boy, Shelly should have told Rumpy that he had no legal claim to the child but was free to investigate legal recourse.

Perhaps a couple years in our legal system's lingo could stop the relentless Rumpelstiltskin. Rumpy sitting around in the lobbies of government buildings would have been about as entertaining as this film.

* *

LEPRECHAUN 4: IN SPACE
Directed by Brian Trenchard-Smith
1996, 95 minutes, Rated R
Going where no Leprechaun has gone before.

How deep must a horror franchise go before it surrenders to full-on buffoonery? Six movies? Eight? Not if you're talking about the *Leprechaun* films. Apparently three films was all it took to drain the creators of all their earth-based ideas. But to be fair, the idea of a tiny, Irish imp killing people while prattling on about "protectin' me gold" was already pretty absurd.

We immediately start off in Space, with the Leprechaun trying to win over an intergalactic princess. I'm sure you're already full of question like "How did the Leprechaun get into Space?' and "An intergalactic princess?" and "Why does this movie exist?" Neither the movie nor I have any answers. Sorry.

Here's one question I can answer: How is a nasty little toad like the Leprechaun supposed to win over an intergalactic hottie? Same way today's nasty little toads land hotties now: with lots and lots of cash.

Have you guessed that there are space marines are out to get the Leprechaun? Oh. Well, there are. I particularly love how the roughnecks all are equipped with face visors, and all insist on keeping the visors up. One of the roughnecks shoots a Muppet alerting the Leprechaun to their presence. That gives him a chance to use his loot to lay a trap. When one of the space marines starts helping himself, the Leprechaun sneaks up behind him and OMIGOD HE HAS A WEE LITTLE LIGHTSABER! The Leprechaun cuts him down to size, heh heh.

Shoot out! Zap zap! Pew pew! Somehow, the roughnecks can't hit the less than fleet of foot Leprechaun as he scampers for cover. A grenade makes short work of the Leprechaun, but when the grenade-lobber opts to relieve himself on a smoldering Leprechaun limb, he gets a jolt to the wanger for his efforts. That turns out to be important later. Particularly to the grenade-lobber, when during an inopportune moment on the ship, the Leprechaun comes bursting out of him, *Alien*-style. Only instead of bursting out of the chest, the Leprechaun bursts out... well, let's call it "kidney stone-style."

From there, the movie becomes *Alien* except with the Leprechaun, who is allowed the occasional soliloquy about how he's going to kill everyone. And an abundance of "running down the hall" shots. And with zero tension.

Two sub-plots fill the ample spaces in-between. One involves our lead marine, "Books," trying to score with the sexy scientist. He crashes and burns in ways that make me feel like I was a real smooth operator back in the day. The other involves a very strange mad scientist named Dr. Mittenhand who ultimately turns himself in a giant mutant spider-Muppet.

I have to admit, I'm a bit jealous that I didn't come up with the name "Dr. Mittenhand." Unfortunately, that name is probably the best thing about *Leprechaun 4: In Space*.

* *

BIG MONEY HUSTLAS
Directed by John Cafiero
2000, 97 minutes, Unrated
Featuring Mick Foley, Harland Williams, a guy in an ape suit, and a heap of f bombs.

This film stars the Insane Clown Posse, which is probably enough to make some of you skip to the next review. I'm not familiar at all with the musical stylings of the Insane Clown

Posse, but I have it on good authority that "ICP" is a rap band containing circus performers of dubious sanity.

Big Money Hustlas opens in a church during a funeral service, where a preacher is carrying on about how everyone must givegivegive and give some more to the Chur—uh, "Lord." Damn, this scene is every Catholic sermon I ever sat through as a kid. And there, in the pews, is one of the members of ICP. No, I don't know which one – he's one of the ones in clown paint. By the way, I now totally want to wear clown paint to church this Sunday. ICP Guy #1 tells us via internal monologue that he knows the deceased and that it saddens him that the deceased is deceased because of some "bitch-ass money." Hit the Waves of Flashbackery!

…where we meet ICP Guy #2, who plays a crime lord named Big Baby Sweets. We know he's a crime lord because of the cigars, the henchmen, the excessive amounts of gold and leopard print, and the fact that the movie tell us so. His two henchmen, Lil Poot and Big Stank, aren't cool enough to get face paint.

Two things are obvious about the movie at this point:

1. The excessive use of action coming to a record-scratching halt in the first 10 minutes of the film points to just how ham-fisted this movie is.

2. When in doubt, the screenwriters simply inserted either "bitch" or some variation of "motherfucker" into the dialogue. Big Baby Sweets alone must ask for his "mutherfuckin' mon-NEY" at least 400 times in the film.

(That's an exaggeration. But 86 utterences of "motherfucker" – not "fuck," but either "motherfucker" or "mutherfuckin'" – is not an exaggeration. I counted.)

(In contrast, "bitch" is only used 51 times. Restraint?)

Enter ICP Guy #1, one "Sugar Bear," a super cop newly transferred into New York City to take on Big Baby Sweets.

Sugar Bear is something of a blaxploitation superhero, speaking almost exclusively in rhyme. Aiding him is Harland William's dorky Harry Cox (sigh) and a truckload of cops-eating-donuts gags.

I was starting to think this film would be one decrepit knee-slapper after another when a foiled robbery scene kicked things up a notch. Sugar Bear and Harry Cox are grabbing a snack in a donut shop (sigh) when a guy in an ape suit (!!) busts in, holding everyone at gunpoint. "I'm wearing an ape suit! That means I don't give a fuck!" There's no denying that logic. Sugar Bear, unimpressed, saunters up to the guy in the ape suit and takes him out with my all-time favorite wresting move, the DDT. That won some good will.

But that's the double-edged sword of *Big Money Hustlas*: It's not-so much a coherent crime story (humorous or otherwise) as a collection of off-beat wackiness. Sure, some of the jokes go over like a stale fart. Yes, the obese stripper comes hand-in-hand with a slew of tired fat-people-eating jokes, but it's almost worth it to hear an old man call for her to show off her "family meatballs" or for the sex scene.

The same holds true for the film's cameos. As a member of Big Baby Sweets' crime syndicate, Fred "Rerun" Berry does give an obligatory "Hey-HEY-Hey," but I really dug the idea of a specialist of such brand knock-offs as "Adidass" apparel. Rudy Ray Moore shows up as Dolemite, and yes, he does tell Sugar Bear to "Put your weight on it, put your weight on it, put your weight on it!", but the cameo by pro wrestler and best-selling author Mick Foley disappoints. Foley is a charismic personality, but his "Cactus Sac" felt more forced than fun.

So while the film gets lazy in parts – there are recurring gags about the script or the film's budget, and nearly everyone mugs the camera at some point – *Big Money Hustlas* is still lots of fun. Big Baby Sweets spends the entire movie channeling every villain to appear on the '60s *Batman* TV show… and I mean that as a complement. Sugar Bear is just off-beat enough of a throwback hero to keep him from being completely predictable. And the twists at the end are appropriately outlandish.

Long story short, this is a pretty good movie to watch while kicking back with some brews... even if you're not a Juggalo.

* * *

MONSTER MAN
Directed by Michael Davis
2003, 95 minutes, Rated R
Monster, monster man! I wanna be a monster man!

Talk about a swerve: We kick off with the opening credits accompanied by that sound all the cool horror flicks just love these days and a guy getting his head crushed in a vice. We then spend the next hour in a Kevin Smith film.

I'm not complaining – I generally like Kevin Smith's films – but it's definitely not what I was expecting. Bland wussie Adam is taking a road trip to crash the wedding of an ex-girlfriend he's still hung up on. Tagging along – more or less against Adam's will – is his buddy, Harley, who comes off as the diet cola version of Jack Black. The first third of the movie is almost entirely spent steeped in *Clerks*-esque banter: Diet Jack Black carries on about the sluttiness of Adam's ex, ogles women like a 13-year-old, makes a variety of genital jokes, etc. Even after Diet Jack Black shoots his mouth off in a hick bar and the two are run off the road by a monster truck – no, it's *more* than a monster truck, it's like something out of *Road Warrior*. After that, it takes an additional half hour for the two to realize they're in a horror movie.

You might think this gets old, and for a while, it does. But over the course of the movie, particularly after a hottie hitchhiker causes some friction between the duo, their act gets a bit more depth and the characters do start to grow on you. The action builds nicely, and even when we discover that the monster truck is driven by a monstrous-looking man with a mouth stitched together in a most impractical manner (great for being scary, not so good for eating a chalupa), this turns out to be a much better movie than it should be.

There are even a few good twists. And then the bottom falls out when we meet the Torso-less Man of Exposition.

It's such a disappointment. For you potential screenwriters out there, if you need to have a character explain your whole ingenious plot like some kind of second-tier Bond villain, you're doing something wrong.

Yes, even if that character is lacking a torso.

* * *

SANTA'S SLAY
Directed by David Steiman
2005, 78 minutes, Rated R
"He's scary, yet educational."

The mere existence of this movie boggles my mind. I mean, Christmas-themed horror movies have been done plenty of times. And the idea of a demonic Santa can be fun. But it took someone with far more vision than I to look at Bill Goldberg and think "Santa."

For the uninitiated, Bill Goldberg is a pro wrestler who was extremely popular in the late '90s. Goldberg, 6-foot-4 and

285 lbs. of muscle, knows exactly two wrestling moves and was most notable for his ability to snarl and then pulverize his opponent in roughly the same amount of time it will take you to finish reading this sentence.

So: Santa Claus.

Equally mind-boggling to me was the number of cameos in the opening scene alone. The Noxzema Girl! Chris Kattan! The Nanny! James Caan?!? What the hell are you doing, James Caan? You were Sonny Corleone!

The opening scene is not a taping of *Hollywood Squares* but of a highly dysfunctional family about to have Christmas dinner. The scene features the first of many shots across the bow of the Culture War with this heart-warming prayer, straight out of the Supply-Side Jesus playbook:

```
Dear Lord, thank you for the bountiful
food that you've provided for us, and that
our loving family can be together this
Christmas. Also, thank you for not making
us poor or Samoan. Thank you for Maxim
Pharmaceuticals, the latest M-Class and
let those that are less fortunate work
harder.
```

Then Santa busts through the chimney like the Kool-Aid Man and kills everyone to the tune of *The Nutcracker Suite*.

It's that kind of movie, and that's my main beef with the film. Films like *Scream* and *Shaun of the Dead* prove that it is possible to make a film that excels in both horror and comedy. *Santa's Slay* tries to walk that line, too, but is far more wobbly. Goldberg's Santa spends much of the movie stomping around town looking like a deranged Viking, distributing creative deaths and witty wisecracks. Perhaps I've become a fart in my old age, but... are we supposed to be cheering *for* the demonic, psycho killer Santa? Is the audience supposed to think, "Look! He's killing indiscriminately! Wee!"?

It's not like we don't have anyone in the movie to cheer for. Our hero is 16-year-old Nicholas, who works in a Jewish deli with Claire from TV's *Lost* and lives with his paranoid Grandfather (Robert Culp) who is forever having "wacko inventing binges." Turns out there's a good reason why Grandpa is so paranoid – in a scene awesomely told in stop animation, Nicholas learns that Santa is the spawn of Satan, forced to spend his birthday giving gifts to kids for 1,000 years when he lost a bet to an angel.

Of course, you've already guessed that Santa's 1,000 years are up. But did you guess that the bet was who would win a game of curling? Like I said, it's that kind of movie.

* * *

THANKSKILLING
Directed by Jordan Downey
2009, 67 minutes, Unrated
"Thanksgiving break! Woo!"

There are only so many Thanksgiving-themed films out there, so when November rolled around, it seemed like an appropriate time to check out *Thankskilling*. And that might be the only way the word "appropriate" can be applied to this film.

Thankskilling is an intentionally bad, spoof-y horror film. Making a film intentionally bad is a tough line to walk, and it's rarely done successfully. Will it be successful here in this cheap indie film? Ha ha ha…

After some intro text that takes us to the first Thanksgiving, we open on boobies. Literally. Just a close-up of some naked breasts. Cuz nothing says "Happy Thanksgiving" like some naked breasts.

The boobies belong to a topless pilgrim lady, who is topless because… um… Anyway, she's running through the woods, clearly being chased by something. Every third or fourth shot is a close-up of her nakedness, because that's the kind of classiness this film is going for. Eventually, our topless pilgrim trips over a small boulder, and is attacked by an Angry Turkey Puppet.

Seriously: the villain of this film was clearly made by the same manufacturer who gave us Comic the Insult Dog. In fact, I wouldn't be surprised if "Comic the Insult Dog: The Horror Movie" was the initial elevator pitch for this movie. Anyway, the Angry Turkey Puppet says, "Nice tits, bitch," raises an axe, and cut to opening credits.

So yeah, you know it's going to be like that. After a surprisingly well-done opening credits sequence, we fast-forward to present day where a college is letting out for Thanksgiving break. "Thanksgiving break! Woo!" yelled no college student ever until this movie. Let's meet our cardboard cannon fodder:

JOHNNY FOOTBALL. A generically handsome jock, he walks out of the school spinning a football around in his hand. After I dub him "Johnny Football" in my notes, I'm stunned to find out his character's name actually is Johnny. Not John, "Johnny."

FAT BASTARD. He's the one Chris Farley-ing around, yelling "Thanksgiving break, woo!" and sporting redneck chic. Would you believe he likes to eat and party? Of course you would.

THE PORNORIFIC SLUT. She doesn't so much talk as she purrs. How she made it through the film without literally sitting on Johnny Football's face is beyond me.

THE CRANKY PRUDE. Johnny Football's all into her, despite the fact that she's kind of a headache. She's a prudish stick-in-the-mud, which means she's our Final Girl.

NERD! This creepy tag-along is somehow good friends with Fat Bastard, mostly because the film needed a nerdy type.

Our fivesome piles into a jeep and head out for Thanksgiving break. The jeep breaks down that evening, and they need to camp out overnight to let the engine cool. Is... Is that really how car engines work? I'm not a car guy.

Over the campfire, NERD! tells them all the story of the cursed evil turkey, complete with historical sloppiness and bad math ("every 505 years!"). I have to give props to actor Ryan E. Francis for saying stuff like "turkeyologist" with a straight face. Later that night, the Cranky Prude encounters the Angry Turkey Puppet (resurrected when a dog pees on his grave) in the woods, and then... it's the next morning and everyone's fine and they hop in the jeep and go home.

So that was unexpected. Instead of your traditional "cabin in the woods" arrangement, the Angry Turkey Puppet carjacks his way in pursuit and does his killing in the suburbs. Along the way, we get Cranky Prude's sheriff dad in a fake moustache and turkey costume, some weak melodrama at Johnny Football's house, a "find the book in Dad's garage" montage and an extended sequence where none of our characters recognize the Angry Turkey Puppet because he's wearing someone's face like a Halloween mask.

Surprisingly, the film's cheekiness is more hit than miss – at least for the first half. The movie does take an ugly turn about halfway through when the Angry Turkey Puppet kills a guy plowing the Pornorific Slut from behind and then takes his place behind her (before killing her). That's not funny-awful, it's just awful-awful. By then, the novelty of a murderous turkey puppet starts to wear off and much of the humor becomes a bit too knowing, a bit too nod and wink at the camera. It also doesn't help that *Thankskilling* has about as many endings as *The Lord of the Rings: Return of the King*.

Let's get real: By the time I got to "Angry Turkey Puppet," you were either on board or you weren't. If you were, then you should check out *Thankskilling*. Besides, there are worse ways to stall the annual onslaught of Christmas movies...

* * *

FDR: AMERICAN BADASS!
Directed by Garrett Brawith
2012, 93 minutes, Rated R
"The Delano's gonna fix this shit."

When I was a young lad and learning about American history, I'd sometimes ask my grandmother for her take on the events I was learning about. It made sense: As a member of The Greatest Generation, she had a front-row seat to The Great Depression, the home front during World War II, and so on. Even as a young lad, I had a sense that her experiences would give her a perspective on the day's current events that I could never have.

One thing that jumped out at me was that, for as much respect as she had for President Reagan, there was only one "Mr. President." And that would have been Franklin Delano Roosevelt, he of the fireside chats and the New Deal and the unprecedented four terms in office.

I have no idea what my grandmother would have thought of *FDR: American Badass!*

The film opens with this message from FDR:

```
Badassery is not born, but often thrust
upon you. The film you are about to see
is dedicated to Badasses everywhere. If
you have to ask yourself if you are one,
you're probably not.
```

I'd say that sets the tone for *FDR: American Badass!*, but not quite. No, that comes immediately after, with a whirling transition screen straight out of the '60s *Batman*. Only instead of the bat-symbol, the middle of the screen shows the Presidential Seal. Needless to say, I loved it.

What we quickly learn is that *FDR: American Badass!* provides a rather ridiculous alternative history, one that starts with New York Governor Roosevelt (Barry Bostwick, having a ball) and his friends (including Bruce McGill!) encountering a werewolf during a hunting trip. Yes, a werewolf – and not the hulking, check-out-the-awesome-transition kind, but the low-rent "guy with fangs and hair on his face and hands" kind. The *Teen Wolf* kind.

The werewolf rips out the heart of one of the hunters and throws it at McGill. "Why even bother to take the time to do that?" McGill complains, and that answer is simply because it's exactly that kind of movie. FDR is having none of this, and proceeds to box the werewolf. FDR eventually kills the werewolf, but not before being bit in the leg and contracting "the polio." Because werewolves are known carriers of "the polio," you see.

FDR is distressed to learn that he'll spend the rest of his life with "tiny little polio legs" – Eleanor can't even bear to look at them – but the people love him for his badassery and urge him to run for president. And run he does, leading to scenes like this:

Once in office, FDR begins "free-stylin'" directly to the American people, giving them his own brand of hope. Soon FDR learns a horrible truth: The werewolf who bit him wasn't just a polio-carrying werewolf, but a Nazi werewolf. Turns out that Hitler, Mussolini and Hirihito are all werewolves bent on teaming together to take over the world.

The Axis of Werewolves' plan involves infecting the American people with imported beer, wine (and sake, though Hitler and Mussolini don't think anyone will care) spiked with werewolf blood. This forces FDR to not only extend Prohibition, but close down our borders until he can get the tainted booze under control. Personally. General Douglas McArthur (the always awesome Ray Wise!) has outfitted FDR with The Delano 2000, a wheelchair death machine outfitted with dual silver-bulleted machine guns, rockets, classic Atari controllers and more.

Still, the world is marching towards a war that FDR would just as well avoid. After a soul-searching evening of smoking pot with the ghost of Abraham Lincoln (Kevin Sorbo!) on the roof of the White House, FDR decides the only thing to do is to take the werewolf menace head-on by storming the beaches of Normandy. Personally. He is our Badass in Chief, after all.

Needless to say, *FDR: American Badass!* is ridiculous. And purposely so, from the way FDR is portrayed as something akin to a blaxploitation hero to its casual approach to a world where werewolf dictators exist. It's an alternative telling of history, as by a 12-year-old over-caffeinated fanboy of FDR.

That immaturity means that the film isn't very culturally sensitive, but at least its stereotyping comes across knowingly – almost like the script is a couple re-writes away from being a solid Mel Brooks movie. And like in almost any comedy, there are bits that don't quite work. The sequence at the Beufords' residence easily could have been halved, and the mixing 'n scratching behind FDR's fireside chat is a neat idea on paper but just doesn't work.

But that's all good, because *FDR: American Badass!* just wants to be cheeky. The movie has fun with its historical figures (the repeated "Shut the fuck up, Einstein!" is far funnier than it should be) and there are plenty of wacky moments that come out of left field, such as a sex scene where FDR gets a "legs job" that somehow involves ketchup and mustard. Even the film's lack of budget works in its favor, from the pointedly bad CGI explosions to making it look as if the Invasion of Normandy consisted of a dozen people.

At the end of the day, *FDR: American Badass!* is a goofy movie, and everyone involved seems to be having a great time with it. You probably will, too.

* * * *

WELCOME TO THE JUNGLE
Directed by Rob Meltzer
2013, 94 minutes, Unrated
We've got fun and games.

I've started coming around to the idea that maybe, just maybe, we've been taking Jean-Claude Van Damme for granted.

Sure, "The Muscles from Brussels" can make for an easy target: what with his high kicks and his accent and his love of doing splits. But he's also shown a willingness to step outside of his comfort zone, dabbling in comedy and dance, and even showing a surprising amount of self-awareness. I haven't had a chance to check out 2008's *JVCD*, but it's certainly not anything Steven Seagal would do.

Then again, most action stars would stay a country mile away from a goofy comedy like *Welcome to the Jungle*.

We start off in a sitcom-ish office setting, where low level designer Chris (Adam Brody of *The O.C.* fame) is being walked all over by his slick asshole boss, Phil. We also meet a host of Chris' quirky co-workers, including the cute HR rep, the Discount Seth Rogan buddy in IT, the weird girl obsessed with rabbits (Kristen Schaal) and the fatherly yet strange CEO (Dennis Haysbert). It's all pretty much as you'd expect, with Phil's assholishness and Chris's spinelessness amped up to 11.

Haybert's CEO announces that the entire office will partake in a mandatory two-night wilderness retreat, and that's when JVCD enters the scene. In a role only he or Lorenzo Lamas could pull off, JCVD is ex-military vet STORM ROUGHCHILD!, the office's wilderness guide. I wish I could show you Storm's presentation to the office, a flurry of pseudo-inspirational posters of things like JCVD wielding a bowie knife with the screaming headline "LEADERSHIP!" It's one of the best gags of the film.

Chris, a former Eagle Scout, is the only one in the office remotely excited about the retreat (also, bonus time with Lisa the Cute HR Lady). Away they go in an ancient cargo plane to a jungle island, where they partake in a number of silly trust building exercises. Fortunately, this is boiled down to a single montage.

Instead, things pick up the next morning when Chris discovers that their very elderly pilot has passed away. And once a roaming tiger takes Storm out of the picture – and yes, it is that random – the office dwellers are left to fend for themselves. Things start off okay with the group deferring to Chris's wilderness experience until asshat Phil decides to go all alpha male on the group. From there, *Welcome to the Jungle* becomes a comedic *Lord of the Flies*.

I know that "comedic *Lord of the Flies*" doesn't make a lick of sense, but *Welcome to the Jungle* pulls it off for the most part. There are some good gags and nice comedic beats, and JCVD's STORM ROUGHCHILD absolutely steals the movie, and that's all enough to paper over the main weakness of the film: the leads.

I get that there's a cartoonishness to the movie, but both Phil and Chris are ridiculous. Phil is so nasty, so awful, that it's hard to not have complete distain for the office-dwellers who follow his cultish tribe. And Chris is so very, very, very spineless that you want to throttle him instead of pull for him. I kept hoping that JCVD, or the Discount Seth Rogan, or even Kristen Schaal would jump out and roundhouse kick both Chris and Phil in the face. Over and over and over.

In short, *Welcome to the Jungle* is a pretty decent comedy… but nothing you need to go out of your way to see.

* * *

MY ROAD TO BAD MOVIES: THE BACK-BREAKER

Now we fast-forward to 2005. Married, with one baby girl and another on the way. I had settled down, but wasn't completely settled, if you follow. I was looking for a creative outlet, but necessity dictated that it be something I could do from the house at little expense.

I hemmed and hawed, and after much deliberation, I launched a blog called the Bargain Basement Review. That's right: "Basement."

The scope of the Bargain Basement Reviews was specifically straight-to-rental fare. Being enthusiastic and naive, I had created an elaborate rating system based on the film's cheesiness, incoherence and overall gratuity. I thought the idea of a 15-point rating system would be delightfully obtuse.

And the Bargain Basement Review was good. For three whole reviews.

Then something terrible happened, something I was not prepared for. It was only the fourth film I'd ever reviewed, and I was still learning the ropes, still sorting out what works and why it works in a film (good, bad or otherwise). Worse, this film exposed the problems with the Basement's overall approach. This film is quite cheesy, has moments of stunning incoherence, is enormously gratuitous… and is the worst thing I've ever sat through.

The experience broke me. I shut down the Bargain Basement Review, and wouldn't even consider trying again for another year. All thanks to…

ROCK & ROLL FRANKENSTEIN

Directed by Brian O'Hara

1999, 88 minutes, Rated R

A cinematic monstrosity

This film is a tragedy. I don't mean it's a tragic story, like *Romeo & Juliet*. I mean its mere existence is a tragedy.

Rock & Roll Frankenstein has a great premise: A lazy music producer enlists his pre-med nephew to re-create Victor Frankenstein's famous experiment, but with the body parts of rock legends. "Frankenstein in a jumpsuit" – that's as pure of an elevator pitch as it gets. Wouldn't you want to watch that movie? I wanted to watch that movie.

And then the filmmakers screwed it up. Oh, they didn't make a cheap knock-off of *Young Frankenstein* or hold off on unveiling the Frankenstein Elvis until the very end of the film. And they didn't just screw it up with bad acting or porn-quality dialogue or sluggish passing (all of which it has). The filmmakers thoroughly and completely screwed up this movie by making *Rock & Roll Frankenstein* as mean-spirited and ugly a comedy as I've ever seen.

For future reference, the following items are not funny:

- Liberace's penis

- A talking gay predatory penis

- Watching someone argue with his penis

- Watching someone masturbate to pictures of cadavers

- Being gay*

- A pile of dead hamsters encased in condoms, killed by being shoved up a character's ass

- Anal rape (no matter how big the prop is)

*While gay people can be absolutely hilarious, simply being a homosexual isn't inherently funny. Absolutely not hilarious? A talking penis threatening to "cornhole" someone.

It's bad enough that the film implies that Liberace was a psychotic serial rapist and contains a scene where a priest is sodomized with an eight-foot tall cross, but the film thinks those are jokes.

Seriously. Go back and look at that bullet list. This isn't some kind of avant-garde take on a crisis of sexual identity. *All of those are played for laughs.*

I can't imagine why anyone involved with this film would think any of this was funny. I don't even want to imagine it. *Rock & Roll Frankenstein* is an ugly and mean film, an endless, unrelenting assault.

This is one of those films I wish I could un-see. I want those 88 minutes of my life back.

0

5: PAIN, SHEER PAIN

THE INCREDIBLY STRANGE CREATURES WHO STOPPED LIVING AND BECAME MIXED-UP ZOMBIES

Directed by Ray Dennis Steckler
1964, 82 minutes, Unrated
America's Got Talent... Somewhere Else

Any bad movie buff worth their salt has heard of *The Incredibly Strange Creatures Who Stopped Living and Became Mixed-Up Zombies*. In fact, you might not even be a fan of bad movies and still may have heard of *The Incredibly Strange Creatures Who Stopped Living and Became Mixed-Up Zombies*. With a title like *The Incredibly Strange Creatures Who Stopped Living and Became Mixed-Up Zombies*, it's hard not to stand out in a crowd of *The Killer* This and *Atomic* That.

It's quite a movie title. And it was probably inevitable that the best thing about *The Incredibly Strange Creatures Who Stopped Living and Became Mixed-Up Zombies* would be its title. By the way, did you know that *The Incredibly Strange Creatures Who Stopped Living and Became Mixed-Up Zombies* billed itself as "the first monster musical"?

It's okay if you didn't, particularly because this isn't much of a musical. I think that was more of a warning to the audience that the film has been padded with performances from a local talent show. Right after the opening credits, we're treated to the first of a few "elegant" dance numbers at a sad nightclub in a sad carnival. I don't know how many carnivals have nightclubs, but never mind. What's important is that it's just like an episode of *So You Think You Can Dance*, but with people who can't actually dance.

Enough of all that! Let's meet Jerry (played by Ray Dennis Steckler, who also wrote and directed the film). He's a mopey young man who has to be roused out of his gloominess by roommate Harold to go pick up Jerry's girl, Angela. I guess Harold is really excited to be a third wheel, cuz the three of them head off to a sad, rundown carnival for a fun day filled with running and skipping. Yay!

We get another dance number, where alcoholic dancer Marge (we know she's an alcoholic because she's been drinking non-stop in her dressing room since they introduced her) actually falls down in the middle of the number. Hard to tell if that was intentional or not.

Bored with all the terrible dancing, our gang heads over to Madam Mole's Tent of Terrible Fortune Telling. Madam Mole pulls out all the soothsaying stops: Tarot cards, palm-reading, gazing into a crystal ball… I imagine there's a deleted scene where she reads Harold's scalp. Something about Jerry rubs Madam Mole the wrong way, so after the gang leaves, she summons her pet Groucho Marx and begins scheming.

The scheme appears to involve luring Jerry into the carnival's strip club wi— the hell kind of carnival is this? – with Madam Mole's sister, Carmelita. I guess Carmelita is really mesmerizing, because Jerry and Angela soon engage in the time-honored argument about whether or not they should all go to the strip club. In the end, Jerry goes by himself to take in a dance that is… well, not what I would call "erotic."

During the "erotic" "performance," Madam Mole's pet Groucho (named Ortega, like the taco) gives Jerry a note from Carmelita, asking Jerry to meet her backstage. Jerry goes, but instead of getting it on with the stripper, he gets hypnotized by Madam Mole because... I have no idea. I couldn't stop wondering if Madam Mole's mole was growing larger as the movie progressed.

Time for more musical numbers! These stretches of the film feel just like *America's Got Talent (It's Just Not Here Right Now)*. Drunk Marge and her partner come out for yet another embarrassing dance number, but Hypno-Jerry saves us all by stabbing the dancers to death.

It's at this point when I realized that *The Incredibly Strange Creatures Who Stopped Living and Became Mixed-Up Zombies* really was nothing more than a misleading movie title. Back home, Jerry has nightmares full of crappy interpretive dance and people in goofy face paint calling his name. Clearly, Jerry has not "stopped living," nor is he a "mixed-up zombie." No, Jerry is more like a "clumsy Manchurian Candidate." From this point on, we watch Jerry stumble around town. Occasionally, something happens to accidentally trigger his hypno-homocidal tendencies.

And there are more musical numbers, of course. Here's one of the more memorable numbers, titled "Choo Choo Cha Boogie." Sadly, it's one of the better songs in the film. With ten minutes remaining, a pack of reject zombies break out of Madam Mole's closet. They kill Madam Mole and Ortega, then storm a nearby musical number. Our heroes show up just in time to stand around and watch the cops gun down all the zombies. And Jerry? I think we're meant to think his fate is tragic, but only if by "tragic" you mean "absurdly drawn out and silly."

The Incredibly Strange Creatures Who Stopped Living and Became Mixed-Up Zombies has a reputation of being a very bad movie, and it's a reputation the film deserves. I don't think it's quite as bad as others claim, but boy howdy, it's bad. If you really feel the need to check this out, you'll need the *Mystery Science Theater 3000* episode to help you get through it.

*

MONSTER A GO-GO
Directed by Bill Rebane
1965, 70 minutes, Rated PG)
I'll have one Monster a Go-Go, easy on the Monster and hold the Go-Go.

In the show's fourth season, when *Mystery Science Theater 3000* took on *Monster A Go-Go*, the cast and crew immediately felt that it was the worst movie they'd covered to date. I can't say I blame them. The narration that opens the film certainly raises some red flags: "What you're about to see may not even be possible within the narrow limits of human understanding." It's almost like a pre-emptive excuse for the incomprehensible mess to follow.

A cop named Steve and a low-flying helicopter are looking for a space capsule that's landed in a field. They eventually find the capsule, which is roughly the size of a small artificial Christmas tree and apparently made out of tin foil, but there's no sign of the astronaut. Oh, and the helicopter pilot is suddenly laid out, having been "mauled."

At least, that's what we're told. If you're going to watch *Monster A Go-Go*, then you'd better get used having anything remotely exciting, interesting or important that happens described to you rather than, you know, *seeing* it happen. That's assuming you can even understand what's being said. Here's a tip for all you aspiring filmmakers: A quick way to narrow the "limits of human understanding" is to combine extensive exposition with poor sound quality.

The incident brings together a bunch of scientists and military types. They talk and talk and talk. Sometimes they talk in a "lab," sometimes at an airport, and sometimes out in a field over a freshly mauled body... which they leave behind at the end of the scene. Crime scene investigations have apparently come a long way since the '60s.

Rather abruptly, we go to a swingin' house party with a bunch of hip cats doing The Twist. This is the "go-go" portion of our film, so you'd better enjoy it! Also, one poor actress doing The Twist neglected to wear her standard issue torpedo-shaped bra that day — by far the best special effect of the film. Anyway, everyone's having a great except for one Frat Guy Without a Cause — he's way too busy smoking and being surly. He abruptly carts off one lovely lass caveman-style and drives her out to lover's lane. Unfortunately, just like in today's films, Teenage Sexy Time = Death.

We get a quick glimpse of our Monster, and then... it's later, after any action or excitement, with all our characters chatting around the dead body. They find the lovely lass semi-conscious in the woods, and immediately decide to bring her back to the lab (as opposed to, say, a *hospital*).

Hope you're not too emotionally invested in the lovely lass's sub-plot, cuz we never see her again. In fact, a whole bunch of the characters rather suddenly disappear from the storyline.

One character that does begin to actually appear is the Monster. Like many other radiated fellows of the time, the "Monster" is really just a guy Frankensteining around with oatmeal on his face. At least they had the good sense to cast someone who looks like Lurch from *The Addams Family*, making the Monster look like Lurch with oatmeal on his face.

I'm going to do my best to stitch together what exactly happened to create the Monster. Don't think of this as a spoiler. Think of it as a favor:

That missing astronaut was hit with a bunch of radiation while out in space, but was also injected with some kind of radiation treatment before his mission. In addition, one of the scientists gave him a double dose of some other kind of (extra?) experimental radiation. So, lots of radiation, hence the incredible height and oatmeal face. We're then told that one of the scientists actually captured the Monster and kept him in a storeroom for weeks, giving the Monster injections of an antidote. But one day the scientist showed up a few minutes late for the daily injection, which gave the Monster enough time to bust out of the storeroom and trash the lab. Oh, and now the Monster pulsates radiation in a 25-foot radius.

Keep in mind, we never get to *see* any of that happen. The capture, the monster in a storeroom, the monster's escape… all done off-camera. Know what we do get to see? Talking. Talking over paperwork, talking over dinner.

Oh, and this scene: An attractive woman's car has broken down on the side of the road, and a truck driver pulls up to assist. Her tight sweater and torpedo bra makes the trucker a bit nervous as he does his mechanic thing. Turns out she just ran out of gas – go ahead and insert your own "women drivers" gag here. Fortunately, the guy has a can of gas on his front seat, so she's back in business. She gives him a loooong kiss as way of thanks.

And then… Nope, there's no "and then." That scene has literally nothing to do with anything else in the film.

The military finally decides that a giant killer mutant pulsing lethal radiation just might be a security hazard and comes to the conclusion that the Monster must be destroyed. The hunt is on, and then we hit possibly the biggest cop-out of an ending I've ever seen. I'm talking worse than the much-despised "It was all just a dream" ending. This ending knocked *Monster A Go-Go* from "Awful" to "One of the worst films I've covered so far" status. I can only hope that someone was punched in the crotch for coming up with this ending. I'm not even going to dignify it with my own write-up. I'll let the film's narrator tell you about all about it:

> As if a switch had been turned, as if an eye had been blinked, as if some phantom force in the universe had made a move eons beyond our comprehension, suddenly, there was no trail! There was no giant, no monster, no thing called "Douglas" to be followed. There was nothing in the tunnel but the puzzled men of courage, who suddenly found themselves alone with shadows and darkness! With the telegram, one cloud lifts, and another descends. Astronaut Frank Douglas, rescued, alive, well, and of normal size, some eight thousand miles away in a lifeboat, with no memory of where he has been, or how he was separated from his capsule! Then who, or what, has landed here? Is it here yet? Or has the cosmic switch been pulled? Case in point: The line between science fiction and science fact is microscopically thin! You have witnessed the line being shaved even thinner! But is the menace with us? Or is the monster gone?

What? *What?* Wh—oh, who cares.

0

KILLDOZER!
Directed by Jerry London
1974, 73 minutes, Unrated
Sic, Killdozer, sic!

Life is full of disappointments. My car never won the Pine Box Derby, no matter how bad-ass I made it. The first girl I ever asked out said no. And then, the other night, I watched *Killdozer!*.

How could they go wrong with a title like *Killdozer!*? It's part of a long, proud tradition of awesome movie titles: *Snakes on a Plane*, *Sharknado*, *Death Bed: The Bed That Eats*, etc. Visions of a demonic bulldozer busting through walls like the Kool-Aid Man danced in my head. Unfortunately, we get a '70s TV movie.

Killdozer! confusingly opens with a meteor hurdling towards a globe of the Earth swiped from an elementary school classroom. The meteor crash lands on a scenic island beach, where it makes a series of space-y noises.

We jump to some time later, where a construction company is doing all sorts of construction-type stuff for an oil company on the same beach. There's some lip service to the fact that the beach has old WWII bunkers about, and one of the roughnecks, "Dutch," spends some time unearthing old photos of Veronica Lake. It doesn't take long for Dutch's buddy, Mack, to run into the meteor with his giant bulldozer. Mack and the Foreman try to move it, but all that does is make the meteor turn special effects blue. The special effects spread over to the bulldozer, transforming it into Killdozer!

Mack gets flashed by Killdozer (ew!), giving him radiation poisoning or something. Which, I have to say, is most definitely *not* what anyone was looking forward to in a film about a killer bulldozer. None of the other construction guys were present for the flashing, and go about blaming the Foreman for pushing Mack so hard.

At least Mack doesn't seem to hold a grudge, as he tries to warn the Foreman about the blue special effects. Unfortunately, all Mack does is succeed in sounding crazy and giving an over-the-top death bed scene. Even the sourpuss Tommy Lee Jones Lite who eavesdrops on the scene thinks Mack's story is all crap. Or maybe he just always makes that face.

The Foreman decides to work through his grief with a little late night bulldozing. But surprise! The bulldozer is alive! What should be a frightening scene plays out like a scene from *The Love Bug*, all goofy noises and jittery movements. The notable exception, of course, being that the bulldozer is trying to run down the Foreman. Fortunately, the Foreman managed to clip one of Killdozer's cables as he jumped out, saving himself from a serious killdozing. Needless to say, it's pretty disappointing to see the murderous bulldozer neutralized before the movie reaches the halfway mark.

Killdozer is all better by the morning (how? Movie Magic!) and goes about killdozing the crew's radio, about a half mile of brush, and a guy hiding in a drainage pipe. By the time the surviving construction crew members get wise to what's going on, they're scrambling for high ground and watching Killdozer killdoze their entire camp. Yes, Killdozer does gets spunkier as the movie progresses. In one notable scene, the survivors are burying their dead when Killdozer takes the high ground and dumps rocks and gravel down on the men. For that one glorious, unintentionally hilarious moment, Killdozer is more a dick than a killing machine.

But those moments are few and far between. Even the climactic scene, which features a steam shovel battle, plays out like Battlebots on cough syrup.

And that's the biggest problem with *Killdozer!*. Hey, I'm all for a slower paced drama that focuses on the characters (of course, it helps if you're characters are interesting)… but not in a film called *Killdozer!*. That's just wrong, wrong wrong. I wanted to see big, nasty machines whipping around, steamrolling dozens of people while smashing into everything. And if that's what you were hoping for, too, then you're better off skipping *Killdozer!*

*

SURF NAZIS MUST DIE
Directed by Peter George
1987, 82 minutes, Rated R
Surf Nazis! Come out and play-yay!

"Surf Nazis." Has a nice ring to it, doesn't it?

I'm sure the filmmakers thought so, too. Unfortunately, it takes more than just a catchy phrase to make a worthwhile movie. And *Surf Nazis Must Die* is not a worthwhile movie.

This Troma-distributed film is set "sometime in the near future," the kind of near future that looks suspiciously like the one in *Mad Max*. The story is that a large earthquake (finally) shook California loose from the continental U.S., and the isolation has caused a huge spike in crime and gang activity. At least, that's what my podcasting partner told me is the backstory – it's hard to make a lot of sense out of this film.

The film focuses on the Surf Nazis themselves, essentially the '80s version of a gang but with surf boards and swastikas painted on their faces. "I am the Fuhrer of the New Beach!" declares gang leader "Adolf" early on, and he does an impersonation of *The Warriors*'s Cyrus in attempting to unite all the beachside gangs "under the swastika."

That's nice and all, but unfortunately, the Surf Nazis are a bunch of bland dickweeds. They surf and sneer, push people around, maybe steal an old lady's purse. Whatever. Everyone spends a lot of time posturing and talking tough, and as a result, the viewer has little to no idea of what's actually going on.

Breaking up these muddled sequences of Nazi douchebaggery are scenes of a middle-aged black lady settling into a retirement home. She seems awfully young for retirement, but whatever. She grumpily mourns the loss of her war vet husband, and is occasionally visited by her son, Leroy. These scenes seem to have absolutely nothing to do with anything until the halfway point, when Leroy interrupts a purse-snatching and runs afoul with Adolf. We don't see Leroy's actual death – Where's the overly graphic maiming and mutilation? This is a Troma film, right? – but once we see the casket, we know it's just a matter of time before Mama gets all Pam Grier on the Surf Nazis' asses.

Unfortunately, that doesn't happen until the last 15 minutes of the film. Until then, we have to endure endless gangland intrigue. You'll laugh, but you know what annoyed me? There's never any explanation of why these guys are Nazis. I mean, there's a lot more to fascism than swastika face paint. At no point are we shown what it is about Nazism that appealed to these guys. Or that they're a bunch of poseurs – that would have been just as good.

Oh, I know this wouldn't have made this a good film – it still would have been an incoherent mess filled with bad acting, but at least it would have been a sign that there was a brain behind the filmmaking.

But no. Instead, we get the slow realization by the other gangs (and yes, they all have themes a la *The Warriors*) that maybe the Surf Nazis are getting a bit big for their britches.

The other gangs attempt to take out the Surf Nazis, and fail hard. Granted, they didn't bother to coordinate their efforts, but it certainly helps that the Surf Nazis are apparently the only gang to have more than three members.

And then, finally, a middle-aged heavy-set woman is able to do what a dozen or so gangbangers couldn't. I reckon we're supposed to be cheering her on at this point, but I was just cheering for the end credits to appear. After all, film called *Surf Nazis Must Die* should be fun, not an endurance test.

*

ROCK-A-DOODLE
Directed by Don Bluth
1991, 74 minutes, Rated G
Bluth lays an egg.

Cinema Confession Time! I've never cared for the animation style of Don Bluth. I know his work is highly celebrated and all that – it's not like I can't see the talent and skill. I just don't like it. I always feel like Bluth animations look dingy and dirty, as if I'm watching some sort of seedy '70s underground film instead of a cartoon.

But, hey, we're talking about *Rock-A-Doodle*, a film about a rooster who sings like Elvis! What can be more happy and shiny than that?

Oi.

Rock-A-Doodle opens in Space: The Final Frontier. The hell? Isn't this a movie about a singing rooster? As we pan across the cosmos, we listen to the kind of uplifting music you'd expect to find in a pastoral family film. And then we get the '50s-inspired title logo. Yeah, *Rock-A-Doodle* is a mess right out of the gate.

We finally reach Earth, where we witness what I think is meant to be the very first sunrise. Jeez, really? Can't we just get to the singing chicken? We finally zoom from The Dawn of Time to our rock-n-roll rooster, Chanticleer (Glen Campbell). And sure enough, he's very much patterned after a young Elvis Presley. Of this, I approve.

I don't think Don Bluth knows what a rooster looks like. I mean, sure, Chanticleer looks more like a rooster than anything else. He just happens to have the chest and arms of a gorilla.

Our Narrator Dog (classic Disney utility man Phil Harris) – who seemingly narrates non-stop for long stretches of the film – explains how Chanticleer's singing causes the sun to wake up and rise in the sky. That's not how sunrises work, but I'll give him a pass cuz he's just a dog. Then one day, before dawn, some bird thug sent by "the Grand Duke of Owls" shows up to pick a fight with Chanticleer (because... ?). Chanticleer beats his ass, but the fight keeps him from singing to wake up the sun and, le gasp!, all the farm animals learn that the sun actually rises on its own.

How f'n dense are these farm animals? None of them remember a time before Chanticleer? Or when Chanticleer was too young to sing the sun awake? I call "shenanigans" on this movie... All the farm animals make fun of Chanticleer, who leaves for The City because he no longer has a reason to crow. Now it rains all the time (because... ?) and the Grand Duke moves into the area, which the music tells me is Bad.

Still sounds like a hot mess, eh? Just wait.

We suddenly go to a live-action scene of a mom reading her little boy the story of Chanticleer. To his credit, the little boy, Edmund, asks a lot of the same questions I did. Mom pretty much blows off our questions, and is ultimately saved from more probing questions to help out Pa and Edmond's older brothers who are toiling to save their farm from a flash flood. That leaves Edmond to open his bedroom window and shout out into the storm for Chanticleer. Because the lad is deeply, deeply confused.

Then again, Narrator Dog is still narrating, causing me to be deeply, deeply confused, too.

Lightning strikes a nearby tree. A branch that now looks like a g-d demonic claw busts through Edmond's bedroom window. Into this live-action nightmare enters the animated Grand Duke (Christopher Plummer, who apparently lost a bet), ripping Edmond a new one for calling out to Chanticleer by name. The Duke also tells Edmond that he hates rock-n-roll. Oh, that that he's going to *eat* Edmond.

"Not going to eat me!" chirps spunky Edmond, without the slightest hint of being disturbed by anything I just wrote in that last paragraph. So – and I swear this is true – Grand Duke vomits Lucky Charms all over Edmond, turning everything animated and Edmond into a kitten.

Hold on a minute. This movie just gave me a nose bleed.

Okay, I'm back. One thing I almost forgot about that last sequence: The damn Narrator Dog narrates through the entire scene. Worse, Narrator Dog's narration had a definite disconnect to the action on the screen. So while Grand Duke is saying "I'm going to eat you" to Edmond, Narrator Dog tells us how Edmond is about to go on an amazing adventure. And he narrates nonstop throughout the insanity of the sequence, as if to make extra sure your brain can't process what's happening on the screen. SHUT UP, DOG!! SHUT UP SHUT UP SHUT! UP!!

Narrator Dog actually shows up and chases Grand Duke away, which makes everyone grateful because that means he can't narrate anymore. At this point, the water has reached Edmond's second floor bedroom window because this flood is of Biblical proportions, so Edmond and his new animal friends sail out to The City in search of Chanticleer.

I'm not going to give you the blow-by-blow for the rest of the film, because it's as inane and nonsensical as everything I've covered so far. Some stray examples:

- All owls are demonic hellbeasts that spend their off-time playing the organ like the Phantom of the Opera.
- Also, light harms owls the same way sunlight harms vampires.
- The City is a full-sized place built for humans but filled solely with half-dressed animals.
- Chanticleer is now a huge star who goes by The King (wow, this movie isn't even trying), who becomes involved with a strangely sexualized chicken lady named Goldie – because unlike any of the other animals in this universe, chickens are built like Playboy Bunnies.

I guess I should mention the songs. Yes, it's an animated film and therefore the filmmakers feel obliged to provide a handful of music numbers. That's fine for the Elvis-inspired stuff. As for the other songs... I wish they didn't feel obliged to include them.

From top to bottom, *Rock-A-Doodle* is a mess. By the end, I can't tell if the whole story was Edmond's fever dream, part of a splintered reality, or if Edmond is suffering from some kind of psychotic delusion.

Perhaps the film's biggest sin is the way it absolutely wastes Charles Nelson Reilly on a bumbling henchman role. The man deserves better, dammit! In fact, we all deserve better.

*

SURF NINJAS
Directed by Neil Isreal
1993, 87 minutes, Rated PG
Crap Fu Do

If I had to pick one minor character from *The Simpsons* as my favorite, it would unquestionably be Poochie.

What I love about Poochie is that the character skewers everything about a corporate marketing team packaging "cool." The problem is that corporate marketing teams are commonly made up of people like me: white, middle class 40-year-olds who have settled down. Trust me, I have no business trying to tell today's youth what is cool. And yet, countless marketing teams are out there now, grinding away at a futile attempt to package "cool" for their breakfast cereal or pizza place or whatever. Inevitably, this packaging includes buzzwords like "edgy" or "attitude" or "extreme," and inevitably it all reeks of desperation.

It was hard not to think about Poochie while watching *Surf Ninjas*. I'd go so far as to say that *Surf Ninjas* is the Poochie of family films.

Meet Johnny and his kid brother, Adam. They're just typical kids: They surf! They carry around skateboards! They wear their ballcaps backwards! They blow off their homework cuz homework is lame, yo. And they're often accompanied by a wailin' electric guitar. WAAAA-WAAAA-WAAAA-WAAAAAAAAAHH!!

Johnny and Adam like to "smooth talk" their way out of trouble with their foster dad and hang out with their best bud/wacky neighbor/alleged teenager Iggy (Rob Schneider). Are alarms going off yet? Are your "shitty movie senses" tingling?

Our totally rad trio scamper around Los Angeles and make a mess of things in the most unrealistic way possible. Example: Johnny is to give a traditional greeting to some Polynesian wise man or some such, but like he totally forgot about it! Bogus! And the school administrator hasn't thought better of making sure everything is set beyond "you're on in five minutes and don't screw this up." Hey, that's enough time for Johnny to grab the school's a cappella group and come up with a way to springboard the wise man's name into a cover of The Beach Boy's "Barbra Ann." Of course all the kids love it! The Beach Boys are crazy dope, yo!

This leads to my first specific beef with Johnny from *Surf Ninjas*. Johnny is meant to be a delightful cut-up, but he's really an obnoxious screw-up.

In the background, we have the occasional appearance of ninjas in blue camos (no, I don't know why they're in blue camos) trying to attack the boys but being fended off by our eye-patched narrator. We also learn that *The Naked Gun*'s Leslie Nielsen is some kind of cyborg villain.

After their foster dad is kidnapped in a fight at their burger joint involving an unnecessary amount of property damage, Eye Patch Guy finally tells Johnny and Adam (and us) what's going on. The brothers are actually princes of a small nation in the South Pacific, and have been in hiding in L.A. to protect them from the evil Colonel Chi (Nielsen), who led a coup overthrowing the royal family. The boys react to this by... completely berating the eye-patched kung fu master. Because they're little shits.

Look, I get that it sounds far-fetched to them, but they were just attacked by *ninjas*. That kind of thing doesn't happen every day, not even to renowned movie reviewers like myself.

'Course, Eye Patch Guy doesn't do himself any favors by carrying on about how it's the boys' destiny to overthrow Chi and reclaim the throne, saying that Johnny will be a great warrior and Adam a seer. It also doesn't help that the Big Bad is being played by a Leslie Nielson who prat-falls for no apparent reason and is a cyborg who is forever running to get his telephone.

Adam starts getting 8-bit visions on his Sega Game Gear, where he basically has the ability to play *Surf Ninjas: The Game* (in stores now!). After blowing up the boys' home to evade more ninjas in blue camos, Eye Patch Guy takes our dudtastic trio to "Little Patu San," where *everybody* recognizes Johnny and Adam as the crown princes. Okay… We also find out that Johnny is arranged to be married to Kelly Hu. Boo-hoo for him.

Oh, and I almost forgot: Tone Loc is in this as a police detective assigned to find the boys' foster dad. And he… plays it pretty straight up. Kinda feels like he should be in a better movie, or at least a respectable cop procedural show.

To make a long story short (too late), Johnny, Adam, Iggy, Eye Patch Guy, Kelly Hu and Tone Loc all take a ship to the home island to face RoboNielsen. Johnny discovers he has super kung fu powers, and then they find some ancient weapons that give him more super kung fu powers.

And this leads me to my other specific beef with Johnny from *Surf Ninjas*: Everything he obtains is completely unearned. He gets Kelly Hu just because – she's smitten with him, despite the fact that he can barely hold a conversation with her. He suddenly has kung fu skills just because – no training necessary. I defy you to find a film where someone becomes a kung fu master without some kind of training montage. Hell, even Neo had a training scene in *The Matrix*, and all he had to do was download the information into his brain.

Damn, this movie sucks. Oh, I guess that it's a joy for young boys, but for the rest of us it's tedious and annoying and so very not funny. It says something when Rob Schneider's lack of funniness is *not* attributed to Rob Schneider – I can't imagine a single comedy legend would have done any better in that role with those lines. And it says something that I spent most of the movie hoping RoboNielsen would straight up murder Johnny's smug ass.

Do I even need to tell you that there are no actual surfing ninjas in *Surf Ninjas?* Stupid movie.

I'll end this on a more positive note: I was thinking about watching this movie with my girls, so I checked IMDB's Parents Guide for *Surf Ninjas,* just to be sure it'd be okay for them. The site reported that in one scene "Leslie Nielsen masturbates," and while I found that unlikely, we watched a Muppet movie instead. Well, I'm glad to report that Leslie Nielsen does not masturbate in *Surf Ninjas,* and that my children will live a happy life without having seen this movie.

0

HOUSE ARREST
Directed by Harry Winer
1996, 109 minutes, Rated PG
Shock Therapy

There is a common school of thought that believes a film critic or reviewer should be completely impartial, that any expectations or personal experiences should not factor into the critique. I respectfully disagree with this thinking.

Expectations and personal experiences are a natural part of the reaction to any art form. The way I see it, to ignore those reactions in a review is to only tell half the story. And if I only told half the story, it'd be hard for you to understand why I consider the 1996 family comedy *House Arrest* to be one of the most harmful movies I've watched in quite a while.

Let's get on with it... Meet Grover! He's a marble-mouthed lad of 14 who breaks the fourth wall right out of the gate. You can tell by his sunglasses and kool 'tude that Grover is a righteous dude, yet the flashback to the ritual humiliation in the school hall lets you know that he's also a regular kid *just like you*. As for his insistence that we start the story with home movies of his parents' wedding, honeymoon and early married life? I can't tell if that's dorky or weird for a 14-year-old.

Turns out that all the video footage is due to him making his parents a video for their 18th anniversary. And why not – the 18th wedding anniversary is a major milestone! I believe Miss Manners says that the traditional gift for an 18th anniversary is Farberware.

Grover and his Li'l Sis present their gift to their very busy parents (Kevin Pollack and Jaime Lee Curtis) over breakfast, and their parents react like someone just farted really loudly. Uh-oh...

At school later, Grover is doing some heavy duty moping. Even the sight of dream girl Jennifer Love Hewitt can't cheer him up! Speaking of which, here is JLH's introduction to the movie: Grover's best bud Matt spies her in the lunch line through his camcorder, and promptly does a quick zoom in and out on her chest. Way to keep it classy, *House Arrest*.

Grover finally breaks down and tells Matt that his parents announced that they're separating. Matt, whose parents had divorced and remarried, gives Grover some fairly astute tips before off-handedly suggesting that Grover lock his parents in a closet until they worked things out. You see where this is going, right?

Soon Kevin Pollack and Jaime Lee Curtis are locked in their semi-finished basement. Word gets out and soon Matt, school bully T.J. and JLH are over to help... and deposit their parents (who include Shawn Wallace, Christopher McDonald and Jennifer Tilly) in the basement to work out their issues. Along the way, there's all manner of kookiness such as ye olde "kids cook the darndest things" montage. There's also a subplot involving Ray Walston as the retired police chief across the street who thinks Those Kids Are Up To No Good that I wouldn't even mention if it weren't for Ray Walston.

And it's... fine. I mean, much of the comedy is strained and tired, but *House Arrest* is definitely geared towards kids and I could see kids really enjoying the wish fulfilment aspects of the movie. There are a few good lines and moments sprinkled in, including a nod to Jaime Lee Curtis's horror roots when she crawls through the laundry chute and a couple rats scamper down her back. It's always fun to see Christopher McDonald do his pompous bastard act, and Shawn Wallace seems to be having a grand ol' time. And despite the ham-fisted way the kids all come together, they're believable as a makeshift family.

I also appreciated that the film allowed for a certain sadness to creep into the proceedings. Which is appropriate, as *House Arrest* is ultimately about a kid trying to process the fact that his parents are splitting up. As a divorced father of two who watched his daughter struggle with her parents splitting, these moments hit a nerve...

And then we get to the end, where the filmmakers take what was a passable family comedy I would have given a strong two asterisks and screw it up. Screw it up hard. Screw it up in the worst way possible.

(SPOILER ALERT for the movie nobody saw in theaters and critics hated)

So after about five days (!) locked in the basement, the police show up in force and bust the kids. Knowing the jig is up, the kids peacefully surrender, knowing that they did what they could to help their parents deal with their issues. Jaime

Lee Curtis steps out of her front door – outside for the first time in nearly a week – and takes in the ocean of police cruisers and assorted rescue personnel. She turns to Kevin Pollack and points out how "Grover did all this for us" and "we must be doing something right" and reconciles with her husband. Marriage saved!

NO! NOOOOOOO!!! NONONOFUCKITYNO!!

I have no problem with the statistical unlikelihood of Curtis and Pollack's characters staying together. It's a movie – a family film not named *Old Yeller* – and people like their endings happy. That's fine.

But ending your family film by telling kids that they can stop their parents from getting divorced by trying really really hard to keep them together? That's seriously messed up. No, more than that: In a film clearly geared for kids, to have a story about a kid who loves his parents so much that he keeps them from getting divorced (and if your parents got divorced, maybe it's because *you* didn't love them enough) is negligent and actively harmful. And really, really shitty.

Screw you, *House Arrest*. Back to the basement with you.

0

THE PATRIOT
Directed by Dean Semler
1998, 86 minutes, Rated R
The Un-Seagalling of Steven Seagal

I have to admit, I do enjoy the occasional Steven Seagal movie. Well... maybe "enjoy" isn't the right word for it. I enjoy Steven Seagal movies the way you might enjoy watching that one inappropriate relative go off on a ridiculous tirade at a family gathering.

Also, Steven Seagal movies are predictable. You see Mr. Seagal's name in the credits, and you know you're going to get copious amounts of:

- Unnecessarily brutal take-downs
- Non-reactions from our hero
- A cartoonish villain
- Whispery dialogue
- Long overcoats to help hide the bulk
- Sanctimonious sermonizing

But if you remove any of those elements, is it still a Steven Seagal movie? Let's find out.

The Patriot – not to be confused with 2000's *The Patriot* starring Mel Gibson – opens with beautiful spacious skies, the sun rising over purple mountain majesties, and Steven Seagal's name. Subtle! Seagal and his flowing locks are out on the range doing some good ol' fashioned ranching with That Old Coot from *Lone Wolf McQuade*. Seagal('s stunt double) ropes a steer and injects it with something that is *not* antibiotics, he assures us. What it is is never explained.

So it turns out that Steven Seagal is not a single dad who is a cop or a super soldier or a government agent but a single dad who is a farm vet/family doctor/holistic therapist. Oh, and he's willing to provide services on a barter system because he's a Really Nice Guy. Huh. That's... huh.

Meanwhile, the Feds are in the 52nd day of a standoff (!) with a neo-Nazi militia. The head militiaman, Floyd, spends a lot of time strutting around in camouflage and quizzing his army of *Duck Dynasty* fans on famous American quotes. Oh, and all of this is happening *right next door* to Dr. Seagal's homestead.

You think you know what's going to happen next, don't you? WRONG! Floyd takes some kind of pill and promptly turns himself in to the authorities. Floyd then gets an arraignment hearing that very day, where he spits poison from his pill on the judge. Seagal, with his daughter in tow, is called in to treat the rapidly deteriorating judge. When the cop who escorted them in collapses, Seagal *immediately* identifies the culprit as an emergency contagion and calls in his old government colleagues.

And just like that, the little town of Montanaland has an outbreak on its hands. Choppers drop fully armed soldiers in gas masks onto Main Street while someone with a bullhorn bellows: "RESIDENTS! DO NOT BE ALARMED! A STRAIN OF RHUMPHRHUMPH HAS BEEN DETECTED IN YOUR AREA. PLEASE REPORT TO THE HOSPITAL FOR VACCINES AND FURTHER ADVICE." Comforting!

Floyd learns that his antivirus isn't working so after busting out of jail, he sends his army to take out the Army and steal their antivirus, which happens with alarming ease. Steven Seagal magically deduces that Floyd causes the outbreak, and manages to stay out of the fray during the assault. So now you're thinking that this is going to be like *Die Hard* in a hospital, right?

WRONG! Ish! Steven Seagal punches one baddie through a door (!) and launches a quick flurry of random punches and kicks – just like your average farm vet/family doctor/holistic therapist would when faced with a hostage situation – before running off with his daughter and That Old Coot from *Lone Wolf McQuade*, where they…

- Make fake IDs!
- Get That Old Coot from *Lone Wolf McQuade* killed trying to stop a convoy!
- Visit Seagal's father in-law!
- Commune with nature (complete with Native American chanting and an eagle cry!!)
- Wander around the countryside looking for a secret military lab!
- Spend an ungodly amount of time in said lab staring into a microscope and failing to cure the infected soldiers stationed there!

It's worth noting that despite being exposed to countless people infected with an airborne virus, Steven Seagal never ever gets infected himself. That man is magic. It's also worth noting that with f'n 15 minutes remaining in the film, the only action has been the brief and unexplained spurt of martial arts during the four minutes the film became *Die Hard* in a hospital. *That's it.*

In case you're wondering, that's not a good thing. Imagine all the sanctimonious sermonizing of *On Deadly Ground* with the slimmest fraction of the action.

But if Steven Seagal restrains himself from doing a lot of Steven Seagalling, is it still a Steven Seagal movie? I guess, though it's certainly not a *good* Steven Seagal movie. And given how good a "good" Steven Seagal movie is, that's definitely not a good thing.

*

POKEMON: THE FIRST MOVIE
Directed by Kunihiko Yuyama
1998, 85 minutes, Rated G
You're punching yourself! You're punching yourself!

I was too old to get into Pokémon. Oh, I was aware of Pokémon. I knew it was A Thing, the same way I knew *Saved By the Bell* was A Thing without ever having seen it, but that's about it. Sure, I could pick Pikachu out of a line-up, but that's about it.

But hey, this is *Pokémon: The First Movie*, so all of my questions should be answered, right? Ha ha ha ha…

We open with a monologue contemplating the Meaning of Life. Nothing like starting off small. Our narrator talks about how Humans and Pokémons are forever searching for the meaning of life. Right now, I'm just searching for the meaning of "Pokémon."

Some evil scientist type is making a Pokémon clone. It's some kind of mouthless cat thing named "Mewtwo," cloned after "the rarest of Pokémons." So does this mean there are Pokémon breeds? Anyway, it's floating around in a tank when it achieves consciousness, and like any newborn, Mewtwo immediately wants to know what his purpose is. Mewtwo knows he doesn't want to be a lab rat, so he unleashes his immense psychic powers on the lab.

But then there's some other guy, and he wants to team up with Mewtwo to take over the world. He gives Mewtwo some armor, and then there's a bunch of extreme close-ups and I have no idea of what's going on. The other guy says something dickish, so Mewtwo ditches his armor and essentially becomes a supervillain.

Enough of that! Our narrator suddenly gets all cheery and tells us about how young Ash strives to be a world-class

Pokémon trainer, which apparently consists of picnicking and being lethargic. The picnic is interrupted by some random guy looking to challenge Ash to a duel. Is this just an animated version of *Over the Top*?

Okay, so here's how a duel works: Each trainer dramatically throws out a red and white pool ball that spits out a cutesy looking monster. The monsters fight, and the trainer gets credit for the win. In other words, Pokémon is an animated sci-fi version of cockfighting.

I'll sum up, because I'm getting bored and none of this makes a damn lick of sense. Ash gets invited to "Pokémon Castle" on "New Island" (presumably off the coast of Fakelandistan) by the self-proclaimed "strongest Pokémon trainer." Off goes Ash and friends, followed by some comic relief villains. Also, there's a flying white cat…

The Pokémon trainers make their way through a monsoon to New Island and discover that the self-proclaimed "strongest Pokémon trainer" is Mewtwo. Turns out that in the 30 or so minutes since he last appeared in the film, Mewtwo has been cranking out clones of Pokémons. Then there's an endless parade of Pokémons fighting identical Pokémons, broken up with spurts of unironic complaints from people who professionally force these creatures to fight in duels about the cruelty of making these creatures fight clones of themselves.

I don't get it. I don't get any of it, and I really could care less. Apparently, I am too old for this shit.

Just when I didn't think it could get worse, one of the main characters sacrifices himself in an attempt to stop the fighting. It's meant to be tragic, but it's mind-numbingly stupid – he essentially jumps in the middle of a gunfight. But nevermind! Turns out the Pokémon all have Care Bear-like abilities and shower the character with sparkles that revive him, undoing his death even faster than the one at the end of *Star Trek Into Darkness*.

The film ends with Mewtwo deciding that it might be best that everyone forget this ever happened. I couldn't agree more.

0

BALLISTIC: ECKS VS. SEVER
Directed by Kaos
2002, 91 minutes, Rated R
Explosion Porn

This film was directed by someone named Kaos. With a "K." And that's all you need to know about the direction of this film.

The opening shot is a fast pan over water towards the city skyline. How many times have we seen this shot before? I wouldn't mind such a cliché opening our story started at the harbor or on a boat. Nope, we're deplaning at an airport. Sigh.

A MILF and her son are heading, uh, somewhere when DIA agents – yes, that's a real thing – pull up out of nowhere to escort the kid, uh, somewhere else. But then EXPLOSIONS! CAR SMASH! SMOKE BOMBS! The Crystal Method's "Name of the Game"! And out of the smoke comes a hooded figure who is very clearly Lucy Liu. Fighting time! Kick, kick, kick! Soon the boy is the only one left, and we get the world's... slowest... reveal... that it is... in fact... Lucy Liu. No kiddin'.

She takes the kid off to, no joke, the Bat Cave.

Meanwhile, FBI Agent Ecks (Antonio Banderas) is in a bar, dripping wet and wallowing. He's all burned out, John McClane-style, and still tough enough to make a pair of agents look like chumps. Miguel Sandoval shows up to make me feel sad because he's in this film. And to inform Ecks that his long-exploded wife is still alive – cue the EXPLOSIONS!-filled flashback.

Time for a briefing! I'd like to tell you exactly what happened, but everyone was too busy mumbling cuz they're too tough to speak clearly or annunciate. In a nutshell: the boy's dad, Gant, is the head of the DIA and has come up with a microscopic insta-kill machine. So, yeah, he's the Bad Guy. But since Mystery Woman Sever (Lucy Liu) kidnapped Gant's son, it's up to Ecks to find her.

Talk is boring, time for more EXPLOSIONS! We find Sever in the food court of a mall and -- jeez, Lucy Liu can't even go to a food court convincingly – running, shooting, EXPLOSIONS! Even the snipers use rocket launchers, it's a bit ridiculous. Through it all, Lucy Liu maintains her trademark "bored but slightly annoyed" expression.

Poor Vancouver. Often cast as the K-Mart New York City, this film is actually set in Vancouver, which means this glorified turf war between U.S. agencies is taking place on foreign soil. Nice. I'm sure this film was in production during 9/11, causing the filmmakers to change the setting from New York to Vancouver. Because rocket launching snipers firing away in downtown New York would have been tacky. Rocket launching snipers firing away in Vancouver? Not a problem.

Anyway, when Miguel Sandoval gets hit by Sever, he abruptly tells Ecks, "She knows! She knows where your wife is!" The hell? Wasn't she the Mystery Woman no one knew anything about ten minutes ago? And why would someone burden Miguel Sandoval with such horrible lines? Oh well, more running! Ecks and Sever finally face off on a rooftop, where we're treated to some painfully slow fight choreography.

And that will be the only time we actually get Ecks vs. Sever.

Now that I think of it, all of the action sequences feel slow, like the cars are only moving 20mph during the car chases. But that's the least of this film's problems. Literally every other scene features lots of cars skidding around and running and shooting and EXPLOSIONS!, with little sense of what's going on. And since most of the sequences don't move the story forward, you won't care. With all the techno and EXPLOSIONS! this film makes Michael Bay movies look restrained.

The high water mark comes when we learn that Gant's MILFy wife is Ecks's wife (?), making the kid Ecks's kid (!), and that Gant got Ecks and the MILF to believe each other was killed in an elaborate pair of EXPLOSIONS! Damn, this movie is stupid.

I gave this review the subtitle "Explosion Porn" for a reason: The explosions are exciting at first, but then you quickly lose interest.

It's amazing: 91 minutes and not a single thing happens that is interesting, original, clever or entertaining. Hell, I'm starting to think I was too hard on *Killdozer!* and *The Patriot* – at least they contained an occasional amusing moment. But here, I couldn't even make it through the action sequences without checking the clock to see how much longer I had to sit through the movie.

The sad thing is, I *knew* it was a crummy movie. I saw this a number of years ago, long before my bad movie-reviewing days, and remember it being pretty weak. After watching it again, you'd have to put a gun in my mouth to make me watch it a third time.

0

STINGER

Directed by Martin Munthe
2005, 97 minutes, Unrated
Filmed in all-new Confuso-Vision! [TM]

This film was recommended to me by a buddy from college. He's a screenwriter, and as someone who is devoted to his craft, he makes a point of watching everything – and I do mean *everything*. About *Stinger*, he told described the film as "Almost unwatchable, but a classic."

Well, I would agree that *Stinger* is classically unwatchable.

We open in the Bluest Water Ever, where a submarine cruises around. The crew of the sub is at Red Alert – we know this from all the red lighting and the sirens that drown out all of the dialogue, otherwise, everyone is just going about their business. Suddenly, a few bodies are thrown around and – what the hell? A large CGI scorpion? Okay then. Shooting! Looks of terror! Blood splatter! And scene.

In our post-credits exposition dump, an extra from *The Sopranos* debriefs his crack team and the audience: The SS Newark (the sub from the opening) has been MIA for a couple months and has just been located. The sub was apparently carrying some Big Deal cargo – because Navy subs are like the U-Hauls of the Sea, I guess – that belongs to GenericCo. Their mission: Accompany members of the GenericCo staff to the Newark via mini-sub and get the Big Deal cargo. No talk of rescuing any survivors or salvaging what I imagine is a very expensive submarine.

We quickly get to meet some of the main players. From GenericCo, we have the sexy Dr. Carly, the Hairy Rain Man guy, the Slutty Lady and the Tall Bald Guy (Who In No Way Is The Villain). For the marines, we have… a bunch of young bald guys. Sorry, that's the best I can do. I know "Sarge" had a perpetual cigar stump implanted into the lefthand corner of his mouth… there was a guy named "the LT" and "the Rookie"… yeah, that's all I have.

And they're off! To celebrate, we're treated to the only Handi-Captions of the film: "Eighty miles of the cost of California" Handi-Captions, indeed.

After a dramatic "opening of the hatch" sequence – which has all the drama of watching someone struggle with a pickle jar – the roughnecks enter the Newark with "weapons at ready." I can't even imagine why that would be necessary when boarding your own sub which is likely to be filled with your own countrymen. What were they expecting? Giant mutant scorpions?

Oh. Never mind.

The next bit of forever is spent wandering around the darkened submarine that looks suspiciously like the basement of an office space, with the folks from GenericCo aggressively not talking about what their Big Deal cargo is. There's some jocular banter involving "The Dog Whisperer" and strange food combinations, and it's a nice thought but doesn't really work cuz it's trying too hard. Every now and then, some CGI scorpion part makes an appearance and kills someone. Once everyone figures out that there are CGI scorpions on the loose, there's a lot of shooting (always a great idea inside a submerged submarine) and yelling and shooting and scorpions and shooting – either the marines are terrible shots or the CGI scorpions are bulletproof.

And that's about as much as I can figure out from watching the film.

It's bad enough that nearly everything takes place in the dark (despite the fact that the Hairy Rain Man got the generator running by whacking it with a hammer – don't know how that works, but I'm not an electrician). But what really made this film incomprehensible – besides the plot – was that literally every other shot is an extreme close-up. It's as if all the director remembered from film school was "closer = claustrophobic," and demanded extremely tight close-ups on the actors' faces (or parts of faces) at all times.

Yes, even during the action sequences. Especially during the action sequences. I really had no idea of what was going on at any time.

The only scene that wasn't clogged with extreme close-ups was the one where the Slutty Lady gets naked and shows off her extraordinarily perky chest. Best special effects of the film – zing!

Speaking of special effects, *Stinger* sports some of the worst CGI I've seen in a long time. There is absolutely no weight or feel that the CGI scorpions take up any space – they look every bit as super-imposed into the scene as they really are. And the CGI in the final scene of the film? Laugh-out-loud bad. I only wish the rest of the movie was so delightfully terrible.

Talking about terrible, let's re-visit the plot: Mutant scorpions on a sub. Already, the story sounds like it was created by a random word generator. But a closer examination shows just how stupid the movie is: The marines spend a good chunk of the film moving through the sub from room to room, trying to exterminate the scorpions. No one ever suggests that they simply return to the *fully functional mini-sub they arrived in* and leave, then have the Newark torpedoed later. It's not like the scorpions are going anywhere – they're stuck on the ocean floor, and last I knew, giant mutant scorpions aren't particularly adept at operating a submarine.

Of course, if the marines did that, there would be no movie. Trust me; that would not be a bad thing.

0

FIREPROOF
Directed by Alex Kendrick
2008, 118 minutes, Rated PG
The Passion of the Cameron

I really wanted to give this movie a chance. I really did. Sure, it would have been easy to make a few cracks at Kirk Cameron's expense, mention *Growing Pains* and trash the film's piousness. It would have been *really* easy. And it would have been cheap.

So I decided to put on my Big Boy pants and take *Fireproof* at face value. *Fireproof* starts strong, get a bit wobbly, and man, does it botch the landing.

Kirk Cameron plays Caleb, the captain of a fire department in Georgia, and his marriage to Catherine, head of public relations at the local hospital, is falling apart. She accuses him of never being around and wasting all his spare time with all "that trash on the Internet." He accuses her of devoting all of her time to her job and ailing mother and of not "respecting" him. I'll leave it to you to determine what that might mean.

With the couple on the brink of divorce and counseling off the table, it's up to Caleb's friends and family to help him weather the storm. The firefighting allusions come fast and furious: Caleb's Christian co-worker confidant (CCC) is quick to point out that Caleb regularly puts it all on the line to save a stranger's life, but won't make an effort to save his own marriage. Even Caleb himself trots out his own heavy-handed credo, "You never leave your partner – especially during a fire," early and often.

But it's Caleb's father, the Most Beatific Man on the Planet, who gives Caleb the "Love Dare," which I'm sorry to report is not a raunchy party game. Beatific Dad asks Caleb to put the divorce on hold for 40 days and partake in a daily challenge to rekindle the relationship. Challenges start off with such baby steps as "Don't say shitty things" (I'm paraphrasing), then build to the likes of "Make a romantic dinner at home." All of the challenges are accompanied by Bible verses, because how else do you think Beatific Dad got to be so beatific?

So far, so good. Yes, Kirk Cameron is stiff and unconvincing as a firefighter of any kind (let alone a captain), but the rescue scenes work well enough. No one is going to confuse this film with *Backdraft*, but the filmmakers do just fine with what they have.

Many of the other firefighters are there for comic relief, which is serviceable and harmless. There's also a scene that juxtaposes Caleb venting to CCC and Catherine dishing to her girlfriends that's highly amusing. At least, I'd like to think that lines like "And then she starts nagging me, saying I don't listen to her, or something like that" were meant to be funny.

While Cameron can't pull off the role of fire chief, he is very strong in the scenes of domestic un-bliss. I don't know if Cameron is tapping into frustrations with his career or personal life or what, but he's extremely good in scenes that could have played as corny or melodramatic (despite some of the film's dialogue). He's so convincing, in one scene I really thought Caleb was going to haul off and slug Catherine. Equally convincing are Caleb's initial attempts at the Love Dare. Oh, he does 'em, but it's a put-upon, half-hearted effort that gets him nowhere.

And then, about an hour in, the wheels start to come off of *Fireproof*.

Caleb is halfway through the Love Dare and ready to throw in the towel, so Beatific Dad comes over for a pep talk. And by "pep talk," I mean a lecture on how Caleb isn't living up to God's standards, where "hate is the same as murder and lust is the same as adultery" and how Caleb won't be able to love without loving Jesus. There's a lot wrong with that last sentence:

1) The other 2/3rds of the world's population might take offense to being told that they're incapable of love. I'm no Biblical scholar, but my reading is that Jesus taught the nature of God – pledging allegiance to Christ was never required or even asked for. That kind of qualifier seems to fly in the face of a guy who famously broke bread with lepers and tax collectors and prostitutes.

2) I'm endlessly unimpressed with the idea that hate is the same as murder or lust is the same as adultery. Do I really have to outline how checking out someone's bum is different than physically cheating on a spouse? We're not machines – we commonly have emotional, irrational responses and reactions to the world around us. Isn't it more impressive, when faced with the temptation, to *decide* not to commit adultery? Isn't it better to seethe with anger and *choose* not to act upon it?

Caleb and his dad go back and forth, and Beatific Dad steers Caleb into seeing the parallels between his plight and the Passion of Christ. As Caleb has his Come to Jesus moment, Beatific Dad leans oh-so nonchalantly against the conveniently located cross, and he looks so damn smug that I desperately wanted to dropkick him in the face.

Caleb may have found God, but he's lost any emotional perspective. When CCC confides that he too had gone through a divorce, Caleb is shocked – SHOCKED! – as if CCC had just confessed to buggering goats. Speaking of buggery, Caleb decides to address his "porn addiction" the only way he knows how: *to smash his home computer with a baseball bat*. Guess they won't be paying bills online anymore...

Caleb steps up his efforts to win back his wife, but she's having none of it – especially with that smarmy doctor coming on to her. Coming down the stretch, the film falls into the typical rom-com trap where everything could be patched up if only our two should-be lovers would just talk to each other. And then they do! Caleb comes clean honestly and sincerely (and it's fantastic work by Cameron), and… this is where the movie fails.

Catherine still isn't convinced. No, it's not until she finds out that Caleb spent the $24K he'd saved up for a boat to get Catherine's mom that wheelchair she needed – in other words, when Caleb *bought her affection* – that Catherine comes running home, crying, to frantically put her wedding ring back on and take Caleb back.

Gross. I could have forgiven the goofy comic relief, the well-meaning but wrong-headed theology and the Christian rock montages, but not this. *Fireproof* plays it as a grand act of charity, but it clearly isn't – *Caleb is trying to win his wife back*. This isn't an act of love, it's an act of commerce. It's literally something Tony does with Carmela on every other season of *The Sopranos*.

Makes me wonder what day of the Love Dare – which is a real thing – challenges the reader to "Empty out your savings account and buy her devotion." Just like Jesus taught.

*

MANCATION
Directed by Frank Vain
2012, 100 minutes, Unrated
Unworthy!

Before we dig in, a little history:

I'm still close with my childhood friends, and we've all reached an age where we've scattered to the four winds and started families of our own. With kids and family and day-to-day obligations, it's become difficult for us to get together. To remedy this, a couple years ago we established THE MANCATION. This weekend – this glorious weekend – has been meticulously engineered to avoid birthdays, anniversaries and so on, and is etched in stone in our calendars as a time for us all to assemble and unleash all manner of manliness. As you can imagine, we look forward to The Mancation every year.

At a recent Mancation, I was discussing the newly unveiled Mancation Crest (not pictured here, because then I'd have to gouge out your eyes) with Dave, the buddy of mine who designed it. Dave suddenly pulls out his phone to show me something he found in his research: *Mancation*, starring Joey Fatone of N'Sync fame. We laugh, because we had absolutely no idea that a film titled *Mancation* existed, let alone that Joey Fatone has a film career. "You have to review this," Dave said to me, and I promised to do so.

LATER THAT VERY DAY we're breaking up into teams to pick up provisions for the evening, and Dave and I just so happen to be teamed up. We get what we need from the grocery store, and I notice an actual brick-and-mortar video store in the same plaza. "Hey Dave," I say, "mind if we duck into the video store and see if there's any used movies worth picking up cheap?" You'll never guess what I found there…

We open in Club Risqué, Philadelphia's finest gentlemen's club. Never you mind how I know. It's strangely quiet in the club, despite the fact that ECW legend Tommy Dreamer is emceeing. The camera cranes its way over to the booth where our Dudes have set up shop: there's Vince the Vanilla Lead, the Faux Tuff Guy (FTG) and Joey Fatone, and they're all weakly woo-ing over their round of shots. The FTG swats the waitress in the bum, and then has the gall to stand up and taunt the bouncer twice his size without having his head caved in. Which is too bad, because I immediately hate the FTG. FTG celebrates by smashing his shot glass on the floor, because he's trying to make that a thing.

So here's the long and short: Vince is getting married to the boss's daughter, despite clearly having a thing for the florist, Winnie Cooper from *The Wonder Years* (who very clearly has a thing for him, too). The wedding is on a Friday so that the newlyweds can *not* have a honeymoon and Vince can be in the office Monday for the Big Merger with the "Japanese consortium." Vince's bride is played by a porn star, and Boss Daddy is played by Mike Starr in full-on Terrible Person mode. You'll never imagine how this is going to turn out…

…partially because I'll tell you now: Less than 24 hours after the "I do's," Vince walks in on his blushing bride taking the maid of honor from behind with a strap-on. Turns out she's a lesbian and only married Vince so she could access her trust fund, and assumed Vince only married her to advance in Boss Daddy's company. Oh nos! Looks like it's time for a "Mancation"!

So off the lads go to Atlantic City, along with Vince's "younger" brother, Leo, and his collection of sweater vests. Along the way, FTG's mouth gets him thrown through a glass door by a gang, and in one of my favorite moments in the film, Joey Fatone simply sits in his car and watches the gang kick the hell out of FTG.

They arrive at a condo "owned" by FTG's oddly not-present buddy (hmm), where they find a medicine cabinet full of "Bonerall: Ritalin For Your Dick." These are the gags, folks. They do another round of shots, and FTG smashes yet another shot glass. Still not funny, though FTG certainly thinks so. I can't tell you how annoying FTG is.

No, that's not true: I totally can. The Loveable Asshole is a really tough role to pull off. For clarity, I don't mean someone who's a bit dickish, like a Vince Vaughn character, or a delightful villain, like Al Swearigan from *Deadwood*. The

Loveable Asshole character is a full-on, largely unrepentant asshole, yet is so charismatic that everyone loves him anyway. Jack Nicholson used to pull off the Loveable Asshole nicely, and if you've ever seen the show *Misfits*, Robert Sheehan's Nathan is a master class in Loveable Asshole.

FTG is not a Loveable Asshole. He's just a regular asshole, obvious and desperate and without an iota of wit. And he wears thin very, very quickly.

As the guys go about their shenanigans – Vince with his binder in hand! – we get clumsy discussions of over-planning (Vince) versus spontaneity (Joey Fatone) and restraint (Leo) versus a complete lack of consideration for anyone and anything (FTG). There are repeated run-ins with an off-beat Russian named Igor, Vince spends most of Sunday tracking down Winnie Cooper at her flower convention, and Leo begins receiving tutorials in dickishness from FTG.

That training consists of FTG gets a "Prince Albert" at a tattoo parlor. Unfortunately, I'm not referring to a tattoo of a pasta sauce jar. I'm not sure what the point is – other than to freak me out – but Leo seems to learn something.

It all winds up in the strangest climax I've seen in some time, where Vince and Winnie Cooper's Big Moment is juxtaposed with FTG in a gang fight, Joey Fatone running away from elderly sadomasochists and Leo having a "controversial-off" with Igor that leaves most of the spectators vomiting. I'm not sure what the juxtaposition of those things is supposed to mean, other than that the film is mercifully almost over.

I tried to give *Mancation* a lot of leeway. I *wanted* to give *Mancation* a lot of leeway for sentimental reasons. But at the end of the day, this film is not worthy of the "Mancation" title.

*

TEEN BEACH MOVIE 2
Directed by Jeffrey Hornaday
2015, 105 minutes, Rated G
Bogus!

What better way to close out the summer than with a beach movie? I had previously taken on the Disney Channel hit *Teen Beach Movie* and was pleasantly surprised by how watchable it was ("watchability" not being a strong suit for beach movies).

So here comes the inevitable sequel. Will *Teen Beach Movie 2* continue the watchability of the original? Or will it be the *Matrix: Reloaded* of teen beach movies, full of bad CGI and pointless set pieces and convoluted plot points that hint at deep philosophical musings but fail to land?

To recap (cuz the movie assumes you've seen the first movie over and over and over again): Brady and McKenzie are photogenic teens who love surfing and somehow get sucked into Brady's favorite '60s beach movie. There's singing and the upending of gender roles, and then they get home. Post-credits, a bunch of their new friends from the '60s movie wash up on shore in our universe/time-line.

Well, forget that last part, cuz *Teen Beach 2* does. Instead, we get Brady and Mack having a romantic "meetaversary" on a suspiciously empty beach. The two fret about starting the new school year in the morning, because... they just started dating that summer? Did they attend one of those high schools with a zillion students and somehow never met? Is this the end of the same summer as the first movie? Cuz that was at the end of summer, too. My head hurts already. This is not a good sign.

Turns out that their worrying is justified, because they somehow lose the ability to talk to each other in school. Mack is all go-go-getter busy-body gal, and Brady is extra loosy-goosy and never takes anything seriously. But Brady starts getting concerned when some nerdy bohunk starts hanging around Mack and her BFF. Things come to a head when Brady stands up Mack at the college fair (on the first day of school?!) because he's busy building surfboards – something he keeps super-secret for some reason.

Hey, remember that '60s movie? Yeah, that's still a thing. Apparently in that universe, they replay scenes from the movie over and over... but remember their visit with Brady and Mack? Huh? Biker girl Lela keeps thinking about Mack's liberating advice, so she and her preppy surfer boyfriend Tanner wander into the ocean and magically end up in our world. No, it doesn't make any sense to me, either.

In fact, screw this, I'm bailing on trying to describe this mess of a plot to you. We get to see the '60s kids integrate into today's world – cue all the obvious smartphone gags. We also get to see how their musical powers cause all of today's jaded teens to bust out in synchronized dance numbers. This is a musical, after all.

Tensions between Brady and Mack remain as they figure out a way to get Lela and Tanner back to the movieverse, and that ultimately includes straight-up telling them that they're fictional characters. Somehow, neither Lela nor Tanner slit their wrists. Lela decides she doesn't want to go back, but then all the other bikers and surfers from the movie show up... but they're slowly disappearing so they all leave. But then they come back for another musical number at the big school dance! That takes place during the first week of school for some reason!

They successfully get Brady and Mack back together, but now they all have to go back or else the movie won't exist and Brady and Mack will never have met? There's all sorts of faux drama, but somehow sending the '60s folks back does indeed make it so Brady and Mack had never met. Because why not introduce a new plot point in the last 10 minutes of a movie?

I'm at a loss with this movie. There are glimmers of cleverness, but anything and everything that made the first movie interesting has been aggressively scrubbed from *Teen Beach 2*. Even my daughter, who's still young enough to pretty much like everything, though this was a weak waste of time. The story doesn't make a lick of sense, and even half of the songs are re-hashed from the first movie. I'd say this was just a shameless money-grab, *but it's a TV movie.*

Wipeout.

*

MY ROAD TO BAD MOVIES:
THE LAST STRAW

After my experience with *Rock & Roll Frankenstein*, it took a good year to get up the nerve to simply blog again. But I wasn't ready to write movie reviews – and certainly not of bad movies. Instead, I launched a free-ranging blog covering television, movies, politics, religion, current events and more. It was a good experience for me: The blog allowed me to write about a variety of things, develop an online community, compete in good spirited competitions and take in many different styles of writing.

It didn't take too long before I started gravitating towards bloggers who wrote about movies. I'd make sure to read and comment on the reviews they wrote, which eventually meant that I'd read six to eight reviews of the same film in a single sitting.

I read at least that many reviews of one particular film. With all the marketing and merchandizing, it was clearly a tent pole film for the studio, the kind of film that would make or break its fiscal year. And for this Really Big Deal Movie, all of those reviews boiled down to "Meh."

Not "It was pretty good, but I thought it would be better." Not "What a letdown." Just "Meh."

Eight reviews of Meh. That was the tipping point for me, the moment I thought, "This is stupid. Why am I reading countless reviews of the same bland film? I need to get back out there and present films that no one else will touch. At least with those, I know I'll never have a 'meh' experience."

And so the Bargain Bin Review was born. All thanks, unlikely as it seems, to…

FANTASTIC FOUR: RISE OF THE SILVER SURFER
Directed by Tim Story
2007, 92 minutes, Rated PG
Somewhat less than Fantastic

The Fantastic Four are famed in superhero lore for breaking the mold: a family-based team of superheroes with no secret identities who struggle with both super-villains and domestic issues. That was all well and good in the '60s, when the genre needed a spark. But for today, it leads to sitcom banality.

At their best, the Fantastic Four are heroes, adventurers and explorers. So of course *Fantastic Four: Rise of the Silver Surfer* opens with airport shtick and lots of pre-wedding drama, because that's exactly what someone goes to a superhero movie for.

Oh sure, there are environmental catastrophes going on in the background caused by a suspiciously silvery streak. Reed Richards (Ioan Gruffudd) even states at one point that the phenomena are being caused by the same cosmic energy that gave the Fantastic Four their powers. But who cares! Let's head on over to the nightclub so Richards can have his rubbery dance sequence as part of his bachelor party. Everyone loves a superhero dance sequence, right?

Fortunately, Andre Braugher shows up as a no-nonsense general to get the film back on track. Soon the Richards wedding is ruined and Johnny Storm (Chris Evans) is chasing the Silver Surfer (a CGI'd Doug Jones, voiced by Lawrence Fishburne) all along the eastern seaboard. The sequence is quite stellar, a highlight of the film.

And then, we're right back to yukking it up in sitcom territory as Johnny keeps accidentally trading powers with his teammates.

This is the first sequel in a superhero franchise, so we get talk from our heroes of hanging it up and the inevitable reluctant team-up with arch-villain Dr. Doom (Julian McMahon). There are numerous scenes of derring-do and swooping, swirling CGI, and we get a conceptual approach to Galactus. This ticked off a lot of fans, but I thought it was smart. If anything else because there's no way to pull off a purple-clad space giant in a film.

It's all just fine. Put it another way: If you liked 2005's *Fantastic Four*, you'll like *Fantastic Four: Rise of the Silver Surfer*. All of the strengths and weaknesses of the first film are still there: Evans is still great as the cocky Johnny Storm and Michael Chiklis is inspired as The Thing, Ben Grimm. Gruffudd is a smart pick on paper, but his Reed Richards is still kind of a non-entity, and Jessica Alba is still horribly miscast as The Invisible Woman. Worst of all is that Doom, a heavyweight in the Marvel Universe, is still a completely unknown entity – we only know he's the villain in these films because the music tells us so. And the action is all bland and safe and somewhat satisfying, like visual rice pilaf.

Sure, you could do worse than *Fantastic Four: Rise of the Silver Surfer…* but don't you deserve better?

* *

6: THE BEST OF THE BAD

REEFER MADNESS
Directed by Louis Gasnier
1936, 68 minutes, Rated PG
Tell Your Children (That This Movie is a Scream)

Contrary to popular belief, propaganda films aren't limited to World War II. Even back in the '30s, propaganda films were commonly used in another kind of war – the War on Drugs.

Yes, long before Nancy Reagan made a Very Special Appearance on *Diff'rent Strokes* to "Just Say No," there was a War on Drugs... specifically on the "unspeakable scourge" of marijuana. *Reefer Madness*, originally titled *Tell Your Children*, fights that war one ham-fisted scene after another.

The ham-fistery starts right out of the gate with this scrolling text:

The motion picture you are about to witness may startle you. It would not have been possible, otherwise, to sufficiently emphasize the frightful toll of the new drug menace which is destroying the youth of America in alarmingly increasing numbers. *Marihuana* is that drug - a violent narcotic - an unspeakable scourge - *The Real Public Enemy Number One!*

It goes on like that for three whole minutes, even going so far as to describe the effects of smoking up. And while I'm not well-versed in the ganja, it's pretty apparent that the makers of this film have never, ever been anywhere near marijuana.

After those three minutes of reading, we get... more reading! Newspaper headlines tell us all about the evils of dope, and that we should all "Come! Hear! Listen!" to the esteemed Dr. Alfred Carroll talk about "Tell Your Children." Which doesn't make a lick of sense to me, but people come out in droves just the same. After outlining exactly how one can grow, process, roll and even hide pot – just what you want in an anti-drug film – Dr. Carroll tells a tale that happened in this very town.

Mae and her beau (and pimp?) Jack are drug dealers who host parties for potential/current clients. We very quickly see the effects of "the dread marihuana" when a piano player sneaks off for a joint and starts tweaking and twitching like *Seinfeld*'s Kramer on too much Mountain Dew. Jack's new marks include Jimmy, his sister Mary and her boyfriend, Bill. They seem like good, wholesome all-American teens, the kinds who enjoy tennis, hot chocolate and *Romeo & Juliet*, though by "teens," I mean "actors well into their 30s." Good to know that's not limited to '90s television.

When Bill first joins Jimmy at Mae's place, he clearly does not approve of all the decidedly not family-friendly partying but crumples like a paper cup under the slightest bit of peer pressure. Unfortunately for Bill, "the dread Marihuana" is even more addictive than Candy Crush, and seemingly overnight, Bill is cheating on Mary, screwing up in school and acting like Bobby Knight.

Meanwhile, Jimmy gives Jake a lift to his supplier, and smokes up a bunch while waiting in the car. Naturally, that makes him *crazy!* Jimmy drives like a mad man and runs down an elderly gent trying to cross the road, which is more the actions of a street punk from a Troma film than a pothead. What were they lacing their weed with back in the '30s?

Mary goes to Mae's to find out what the Sam Hill is going on with her brother and Bill, and gets assaulted by Jack's creepy buddy, Ralph. Bill hallucinates that Mary is hooking up with Ralph, and goes on one of those crazed pot-fueled berserker frenzies you always read about. Jack steps in, a gun is pulled, and suddenly it's the inspiration for Barry Manilow's "Copacabana."

Yes, *Reefer Madness* aims for *Hamlet*-level tragedy: an innocent life is lost, another hangs in the balance. "Let's make an example of this kid!" shouts the jury foreman, because suddenly this film takes place in Texas. There's even a character who ends up pleading guilty to "fostering moral delinquency" (though I can't imagine how much jail time that would land someone) before committing suicide. Yet another character is sent to a mental institution for life due to his "reefer madness."

So instead of *Hamlet*-level tragedy, with its cheesy performances and bizarro depictions of marijuana use, the film is about as sad as a scantly-clad Will Ferrell running wildly in public. It's no mystery why it's such a popular midnight movie or why NORML latched on to it in the '70s for circulation around college campuses: This movie is pure, un-cut camp.

* * * *

PLAN 9 FROM OUTER SPACE
Directed by Ed Wood
1958, 78 minutes, Unrated
Hail to the King, Baby

There's a reason why this is the most celebrated Worst Movie Ever. Having a reputation is one thing. Having a reputation that stands for over 50 years is something else altogether.

Ed Wood's infamous *Plan 9 from Outer Space* has such a reputation, and is widely regarded as the Greatest Worst Movie Ever Made. I'm confident that even if you're not a bad movie connoisseur or even that big of a movie fan, you have heard about this film. So the question is, can it really be that bad?

Sweet Christmas, yes.

Less than two minutes in, and you know that you're in for a near-religious experience. I was prepared for the hammy acting and the cheap effects, but I wasn't prepared for the dialogue. Here's the opening monologue to *Plan 9 From Outer Space*, delivered with great relish by the Narrator (Criswell). It made me shoot Thai curry out my nose – and you can imagine how hard your body will instinctively fight to prevent that from happening. No amount of quips and snark can do this monologue justice:

> Greetings, my friends. We are all interested in the future – for that is where you and I are going to spend the rest of our lives...
>
> ... And remember, my friends, future events such as these will affect you in the future! You are interested in the universe... the mysterious... the unexplainable... that is why you are here! And now – for the first time ever – we are bringing you the full story of what happened on that fateful day.

We are giving you all the evidence based only on the secret testimony of the miserable souls who survived this terrifying ordeal. The incidents... the places... my friends, we cannot keep this a secret any longer. Let us punish the guilty. Let us reward the innocent. My friends, can your stand the shocking facts about... GRAVE ROBBERS FROM OUTER SPACE?"

Grave robbers from outer space! Not to get ahead of myself, but that's the Plan 9 in Plan 9 in a nutshell. I was going to do a whole thing about Plans 1 through 8, but the Riff Trax guys beat me to it.

Eh, what the hell. Here are my Plans 1 through 8:

Plan 1: Send in a lone representative, disguised as a human, with a cool-ass robot bodyguard to convince the Earthlings to stop behaving like hairy douche bags. They'll listen.

Plan 2: Send in a fleet to blow up national icons and tourist destinations. Hope that the Earthlings don't have Will Smith or any diseases.

Plan 3: Take control of Earth's giant monsters, have them destroy the planet via remote control. Let the monsters destroy all of the national icons and tourist destination. Explain the plan in great detail to a handful of captured Earthlings, including a meddlesome Japanese boy in short shorts.

Plan 4: Send in an adorable botanist with a fondness for peanut butter candies to befriend a lonely young boy. Caution: Law enforcement officers may be armed with walkie-talkies.

Plan 5: Plant pods to grow duplicates of the Earthlings, painstakingly replacing them one at a time. Time-consuming. Also, the pods require plenty of indirect sunlight and frequent watering.

Plan 6: Send in a battalion of foot soldiers to stealthily invade the heartland of the Earthling terrain known as "America." Beware of teenaged guerilla resistance and conveniently placed glasses of water.

Plan 7: Infiltrate Earthling society disguised as physically appealing humans and surround them with subliminal messages. Hope the Earthlings have a steady supply of bubblegum.

Plan 8: Dull the Earthling's minds with an endless barrage of trashy reality television (currently in progress).

Back to the movie. The first portion of the film consists largely of footage director Ed Wood shot of Bela Lugosi before Lugosi passed away. As Lugosi does the kind of things he did on a daily basis – sashay around in his Dracula cape, smelling roses and parading through cemeteries – the narrator strings together something that resembles a plot. Lugosi plays a man who has just buried his wife (Vampira) who, in the midst of mourning... gets hit by a bus. Off-camera. His funeral is immediately followed by the most stupefying exposition ever, as two mourners explain why Lugosi was buried in a tomb while his wife was buried in the ground.

Around this time, an airline pilot who just happens to live next door to the cemetery, sees a flying saucer during one of his flights. The saucer lands in the cemetery and causes our dearly departed (with Lugosi's character now played by Wood's chiropractor holding the cape around his face) to rise from the dead.

Turns out the aliens are a bureaucratic bunch in shiny uniforms. Frustrated with their inability to communicate with our governments, they've decided to unleash PLAN 9: The Resurrection of the Dead! The big idea is to have an army of the undead pave the way for the alien's "other operations." The mind reels as to what those other operations might include.

Much of the film plays out like a drunken storyteller: confused, vaguely inappropriate and often contradictory. Numerous shots flip from day to night and back within the same scene. The police detective uses his revolver to point at things, scratch his head, just about everything else besides shooting. And in one of my favorite scenes, two high-ranking military officers debate the existence of flying saucers several scenes after they drove an entire fleet of UFOs away with stock footage.

It all builds to a talky confrontation between a pair of aliens and our group of plucky heroes that plays out as half science lesson, half hissy fit.

But that's the beauty of a film like *Plan 9 From Outer Space*: Many filmmakers have tried to make an intentionally bad movie, and they almost always fail because you can't fake these kind of movies. The best bad films are projects the filmmakers care passionately about, and everyone involved is genuinely giving their best effort. And I'd take one of those movies over another soulless, cookie-cutter rom-com or bromance knock-off any day of the week.

* * * * *

GYMKATA

Directed by Robert Clouse
1985, 90 minutes, Rated R
Fusing the awesomeness of martial arts with the cheesy showmanship and awful fashion of gymnastics!

I may not be a classically trained film critic, but I like to think of myself as an observer of the cinematic condition. For example, it has not escaped my notice that every so many years, someone will come out with a film that attempts to convince us that gymnastics is totally bad ass.

It happened a decade ago with the Nick Nolte 2006 film, *Peaceful Warrior*, and back in the '80s with *Footloose* (it totally did – watch it again!). Apparently, the gymnastics action in *Footloose* was pushed too far into the background for some movie exec, who had the genius thought: What if we combined gymnastics with the oh-so hot right now martial arts? All the kids will want to be gymnastics ninjas for Halloween! Hence *Gymkata* was born.

The film opens with… a complete mess. Sorry, but it's so confusing that it's not worth describing. Let's just say it's a mash-up of *Planet of the Apes* (with horseback ninjas) and some guy doing gymnastics stuff on the parallel bars in the dark. Let's just move on.

The guy working the parallel bars is Cabot, a professional gymnast with a definite Luke Skywalker vibe. The Feds pick Cabot – over all of the people in the armed forces – for a one-man mission into reclusive Parmistan to… yeah, I know, let me know when you're finished snickering. Parmistan has a plot of land (don't bother trying to find it on a map) that the U.S. wants access to for its Star Wars project. For you kids out there, the Star Wars project was an '80s initiative to protect America from nuclear missiles with a system of satellites armed with lasers, and no, I'm not making that up.

The big plan? Have Cabot compete in The Game (sadly, not a variation of the Michael Douglas movie), which no one has won "in 900 years." The winner gets a wish granted by the Khan of Parmistan and hence can get the U.S. that plot of land. Also, the winner gets to live.

Cabot is introduced to "the Princess of Parmistan" ("She's very interesting," Cabot's handler tells him. "Her mother is Indonesian.") and his trainers. It's time for a montage! The trainers begin schooling Cabot in the deadly arts of Gymkata, a fighting style that fused the martial arts of the East with the timing and power of Western gymnastics. Or something like that. Gymkata seems to include possessing an array of ugly sweaters. Gymkata also seems to include the essential ability to walk up a staircase on one's hands.

Soon enough, Cabot is able to walk up a staircase on his hands and has hooked up with the princess – time to go into the field! In a far-off marketplace, an agent warns Cabot that the area has "just a little bit of anti-American sentiment," and is promptly plugged with an arrow. And when a local gang abducts the princess, it's time for Cabot to unleash a gymkatass-kicking.

And here's where we see the true beauty of *Gymkata*: Nearly all of the major action sequences involve a conspicuously placed item that resembles gymnastics equipment. For example, a bunch of thugs chase Cabot down an alley where he conveniently finds a high bar-like pipe running between the two buildings. Before you know it, Cabot is whirling and twirling as one thug after another walks into Cabot's feet.

Post rescue, Cabot and the Princess eventually make it to Parmistan and meet up with the Khan, who is strangely reminiscent of Mel Brooks. The Khan hosts a big banquet – much akin to the one near the beginning of *Enter the Dragon* – that is a lot like Medieval Times without the jousting. The banquet mostly serves sideways glances between Cabot, the Princess and the Douchey Head Security Guy with the Rat Tail. Guess who the Princess is arranged to marry?

Finally, *finally*, it's time for The Game, which is like a medieval version of *The Running Man*. Or "The Most Dangerous Game" with a set course for the hunted. There are even ninjas with semaphore flags stationed throughout the course to help keep everyone on track – a sure sign that your country has too many ninjas.

"Anyone trying to avoid an obstacle will be instantly killed!" the Mel Brooks-ian Khan joyously tells the contestants. Said obstacles include a rope course, a forest, and the Village of the Crazies, which is filled with booby traps, recordings of Halloween sound effects and, allegedly, insane cannibals. Fortunately for Cabot, the town square has a stone pommel horse so he can Gymakata the entire town! Everyone stands around, waiting for their chance to walk into Cabot's feet as he does his pommel horse routine. It's one of the most glorious action sequences ever put to film.

This film needs to be seen to be believed. Don't walk – run, tumble and cartwheel your way to *Gymkata*.

* * * * *

DEATHSTALKER II
Directed by Jim Wynorski
1987, 86 minutes, Rated R
"Only recently dismissed by Ivan the Terrible for excessive brutality"

One crummy Saturday night back when I was in college, my roommate presented an obviously well-loved VHS for us to watch. "It's *so bad!*" he gushed. "You're gonna love it!" The cover art certainly looked cheesetacular. Our plans made, we promptly set about obtaining a couple bottles of malt liquor and settling in for a magical movie experience. Followed by a nasty hangover.

Years later, when I got it in my head to review bad movies, I'd reflect back to that crummy Saturday night and think, "*That is what I'm searching for. Deathstalker II* will be my gold standard."

To convey just how totally amazing *Deathstalker II* is, I'm going to skip over plot, character, cinematography and all that other standard film review stuff, and go straight to the rules of the drinking game. Here's what you do: Gather a few good friends, some inexpensive booze and copy of *Deathstalker II*. As you watch the movie, take a drink whenever any of the following happens:

- A moment from a much better movie is blatantly ripped-off
- Furniture is broken
- Someone does a spit take
- Random nudity appears
- A character says "Deathstalker"
- The Deathstalker sound effect, a music sting that sounds like a dying synthesizer

If you can still stand by the time you reach the end of the film, you're a stronger person than I.

The full title is *Deathstalker II: Duel of the Titans.* But don't worry, no titans were harmed in the making of this film... primarily because no titans appear. Or are even mentioned. In a pre-credits sequence that largely cribs from *Raiders of the Lost Ark* AND finds a way to shoehorn the title of the film into the script, we meet our hero. Deathstalker (John Terlesky of *Chopping Mall* fame) is described as a barbarian, though here, by "barbarian" they clearly mean "that smirking guy from shop class with the feathered hair."

It's an unexpected anarchism: Terlesky makes no attempt whatsoever to use an accent or behave like a medieval thief living hand-to-mouth. Instead, he plays Deathstalker as a ladies man ambling into a singles bar after a rough work week. And Deathstalker is like that for the entire film, regardless of what's going on. It could have been an irritating choice. Instead, it plays into the cheesy awesomeness of the film.

After the prerequisite bar brawl – I imagine many of you will drop out of the drinking game after that scene – Deathstalker teams up with a pretty "seer" played by *Penthouse* Pet Monique Gabrielle. 'Nuff said there. Our duo head off to free a beautiful princess from the clutches of an evil sorcerer ("Is there any other kind?" Deathstalker smirks) in order to become a legend "even bigger than Conan."

It's hard to say exactly what happens from there, and I was sober this time around. Remember kids, don't drink and review! The film is a hodgepodge of chase scenes through the same section of forest, horrible effects, bad puns, random toplessness, equally random stock footage from the first *Deathstalker*, zombies, explosions, Amazons, a motley crew of assassins and a "match to the death" between Deathstalker and famed Gorgeous Lady of Wrestling Queen Kong. It all comes to a head with an epic battle involving at least... oh, I don't know, 20 or so extras. The Battle of Helms Deep, this is not.

It's more than obvious that the filmmakers aren't trying to make a serious swords-n-sorcery film, and that the bad jokes and general cheesiness are intentional. For many films, this comes off as desperate. I've always believed that it's nearly impossible to make a great bad movie on purpose, but against all odds, it works here.

Perhaps my favorite moment comes during the final battle when one of the main villains, the awesomely named

"Sultana," simply leaves. That's right: Sultana all but says, "Screw you guys, I'm going home," and strolls off in the middle of the climactic battle scene, right out of the movie.

I will evangelize the glories of *Deathstalker II* for the rest of my days. Simply put, *Deathstalker II* is the most delightful film I've ever seen.

* * * * *

HARD TICKET TO HAWAII
Directed by Andy Sidaris
1987, 100 minutes, Unrated
"This ain't no hula!"

The write-up on Netflix loudly proclaims that this film is from the Andy Sidaris Collection. "THE Andy Sidaris?" I say, "I didn't know Gollum made a series of b-movies." He didn't. I had Andy Sidaris mixed up with Andy Serkis.

It's quickly obvious when the DVD opens with a message from THE Andy Sidaris (who looks nothing like Gollum) and Julie Stain. Ms. Stain is wearing too much lipstick, too much black hair dye, and little else. The two pimp out the movie *hard*, which is kinda stupid because I already have the movie in my DVD player.

Hard Ticket to Hawaii is the story of an unspecified "agent" and her friend (Playmates Dona Speir and Hope Marie Carlton) who are sent to Hawaii undercover for... uh, some reason, and stumble upon a diamond smuggling ring while coming up with various excuses to take their tops off. Also, there's a mutant snake on the loose.

We're first introduced to the mutant snake after the strangely entertaining credit sequence. The opening credits run on the side of crates in a busy warehouse. It was unexpectedly fun and actually got me to read the credits, so there's something. When the credits end, there's a labored forklift accident that breaks the straps to a crate labeled "CAUTION! LIVE SNAKE!" And by "live snake," we mean "rubber snake puppet." But never mind, because "It's contaminated!"

Unfortunately, the mutant snake is but a mere supporting player in this film. The first half of the film tries very hard to capture the same sexy, adventurous spirit of *Romancing the Stone*, and fails. There are a few nice moments, like when the girls are surprised by smugglers and retaliate by hurling throwing stars at them, or when the girls decide that the best place to examine evidence is in a hot tub. Otherwise, the first half of the film is as exciting as a stack of rice cakes.

Even the scenes of romantic frolicking on the beach – always accompanied by Muzak and toplessness – can't help the first half of the film. It did strike me odd that despite all the gratuitous nudity, the sex scenes are extremely tame.

Something magical happens around the halfway point of the film: It get really, really, really wacky.

Realizing that they're going to need some help, the girls call in their guy friends: one a boyfriend and fellow non-specified "agent," the other a karate guy with the ponytail to prove it. As they head over in their Jeep, they have the following conversation:

```
Kung-Fu Ponytail

My first wife used to mow the lawn naked.


Agent BF

What did your neighbor say?
```

Kung-Fu Ponytail

He thought I married her for her money!

Agent BF

Ha ha ha ha!... Did you?

It gets better: The smugglers' mole tipped them off to the arrival of the Secret Agent Guys, and have set a trap. And the trap is... original. First, the smugglers send their Skateboarder to skate past the guy's Jeep while performing a handstand. No, I don't know why either. "That guy must have smoked some major doobage," Agent BF notes.

Then Skateboard Man meets up with his cohorts, who give him a shotgun and an inflated blow-up doll. Skateboard Man teleports back up the hill so he can skate past the guys' Jeep again, this time while hiding his shotgun behind the blow-up doll. Once he's close enough, Skateboard Man takes a shot, winging Kung-Fu Ponytail. After making sure Kung-Fu Ponytail is okay, Agent BF slams the Jeep in reverse. Fortunately, Skateboard Man has *not* fled the scene, opting instead to do 360s in the middle of the road because he's a skater, dude. The Jeep slams into Skateboard Man, popping him up into the air, video game-style.

Skateboard Man pops so far into the air, Agent BF has enough time to reach into the back of his Jeep, pull out *a rocket launcher* and shoot Skateboard Man out of the sky. Agent BF shoots the blow-up doll, too, just for good measure. Both explode in exactly the same way

When the smugglers kidnap their friend, our non-specified agents leap into action... after an evening of vodka and nookie. But the next morning, they're all business. The first part of their incredibly elaborate rescue plan is to take out the one guard patrolling the beach. The ruse involves a spontaneous game of Frisbee and some well-placed razorblades. It's so ludicrous that the scene was reenacted shot-for-shot for FunnyOrDie.com.

Things blow up real good, though our non-specified agents totally forget to apprehend the head smuggler before leaving. That comes back to haunt the agents... as does the rubber snake puppet. Through a toilet.

So for as dull as the first half of the movie is, the second half is more than makes up for it. This movie is screaming for a drinking game.

* * * *

MIAMI CONNECTION
Directed by Woo-sang Park and Y.K. Kim
1987, 120 minutes, Unrated
Tae Kwon Don't

When I was a lad, I thought about taking Tae Kwon Do but just couldn't bring myself to do it. It had nothing to do with the amount of work and discipline needed to undertake martial arts – I could handle that, believe it or not. No, it had everything to do with the exhibition held every year at The Tag Sale On The Green.

The Tag Sale On The Green is the biggest social event of the year where I grew up, so big that you had to pronounce the name of the event in proper title caps. For one glorious summer day, the townsfolk would drag their junk out to the town green and sell it to each other. Bands would play, local restaurateurs would sling cheap eats, classic cars would be displayed, and junk would be sold. And right there along with all the other junk was the local Tae Kwon Do school, doing some kind of underwhelming routine to *The Karate Kid* soundtrack. You see, I could handle the hard work and discipline needed to master the martial arts, but I couldn't handle the idea of performing punch and kick routines to the musical stylings of Joe Esposito.

Maybe it's just that Tae Kwon Do, the kickiest of martial arts, has never been able to effectively market itself. I give you Exhibit A: *Miami Connection*.

The opening sequence of *Miami Connection* alone makes it one of the most '80s movies I've ever seen. We kick things off "Somewhere in Miami" with a drug deal featuring synthesizer music, uzis, cocaine, Panama hats and Members Only jackets… and that's all before the deal is busted up by a gang of motorcycle-riding ninjas. How we don't have more movies featuring gangs of motorcycle-riding ninjas is beyond me. Anyway, the ninjas assault everyone with kung fu sound effects and run off with both the drugs and the money. It's safe to assume that the ninjas aren't good guys.

Know who are our good guys? The boys of Dragon Sound, the best Tae Kwon Do rock band to ever hit the Orlando music scene! Dragon Sound is the new house band at a hip nightclub where Orlando's trendy jet set rocks out to such lyrics as:

```
Friends through eternity,
Loyalty, honesty,
We'll stay together,
Through thick or thin.
Friends forever,
We'll be together,
We're on top,
Cuz we play to win.
```

Like all good bands from the late '80s, Dragon Sound consists of a perfect cross-section of ethnicities:

- Mark, the Korean One!
- John, the Tall One!
- Jim, the Black One!
- Jack, the Jewish One!
- Tom, the One who looks like John Oates!

Not only are the boys of Dragon Sound the hottest Tae Kwon Do rock band in Orlando, but they're also all orphans and Tae Kwon Do masters! That becomes a bit of an issue (the martial arts mastery, not the lack of parents) for crime lord Jeff when he discovers that his sister, Jane, is dating John. Jane introduces the two, and Jeff – who we quickly learn is strangely over-protective of his college-aged sister – greets John with a knuckle sandwich. Back with his motorcycle ninja associates, Jeff announces that they "need to get rid of that band" in order to take control of Orlando. Nonsensical, sure, but if that's what it takes to get us to the fight scenes.

About those fight scenes… they're competent enough, if a bit repetitive, as they usually consist of Mark (co-creator of the film and an actual Tae Kwon Do master) fighting, John running away and then fighting, and the others flailing around. More interesting are the scenes *around* the fight scenes.

Take one of my favorite sequences: the beach scene, where the boys of Dragon Sound head to the beach to blow off some steam. We get a montage of ass shots as the Dragon Sound gang takes in the scene. Then Tom falls onto a blanket with some girls, who promptly pummel him with shoes. Then John and Jane make out awkwardly in the surf. And scene!

You're guess as to the narrative value of the scene is as good as mine.

Then there's the extended Tae Kwon Do sequence, where Mark, John and Jack demonstrate their mastery of the martial art. All that's missing is a phone number running at the bottom of the screen so you can sign up your little tyke for lessons.

It all leads up to a confrontation with the motorcycle ninjas (Jim sees the approaching motorcycle gang approaching and groans, "Aw... ninjas!"), where Mark and John flat-out murder everyone in sight. It made me wonder what part of Tae Kwon Do involved slashing multiple ninjas. Fortunately for them, Mark and John are the protagonists in an action movie, so no legal ramifications for the mass slaughter!

And it certainly adds an extra layer of irony to the final shot, the quote "Only through the elimination of violence can we achieve world peace." Who would've guessed that the Tae Kwon Do enthusiasts behind *Miami Connection* meant for the elimination of violence by any means necessary?

* * * * *

TROLL 2
Directed by Claudio Fragasso
1990, 95 minutes, Rated PG-13
The best dysfunctional family/road trip/horror movie the beef industry has ever made.

I'm going to let you in a little secret: There's only a few things you NEED to do to raise kids. Hey, if you can't get parenting advice from a book of bad movies, where can you get it? TV or no TV? Junk food or healthy snacks only? Doesn't matter. So long as you're consistent – when you say "no," that must mean "no" – and have some kind of routine, you'll be in good shape. Of course, you'll also want to actually spend time with the little ones: playing, coloring, reading, etc. I'm a big believer in reading to kids, been doing it since my little ones were just hours old. Not only do you get to bond, but you also start developing their imagination and story-telling abilities.

The grandfather in *Troll 2* is also a big believer is reading stories to children. Unfortunately, he uses his stories to scare the shit out of little Josh. The movie opens with Grandpa telling thoroughly inappropriate story of how Peter and his stupid pointy hat was terrorized by "haughty creatures, spiteful and impudent"... "the little people of the night." When Josh, on the verge of wetting himself, asks Grandpa if there are such things as goblins (yes, *goblins* – the word "troll" is never used in *Troll 2*), he says YES.

In a twist worthy of an M. Night Shyamalan movie, we quickly find out that Grandpa *isn't really there*! It comes to light that Grandpa passed away in a wonderful bit of clunky exposition, courtesy of Josh's perpetually alarmed-looking mother:

```
Grandpa Seth has been gone for more
than six months now. You were at the
funeral and I know it was very
difficult for you. It was also very
difficult for your father and for Holly
and for me, his daughter.
```

Yes, a major highlight of this gem is the incredibly clunky dialogue. Here's another chestnut from mom:

```
Grandpa Seth will remain in all our
hearts, but you must banish him from
your mind.
```

My own grandfather passed not too long ago. Something tells me that if I tried to pass this advice along at the wake, my grandmother would not have appreciated it.

Elsewhere in Clunky Exposition Central, teen queen and future American Gladiator Holly tells her boyfriend, Elliot, a bunch of stuff he probably already knows:

```
If my father discovers you here, he'd
cut off your little nuts and eat them.
He can't stand you... I like you, but
my family doesn't like you. They say
you're good for nothing and that you
spend way too much time with your
friends.
```

Awesomely, Dad repeats this almost verbatim two scenes later.

Anyway, the fam heads out to the country "to live like peasants" for a month. Mom makes the car ride special by demanding – really, *demanding* – little Josh sing for her amusement. If there's anything more painful than participating in a rousing round of "Row Your Boat," it's watching other people joylessly sing it.

The fam arrives at the farmhouse and meet the family they'll be swapping abodes with. The other family appears to be straight out of *The Twilight Zone*, or are they simply... trollish? They've left a banquet of day-glo pastries for our fam to enjoy, but Grandpa materializes to warn Josh not to let anyone eat the goodies. Grandpa even *stops time for 30 seconds* to allow Josh to come up with a brilliant plan. That plan? Hop on the table and piss on the food. Nice.

To make a long story short (too late), the entire town is populated with non-troll goblins and led by a woman who was cast straight out of a dinner theater production of *The Rocky*

Horror Picture Show. This witchy woman claims that her ancestors came from Stonehenge. Okay, here's the thing: for as interesting as Stonehenge is, it's basically an ancient man-made rock formation. It's not like Stonehenge is a town or anything. Hell, it sits on the side of a highway. Claiming your ancestors came from Stonehenge is like claiming your ancestors came from Madison Square Garden.

Being from Stonehenge, Witchy Woman and her not-troll goblins are avid vegetarians who trick their victims into eating phony-looking pastries. The pastries cause people to vomit green corn syrup and turn into plants... or be eaten... or turn into a not-troll goblin. It kinda depends on what the plot requires at the time. Naturally, they're all undone by the power of bologna.

Other highlights? Rampant overacting, making your buddy run into town to buy food even though you're camping in an RV, a sex scene involving that same RV filled with popcorn and the mere idea that some production lackey had to seek out a platoon of little stuntpeople to abuse.

In the course of the extensive research I do when writing these reviews (ahem), I discovered a number of claims that *Troll 2* is the "the best worst movie" ever made. I don't think it's the best, but it certainly in the top ten.

* * * *

SAMURAI COP
Directed by Amir Shervan
1991, 97 minutes, Rated Unrated
"Yes, it burns! And it's going to burn more!"

Just what makes one a samurai? According to most common definitions, one would need to be a member of Japan's medieval warrior class – a Japanese knight, for all intents and purposes – who follows a strict code of honor, disciple and morality. According to 1991's *Samurai Cop*, all you need is flowing long hair and to have everyone constantly refer to you as "Samurai."

Samurai Cop many have been released in 1991, but it appears to have been shot and edited solidly in the 80s. The synth music, the high-waist undergarments and bathing suits, the plethora of double-breasted suits and mullets... Truly, *Samurai Cop* is a visual feast, sponsored by Good Will.

Let's dig into this epic: Mr. Fujiyama is a Yakuza boss who is looking to unite the gangs of Los Angeles under his banner – by hook or by crook. Doing the heavy lifting for Fujiyama is the big, bearded Yamashita (*Maniac Cop* Robert Z'Dar) and Okamura (the immediately recognizable Gerald Okamura), who also double as the "big name stars" of this epic.

To help combat the rise in organized crime, the LAPD bring in a ringer. Here's the skinny, according to Yamashita:

```
His real name is Joe Marshall. They call
him 'Samurai.' He speaks fluent Japanese.
He got his martial arts training from the
masters in Japan. He was brought over here
from the police force in San Diego to
fight us!
```

I'm happy to report that none of that skill or ability is displayed at any time during the film.

Instead, we get lots of Joe Marshall running around with his partner, Frank Washington, like a Discount Riggs and Murtaugh. Together, they engage in a number of inept action sequences that usually consist of one unnecessarily telling the other what to do. Moments like Joe yelling at Frank, "Shoot! Shoot him!" while Frank is actively firing his gun are very much the norm.

I know I throw out the "Discount" This or That on a pretty regular basis, but this time it's very on the nose – Joe and Frank even dress like *Lethal Weapon*'s Riggs and Murtaugh. I'd have a very, very, very hard time believing that writer/director Amir Shervan's script for *Samurai Cop* didn't start off as *Lethal Weapon* fan fiction. At times, *Samurai Cop* feels like the *Lethal Weapon* movie the Gang made on *It's Always Sunny in Philadelphia*.

And that includes the abrupt and awkward sex scenes. The scenes themselves seem to be put together by a preteen's conception of sex: there are boobies and lots of drowsy, passive kissing and that's about it. Also, I had no idea that the Bushido Code included scoring as much as possible, but our Discount Riggs easily spends more time hitting on and bedding women then doing any actual police work. These moments spring up at the most random and inappropriate times, adding a nice layer of surrealism to the film.

I had a blast with *Samurai Cop*, but the movie is also something of a conundrum: This may be the first time where I can't tell if the film is aware of how bad it is. There aren't any obvious winking, knowing moments in *Samurai Cop*, but there's definitely a strain of Fozzy Bear-esque humor throughout, and scenes like the one featuring the "horny nurse" are definitely meant to be funny.

On the other hand, Joe suddenly sporting a women's wig in scenes was not part of the game plan (actor Matt Hannon cut his hair after shooting, then found out months later that he was needed for extensive reshoots). I can't imagine that some of the more bizarre moments, like the police captain directly ordering Joe and Frank to straight up murder the entire gang, was meant to be funny. And what are we to make of dialogue like this?

> *Yamashita has broken into the house of a cop, and begins torturing her for information by pouring a seemingly endless frying pan of hot eggy water (?) on her off-screen belly.*
>
> YAMASHITA: (pouring) This thing burns, you know.
>
> COP: No! No, stop! You're burning me!
>
> YAMASHITA: Yes, it burns! And it's going to burn more!

Okay, so I can't tell if *Samurai Cop* is intentionally bad... but I can tell that I love it. Bring on *Samurai Cop 2: Deadly Vengeance*!

* * * *

UNDEFEATABLE
Directed by Godfrey Ho
1993, 95 minutes, Rated R
Featuring the Best Worst Fight Ever

You might not guess it, but reviewing bad movies requires a lot of wisdom. The wisdom to find the beauty in stupidity. The wisdom to contemplate such universal questions such as "If a tree falls in the woods and no one is there to hear it, does it make a sound?" and "What would a Jackie Chan movie without Jackie Chan look like?"

The answer to that last question is *Undefeatable*.

Anna has a problem: Her boyfriend, Paul, has given up his steady career in auto maintenance to participate in underground "death matches," which are just like kickboxing matches without refs. Actually, Anna has two problems: the second being that Paul is a complete psycho.

Another underground brawler is Kristi, played by martial arts superstar Cynthia Rothrock. She and her Asian gang of Janet Jackson back-up dancers meet up with some vaguely tough types – you can tell they're tough by their chains and bandanas and studded collars. Kristi gets in the face of one of the toughs, bets are made, and it looks like we're getting our first taste of Street Fighter action.

And then the two gangs have to ruin it by clapping and stomping rhythmically. I wouldn't have been surprised if they all started breakdance-fighting.

They do actually fight, and I don't mean to bury this in the middle of the review, but martial arts superstar Cynthia Rothrock is considered a martial arts superstar for a reason – she doth kicketh much ass.

Unfortunately for her, the cops show up about two seconds after she wins, arresting her and taking her well-earned cash. That leaves it up to the Janet Jackson back-up dancers to get Kristi's pre-med sister to bail Kristi out. Here's the line they use to smooth-talk sis – it's meant to be flirty but is delivered as if our gang member was a soft-spoken teenage girl: "Anyway, once the cops meet you, and see how you're her beautiful sister and a terrific student and all, they'll [something] let her go."

Somehow, that actually succeeds in getting Sis to go down to the police station. Turns out that Kristi is only doing the street-fighting to put Sis through med school, and we get a shoehorned backstory that sounds like a testimonial arguing for health care reform (back in 1993!). Kristi is also released, and there, it certainly helps that the cop clearly has a thing for Kristi.

Let's talk about the cop for a minute, because he's actually a major character. He also appears to be a martial artist – it's the kind of film where everyone is a martial artist – and perhaps the only detective out on the streets of Los Angeles. Seriously, he arrives to break up Kristi's street fights on at least three different occasions throughout the film. Unfortunately, I forgot to write down his name, so let's call him Barry.

While Kristi and Barry the Cop Whose Name Isn't Really Barry are learning about each other at the police station, Anna and Psycho Paul are learning about each other, too. Anna learns that she doesn't enjoy those pre-dinner rapes (it's a rough scene to sit through, but it's mercifully short), so she beats feet, leaving Paul a Dear John letter and a delicious steak to soften the blow.

Paul takes it about as well as you'd expect a complete psycho to take being walked out on. Paul literally hulks out before our eyes, and we get a quick flashback showing that he has just a few mommy and abandonment issues. Back in the present, Paul bug-eyes into a mirror as he spray paints his permed mullet and vows to find Anna.

Instead, Paul finds a couple making out in a parking garage. He's an Asian fellow in a bad suit, she's a brunette in a gaudy floral print dress. Paul pulls them apart and starts calling the lady "Anna," even though it's clearly not her – this lady and Anna have the same hair color and same taste is terrible dresses, but that's about it. That doesn't stop Paul from karate-ing the guy to death (he puts up a fairly good fight – like I told you, everyone in this film is a martial artist) and dragging the lady off for a fate worse than death, followed by actual death.

Because Barry the Cop Whose Name Isn't Really Barry and his partner are the only detectives in Los Angeles, they investigate. Turns out the Asian guy was a karate champion (I told you!), and both he and his lady friend have had their eyes plucked out. Ew. We also learn that there have been a string of similar killings of late, with all of the victims being young brunettes in floral print dresses. And if I'm being honest, I could see how early '90s fashion sensibilities would drive someone into a psychopathic rage.

After a few more random street fights and eye plucking, we catch up with Sis, who apparently has been shopping at the same store as all Anna. Uh-oh.

Kristi swears revenge, and takes it to the streets. She beats the snot out of a number of non-threatening gang types (including one extra bouncy guy in an orange ninja suit) before teaming up with Barry. Because in L.A., it's completely by the book for family members of murder victims to accompany detectives during official investigations.

They finally get a major tip from Anna's psychiatrist. Unfortunately, that's right around the time that Paul gets tipped off to the fact that Anna was seeing a psychiatrist. Paul abducts the psychiatrist, who nearly escapes his lair by using her super-psychiatry powers. Kristi shows up, and she and Paul engage in the first of two climatic battles. The fight consists of lots of posing and leaping and tumbling, and it's actually pretty exciting though a bit silly.

But that's just an appetizer for the big fight between Paul and Barry (Kristi joins later), which is generally regarded as the Best Worst Fight Ever. The posing. The yelling. The clumsy shedding of shirts. The slow-motion punches to the face, complete with out-of-synch facial reactions. It's utterly hysterical. I don't want to give the ending away, so I'll only say that the fight ends in as gruesome and as corny as possible.

The happy ending? Everyone gets enrolled in college. How's that for a public service announcement?

* * * *

SHOWGIRLS
Directed by Paul Verhoeven
1995, 131 minutes, Rated NC-17
So You Think You Can Dance?

The tagline for this movie is "Leave Your Inhibitions At The Door." I'm surprised it's that subtle.

Certainly, subtlety isn't the strong suit of director Paul Verhoeven (*Robocop*, *Starship Troopers*). This is the kind of film where, on numerous occasions, characters seduce each other with the power of dance. The kind of film where almost all of the main characters behave in the most erratic and over the top fashion, because that's "drama." The kind of film where there's a dance-fight.

No, if the advertising were honest, the tag line to this film would have been "Come for Elizabeth Berkley's boobies, stay for everyone else's boobies." I was a tad too old for the heyday of *Saved by the Bell*, so I came into this movie lacking the crucial Jessie fetish that was so obviously used to sell the film. For me, Berkley is merely a barely competent actress who is nowhere near as hot as I'm supposed to think she is.

It takes a whole five minutes for Berkley's Nomi to pull a switchblade on the guy who picked her up hitchhiking, score big on a slot machine, get propositioned by a random tourist, have all her worldly possessions stolen, meet her new bland black BFF (BBBFF?) and annoy the living crap out of me.

Nomi behaves like a feral cat throughout the film – making for a very, very long movie.

Nomi has come to Las Vegas to be a dancer. There are a number of problems with this plan:

1. Nomi has a gigantic, unjustified chip on her shoulder;

2. Nomi aspires to dance in the kind of contemporary performance art that routinely leaves me scratching my head when I see it on *So You Think You Can Dance*; and

3. Nomi is a terrible dancer.

Oh, we're not meant to think that Nomi is a terrible dancer – certainly, all of the other characters think she's a remarkable talent. But the truth is, she dances like an angry epileptic. I don't know if the choreographer is to blame or it's just Elizabeth Berkley's natural dance style, and I don't care. All I can tell you is that in a film about a dancer trying to find her way in Vegas, it's particularly unfortunate if the audience starts cracking up every time that dancer rips out some of her "raw" and "amazing" dance moves.

Among those who think Nomi is amazing/raw/incredibly sexy are Kyle MacLachlan's incredibly bland Entertainment Director (though he gets style points for not cracking up during the scene where Nomi rides him in his pool), one of the Fratelli brothers as a strip club owner with a heart of gol- eh, copper, and Unnamed Black Guy.

Poor Unnamed Black Guy. He's listed as "James Smith," but I never heard his name in the film. Nomi gets him fired from two jobs, but because Unnamed Black Guy had formal dance training in New York, he sees Nomi's "talent" and wants to help her. I think he's supposed to represent "keeping' it real," which makes his fate both extra sad and extra hilarious.

Also riding the amazing/raw/sexy Nomi train is Gina Gershon's Crystal, the star of the big-deal dance revue in town. With Crystal "getting older" (i.e., over the age of 28), she takes sport in becoming her frenemy and messing with Nomi's head – made all the easier with Nomi's hair trigger temper. Gershon plays Crystal like a comic book super villain and has plenty of topless scenes herself. Needless to say, she is by far the best part of the movie.

Ultimately, the film plays like a 1990s-era fairy tale, and a really crappy one at that. Much like the '90s, *Showgirls* is nowhere near as witty or sexy as it thinks it is, leading to lots in unintentional comedy. Per the rules of the decade, Nomi even has her own catchphrase: "It doesn't suck."

Oh yes it does, Nomi. Yes, it does.

* * * *

BATTLEFIELD EARTH
Directed by Roger Christian
2000, 117 minutes, Rated PG-13
You're in the Psychlo Circus / And I say welcome to the show

This film might qualify as a "Modern Cult Classic," largely because its infamy practically begs movie fans to check it out. Here we have one of the biggest Razzie Winners in history, a film widely regarded as the Worst Film of the 20th Century. Years later, the mere mention of the film's title is still enough to generate shivers or snickers. And while I wouldn't call *Battlefield Earth* a film that "so bad, it's good," I would definitely say its badness must be seen to be believed.

As is required of every sci-fi adventure romp since 1977, *Battlefield Earth* opens with scrolling text. It is the year 3000 AD. An alien race called the Psychlos invaded Earth some 1,000 years before and have been mining the planet of all its minerals since. Apparently they're really taking their sweet old time. For reasons left unexplained, gold is the incredibly precious to the Psychlos. But for as much as they love gold, we'll learn later that the Psychlos aren't very good at finding it.

After the title splash, we get a shot of Majestic Mountains… and then more text. "Man is an endangered species"! Yes, we get it, and thank you for insulting your audience within the first five minutes of the film. You might think that our endangered species label would afford us certain protections, perhaps have us put up in habitats where we're fed and encouraged to procreate. No such luck here: Humans have basically gone back to being cavemen.

Our hero – a "Captain Caveman," if you will – is Barry Pepper, the Defiant One of the tribe. We know he's the hero because he gets a grand, virile entrance, galloping into camp on his steed well after closing time. His hottie is on hand to tell him that he's too late with the medicine, dad's dead. And would you believe it, Barry gives us a slow-motion "Noooooooooooo!"

In direct defiance of his cave-dwelling tribe, Barry defiantly heads out in search of a place with more food. He comes across an overgrown mini-golf course and a pair of hunter dudes – they become his buddies, and despite appearing throughout the film, I never knew their names. They talk a lot about how the gods leaving caused their lot in life, or how the gods have been frozen (referring to some giant statues) and… really? I get that they've been running on oral history for generations, but they really have no idea that their planet was conquered by the Psychlos? I'm not buying it.

Maybe that's why it's such a shock to Barry when the Psychlos show up and capture them. Or perhaps that was just the dozen plate glass windows Barry ran through while running away.

Off they fly to a giant dome, and a cameo by the Handi-Captions tell us that it is the "Human Processing Center - Denver." Thanks, Handi-Captions! It's time to meet the Psychlos, and I swear, it's like the costume designer was blindfolded and told to raid the studio's prop shop. The Psychlos are dressed like Gene Simmons from KISS, have Klingon-sized foreheads, dreadlocks and Predator hands. The total effect is less than menacing.

Our starring Psychlos are played by John Travolta and Forest Whitaker. Poor Forest Whitaker looks particularly pooch-like in his Psychlo get-up. It's tragic: He's Forest Whitaker, and he deserves better.

Not deserving better is producer and star John Travolta as Terl, the Psychlo Chief Security Officer. For reasons I don't understand, Travolta seems to be channeling Tim Curry's Dr. Frank-N-Furter from *The Rocky Horror Picture Show* – all that's missing are the fishnet stockings. Travolta's Terl is camp incarnate: He struts around, and laughs and laughs and laughs when he learns that "man-animal" Barry was smart enough to figure out how to use a Psychlo gun. Because your typical Chief Security Officer would find that kind of thing hilarious.

Strangely, the film all but forgets about Barry for a while, focusing instead on the oh-so interesting office politics of the Psychlos. Long story short: The other Psychlos find Terl as ridiculous as we do, which means Terl is stuck on Earth.

Despite his constant boasting of his intelligence, his standings at "the academy," his marksmanship and his upbringing, Terl proves himself to be terrible at this job and one of the weakest villains ever. Everything that leads to the downfall of the Psychlos [spoiler?] is directly caused by Terl's complete stupidity.

Terl wants to use the "man-animals" to mine gold for him, so he plugs Barry into *The Matrix* and teaches him every nuance of the Psychlo's language and culture as well as advanced math and science. What, modern warfare and jujitsu weren't available? Wouldn't it have been better to learn (or have lackey Forest Whitaker learn) English? Apparently not. Instead, Terl teaches Barry all about Psychlos, and teaches him how to fly aircrafts and taunts him by letting him read the Declaration of Independence in a library. Good thing Barry found that document. I imagine things would have turned out differently if Barry picked up *50 Shades of Grey* instead.

And then, Terl leaves Barry and his buddies unsupervised at a mine *for 14 days*? I get that it's supposed to be Terl's hubris that leads to his downfall, but c'mon.

It's a good thing that Terl gave Barry so much unsupervised time, because he and his cavemen need every minute of it to 1) empty Fort Knox of all the gold that the gold-loving Psychlos haven't found *in 1,000 years*, 2) learn how to fly 1,000-year-old fighter jets that are fully-fueled and still in perfect working order, 3) obtain and learn the use of a nuclear weapon and 4) come up with a strategy to take out the Psychlos. It's just the Rebel Alliance vs. the Empire all over again!

In fact, it's obvious that *Battlefield Earth* very badly wanted to be the next *Star Wars*, right down to the use of the same vertical, center-out wipes. Though the film does make the likes of *Phantom Menace* and *Attack of the Clones* look nearly entertaining, I've seen *Star Wars*. And *Battlefield Earth*? You are no *Star Wars*.

* * * *

KARATE DOG
Directed by Bob Clark, 2004
104 minutes, Rated PG
A kung-fu film that's gone to the dogs.

Between all the mindless creatures and kung-fu mayhem and gratuitous nudity and toilet snakes, this hasn't been the most family-friendly chapter, eh? Well, I aim to fix that with a tale of family bonding… Friday night is usually Movie Night at my house, so when my folks came up the other weekend, they and my daughters and I all settled down for some delightful family entertainment that I'd picked out special: 2004's *The Karate Dog*. Because I'm twisted.

We open with *The Karate Kid*'s Pat Morita doing a little breaking-n-entering into some kind of high-tech lab, where he steals a canister of the ooze from *Teenage Mutant Ninja Turtles II: The Secret of the Ooze*. Back at his appropriately Asian-themed abode, Pat Morita explains nothing to his student, Cho-Cho. Who is a dog. That can talk. And, because this movie was mostly created with Mad-libs, is voiced by Chevy Chase.

Pat Morita must've known that they were about to have company, because he keeps shushing the motor-mouthed Cho-Cho. Sure enough, ski-masked baddies come busting into Casa de Morita, and soon everyone is kung fu fighting. Things are looking bad for the very outnumbered and very elderly Morita when Cho-Cho jumps into the fray, *stands up on his hind legs*, and CGI-fus the crap out of the baddies to faux *Matrix* techno.

It's a delightfully ridiculous moment, made all the better by the full-scale incredulousness of my daughters. With this scene, I think they now truly understand what it is I do.

With the ski-masked baddies running off with the Secret of the Ooze and Pat Morita mortally wounded, the only thing left for Cho-Cho to do is call in the cops. At the crime scene, we meet nerdy Det. Fowler and his super crime-solving laptop, COLAR. Fowler is so dorky, all the other officers pick on him for not being a "real" cop, which these days presumably means Fowler doesn't get to wear riot gear or assault unarmed African-Americans. Fowler does get to meet cute with cadet Jaime Pressly, so there's that.

Also barging into the crime scene is the world's most militant animal control officer. Seriously, the guy all but kicks the door in, stomping around *an active crime scene*, in search of the departed Morita's pooch. Cho-Cho, being no fool, stows away in the back of Det. Fowler's vintage, candy apple red convertible. Did I need to tell you that Det. Fowler drives a vintage, candy apple red convertible? Nah, you probably just assumed as much.

Likewise, you probably see where this is all going. Cho-Cho stuns Fowler with his ability to speak. This takes quite a while (understandably), and is given a half-assed explanation that boils down to "because karate." I'm pretty sure that's not how karate works. Then the two do the buddy cop thing to find Pat Morita's killer. Think *Turner & Hooch*, but with infinitely less slobber and 100% more Chevy Chase phoning it in.

So while you can see exactly where things are going, there are still some great moments along the way. There's a surprisingly deft scene early on where Fowler is trying to convince the other cops that Cho-Cho can speak. Fowler sets up Cho-Cho in an interrogation room with the other cops behind the two-way mirror, but Cho-Cho is too smart for that and keeps quiet. We stay in the observation room with the other cops, listening to them peel off zingers like, "Dog won't talk till his lawyer gets here," and the whole scene plays out so much better than it should have. We also get some *Cyrano de Bergerac* action as Cho-Cho feeds lines to Fowler while he's on his dinner date with Jaime Pressly (that goes about as well as you'd expect), and a doggie rager in Fowler's apartment.

And then we have Jon Voight.

I've come to the conclusion that Jon Voight is your parents' Nic Cage. Here we have an Academy Award-winning actor who has spent the majority of the past 20 years focusing his considerable talents to chewing as much scenery as humanly possible. And not in an Al Pacino "Hoo-AH!" kind of way – I mean it's almost as if he's trying to sabotage his own career.

Here's just a sampling of Mr. Voight's career since his, uh, memorable performance in *Anaconda*:

- *Pearl Harbor*
- *Lara Croft: Tomb Raider*
- *Superbabies: Baby Geniuses 2*
- *National Treasure* (with Nic Cage!)
- *Transformers*
- *Bratz*
- *Four Christmases*
- *Baby Geniuses and the Mystery of the Crown Jewels*
- *Baby Geniuses and the Space Baby*

In *The Karate Dog*, Voight is a southern entertainment mogul who is deeply fascinated with Japanese culture. That means he spends most of the film drawling at other characters while wearing a kimono.

You don't need me to tell you that Jon Voight is the villain of this piece. Likewise, you probably don't need me to tell you that the film builds up to a gloriously absurd karate fight between the nearly 70-year-old Voight and a CGI'd Cho-Cho that's choc-full of fixings from *The Matrix*... but you're probably glad I verified that for you.

Even after experiencing *The Karate Dog* with my family (my mother, bless her, loved it without qualifications), I'm still left with so many questions. How exactly does the awesomeness of Pat Morita's martial arts enable a dog to gain intelligence, develop its vocal chords enough to speak English, or defy its own physiology by walking around on its hind legs? What kind of drug regime is needed to make one associate a karate-fighting dog with Chevy Chase? And what's the deal with Jaime Pressly's partner? Apparently, his sole purpose is to drive Ms. Pressly to wherever Det. Fowler is so the two can flirt awkwardly – what's his story?

I guess we'll never know. *The Karate Dog* is an enigma, wrapped in a conundrum, baked inside a bacon-flavored dog biscuit of absurdity.

* * * *

THE WICKER MAN (2006)
Directed by Neil LaBute
2006, 102 minutes, Unrated
"Oh no, not the bees!"

The original version of *The Wicker Man* starring Ed Woodward and Christopher Lee, tells the story of a devout Catholic cop searching for a girl reported missing in a secluded pagan community. Moderately successful when it was released in 1973, the film is a taut psychological thriller that has grown in critical esteem over time and still holds up well today. Even knowing the twist at the end doesn't rob the film of its effectiveness – how many movies claim that?

The 2006 remake of *The Wicker Man* is none of these things. It's not even a pale version of the original. It's more like a feature-length version of prank show with Nicolas Cage.

Cage stars as CHiPs patrolman Edward Malus, largely as an excuse for Mr. Cage to ride a motorcycle and stomp around in big boots. Malus is on hand for a horrible (and highly improbable) roadside accident that results in the death of a woman and her bratty daughter. This makes Malus a Cop On The Edge, which is unquestionably the best kind of cop.

So when Malus receives a letter from his long lost ex-fiancé asking him to come to her remote island commune and find her missing daughter, it's just the kind of redemption he needs. Malus does what any of us would do and hits the world famous Health Foods Metropolis Organic Food Suppliers search engine (how's that for product placement!) to do some research on the island of Summerisle.

No phone, no lights, no motor cars. Not a single luxury. In fact, the community is so closed off, Malus has to bribe his way over. Adding to the alleged spookiness is Malus thinking he sees the bratty girl-turned-roadkill every so often. If you think these "haunting moments" will lead somewhere, you'll be disappointed.

Finally at Summerisle, Malus finds the place to be like *Little House on the Prairie* by way of *The Twilight Zone*. This is where the film really beings to feel like one endless prank show, with the camera catching every one of Nic Cage's overreactions as townsfolk (almost all women) claim the missing girl is either not missing or doesn't exist. It quickly begins to feel like everyone is playing a giant practical joke on Malus, and in this case, the film tips its hand a little too much.

It takes shockingly little time for Malus' investigation to go off the rails. In one priceless scene, he barges into a schoolroom run by Molly Parker (TV's *Deadwood*). Despite not having a shred of jurisdiction, Malus commandeers the classroom, rips the gradebook out of Parker's hands and starts giving the kids the third degree. It made me wonder if I missed a scene of Malus eating paint chips.

Malus later stumbles upon a giant bee yard, which means we're treated to a patented Nic Cage freak-out as he swats the bees away. Non-sequitur moments like these launch the film straight into Accidental Comedy territory

Sadly, much of the movie isn't as strange, settling instead for such pseudo excitement like breaking through the floorboards of the old barn and having a nightmare within a nightmare. And then there's brain-busting dialog like this:

```
Willow (Malus's ex): I can't let them do
this to me.

Malus: Do what? What is it you're not
telling me?

Willow: Forgive me?

Malus: Forgive you for...? I'm lost.

Willow: I don't know.

Malus: Don't worry, it's... you know?
```

No, I don't know. *What the hell are you two blabbering about?*

Know what? It doesn't matter. What matters is that by Chapter 18 on the DVD, Malus has officially lost the plotline. As the community prepares for a festival, Malus runs around like a maniac, kicking in doors, yelling and screaming and flipping masks off kids. He commits what might be the world's first armed bicycle-jacking. Malus then punches the woman who runs the tavern in the face for absolutely no reason and drop-kicks Leelee Sobieski, presumably for her participation in *Jungle 2 Jungle.*

And that's all before Malus starts running around in a bear costume. We still get the famous twist ending, but the impact of the original is replaced with Nic Cage yelling, "Oh no! Not the bees!"

So let's review: This film features the following:

- Nic Cage as a CHiPs On The Edge
- Nic Cage giving a clinic on how *not* to conduct a missing person investigation
- Nic Cage flailing around at bees
- A bike-jacking
- Nic Cage punching a woman in the face
- Nic Cage dropkicking LeeLee Sobieski
- Nic Cage running around in a bear costume

As long as you're not expecting this film to give any kind of justice to the original, it's comic gold.

* * * *

THE ROOM
Directed by Tommy Wiseau
2003, 99 minutes, Rated R
"Leave your stupid comments in your pocket!"

There are plenty of films with bad reputations, and it seems that just about every year another film gets rolled out as the Worst Thing Ever. As a reviewer of bad movies, I quickly learned to take these kind of things with a big ol' lump of salt.

But when it came to *The Room*, one of the most hyped bad movies to come out in a generation? No salt necessary. Like a velvet Elvis or a well-timed zinger, *The Room* is a thing of beauty.

We open with the swelling sounds of the Oscar Bait Orchestra. Johnny and his Rockin' Strands of Artisan Hair have just come home after a long day at the office. In his strange, possibly made-up accent that sounds like Jean-Claude Van Damme bit his tongue, Johnny surprises his "future wife" Lisa with some lingerie. Lisa, with all the grace of a drunken moose, says that she's going to try it on right now, and where's the porn groove?

The movie is certainly heading in that direction when Denny, the Eddie Haskel of our story, waltzes in sitcom-style. "Oh, hi Denny," Johnny says, nonplused by the fact that his lovin' was just interrupted by the neighbor kid. I keep waiting for a laugh track, but it never comes.

After chiding Denny for wanting to watch (!), our two lovebirds eventually do start to get it on, and suddenly we're in a Keith Sweat video: the slow jam is jammin', rain is pouring down the window pane and there's white satin and rose petals everywhere. It is unquestionably the cheesiest sex scene I've ever seen. It carries on far too long, and the fact that it ends with Johnny mounting Lisa and making sweet, pumpy love to her bellybutton is just icing on the cake.

Just in case you didn't get enough of that sex scene, shots of it are edited into later love scenes.

So it seems that everything is cool in Johnny's world... OR IS IT?? Because only a scene or two later, Lisa is lamenting to her mother (cast straight out of Sitcom Purgatory) that she's sick of Johnny and wants to leave him. This revelation, like many others throughout the film, comes absolutely out of nowhere. At least this one actually drives the story along. Later revelations like the fact that Lisa's mom "definitely" has breast cancer are mentioned once and promptly forgotten about.

Turns out that Lisa isn't too crazy about her mom, either. In a priceless bit of dialogue, Lisa complains:

> [My mom] wants to control my life. I'm
> not going to put up with it. I'm going to
> do what I want to do, and that's it. What
> do you think I should do?

Lisa opts to seduce Johnny's best friend, Mark, and comes on to him with all the subtlety of a kick in the nuts. Mark protests, but it doesn't take long for them to start slow jammin' on the staircase.

From this point on, the plot becomes unstuck in time. Johnny states his overall happiness in life with such odd, ironic statements as "I'm so happy I have you as my best friend, and I love Lisa so much." Lisa continues her Jeckyll/Hyde routine. Mark laments the fact that he's carrying on with his best friend's girl, pausing long enough to shag Lisa and make a few random Hyde turns of his own. Wash, rinse, repeat.

Nearly all of the action takes place in Johnny and Lisa's apartment ("The Room," I suppose), with a few breaks in the action to go "throw the ol' pigskin around" in an alley or to have a chat on the Roof of Heart-to-Heart Discussions. My favorite scene takes place on the roof: A ruffian is hassling Denny for money from some prior drug transaction, and all our main characters show up (or, in the case of Lisa and her mom, teleport in) for Big Exciting Drama. The scene achieves a level of cheese that most folks can't imagine – it's like a parody of an afterschool special.

My lone knock against this film is that because there's only one way for this story to end, it feels like it takes forever to get to that moment. Until then, we're in an endless loop of odd declarations, wild mood swings and slow jam grinding. Plot points come and go with little to no impact. Time lines are jumbled. Characters are introduced and promptly disappear while other characters who have not been introduced at all suddenly have key moments.

In short, the film plays like a soap opera made entirely by people suffering from concussions. It's a beautiful mess.

This cinematic achievement is the work of a Mr. Tommy Wiseau (who writes, directs, produces and stars as Johnny). While promoting the film – it has quite the following in L.A., where midnight showings of *The Room* are quite common – Mr. Wiseau has claimed that the movie is intentionally bad and meant to be a comedy. I'm not buying that. Even if he purposely kept his actors in the dark (which he claims), movies this bad can't be faked.

In this regard, the comparisons to Ed Wood are totally appropriate. Bravo, sir!

* * * * *

EPILOGUE:
WHY BAD MOVIES?

Congratulations, you've just waded through 90 reviews of terrible movies! And as you let that reality sink in, you might be asking yourself, "So why does he do this again?"

It's a fair question. You read over and over again about the bad acting, the lazy production values and the incoherent plot... movies that are, at best, labeled "so bad, it's good." So why bother? Am I a sadist? Am I really that bored? Or is it a need to inflate my own self-esteem and compensate for my professional failings by picking on easy targets?

Maybe, but that's not the real reason. The real reason is that I think bad movies are great.

Seriously. I know you don't often hear film critic expounding on the virtues of bad movies, but consider this: Movie fans have been complaining forever about how unoriginal Hollywood has become, how dependent the studios are on remakes and reboots and comic book franchises and adaptations of TV shows. What they don't consider is that, unlike for you and me, movies are a *business* for Hollywood. The studios aren't in it for fun – they're in it to make money. And just like any business model, the studios are looking for the safest way possible (established brands, strong name recognition, proven story formulas, etc.) to maximize their investments. Not exactly the most romantic notion of Hollywood, but again, we're not talking about Santa's Workshop – we're talking about moviemaking as a business. If Hollywood is a Dream Factory, then the modern-day emphasis is on "Factory."

Most bad movies, like many of the films in this book, don't play by those rules. These movies aren't driven by proven formulas and test audiences, giving them the ability to surprise us in a way that today's vanilla action movies or rom-coms can't. The blockbusters may have all the money and star-power and special effects, but they often lose a bit of heart and creativity of films made with nothing but gumption and pocket change.

And determination. You can't discount the fact that the vast majority of the films in this book are passion projects, helmed by one person or a small group chasing a dream. Okay, sure, that dream often turns into a nightmare to watch, but it's also frequently unpredictable, commonly imaginative and every once in a while… admirable.

ACKNOWLEDGEMENTS

You can't devote this much time and effort to bad movies without being weird.

Clearly I've been pretty weird my whole life, but it wasn't until writing those "My Road to Bad Movies" pieces that I fully, truly recognized it. So I want to give my thanks and appreciation to all of those who enabled my weirdness: my family for feeding my Godzilla fixation; the Jack Jackter Elementary School library in Colchester, CT for having a surprising number of books about movie monsters for a relatively small school; my dad for staying up through the always-painful last half-hour of *Saturday Night Live* to tape *It Came From Hollywood*; Greg Stout for introducing me to the magical combination of *Deathstalker II* and malt liquor; and all the friends and readers who recommended bad films for me to check out.

As grateful as I am to all of those people, I have to admit that I probably wouldn't have kept writing movie reviews for so long if it weren't for the Large Association of Movie Blogs. The LAMB is the premiere film blogging community, consisting of nearly 1800 members as of this writing. More than just a directory of movie blogs, the LAMB offers a host of features, aggregate movie ratings and an entire podcasting network. You can check it out at largeassmovieblogs.com.

But the best thing the LAMB has to offer is the simplest: the opportunity to meet fellow movie reviewers. I can't emphasize enough how encouraging it is to discuss, debate and collaborate with fellow movie reviewers, and know that you're not the only one who's way too into movies.

I've met a lot of great folks through the LAMB over the years, but I want to give a special shout-out to two of them. First to Steve Honeywell for editing this book. Steve also happens to be one of my favorite movie critics, so make sure to check out his stuff at 1001Plus.blogspot.com. And to the Internet's own Jason Soto, my podcast partner on The Lair of the Unwanted (lairoftheunwanted.com, free on iTunes). He's the best podcast partner anyone could ever ask for, and the only person I've ever met who loves bad movies more than I do.

Finally, I need to give a special thanks to my daughters, Natalie and Olivia, for not revolting whenever I subjected them to the types of family films described in this book, and Michelle Ward for finding my weirdness cute and encouraging me to chase this particular windmill.

A most heartfelt thank you to you all for your support, encouragement and patience with my weirdness.

ABOUT THE AUTHOR

A lifelong fan of monster movies, Scot Nolan began reviewing bad films in 2007 and soon after became a member of the Large Association of Movie Blogs. Nolan's reviews also appeared in Utica's *Observer-Dispatch*, and led him to hosting WPNY's weekly televised program, *Magnificent Movies at 8*.

Nolan currently cohosts *The Lair of the Unwanted*, a podcast dedicated to bad movies, and resides in Little Falls, New York with his two daughters.

INDEX

32954214R00154

Made in the USA
Middletown, DE
24 June 2016